Scenic Driving

NEW YORK

Including the Adirondacks, the Catskills, and the Finger Lakes

RANDI MINETOR
PHOTOS BY NIC MINETOR

Globe Pequot

Guilford, Connecticut

Globe Pequot

An imprint of The Rowman & Littlefield Publishing Group, Inc.
4501 Forbes Blvd., Ste. 200
Lanham, MD 20706
www.rowman.com

Distributed by NATIONAL BOOK NETWORK

British Library Cataloguing in Publication Information available

Library of Congress Cataloging-in-Publication Data available

ISBN 978-1-4930-5822-8 (paper : alk. paper)
ISBN 978-1-4930-5823-5 (electronic)

∞™ The paper used in this publication meets the minimum requirements of American National Standard for Information Sciences—Permanence of Paper for Printed Library Materials, ANSI/NISO Z39.48-1992

CONTENTS

Adirondack Park Scenic Drives

Catskill Mountains Scenic Drives

Central New York Scenic Drives

Finger Lakes Scenic Drives

Great Lakes Scenic Drives

Hudson Valley Scenic Drives

Long Island Scenic Drives

Southern Tier Scenic Drives

About the Author

Randi Minetor has just traversed the beautiful routes and byways of New York state while writing *Scenic Driving New York* and now brings you this gorgeous volume for Globe Pequot. Her books include the tenth edition of *New York Off the Beaten Path, Hiking Waterfalls in New York, Hiking Through History New York, Backyard Birding: A Guide to Attracting and Identifying Birds* for Lyons Press, five books on hiking in New York State in the Best Easy Day Hikes series, and six books in the Death in the National Parks series. She is also the author of *Birding New England, Best Easy Bird Guide Cape Cod,* and *Best Easy Bird Guide Acadia National Park.*

About the Photographer

Her husband, photographer **Nic Minetor,** is a professional lighting designer for theater, film, opera, dance, and television, including twenty-eight seasons of the Eastman School of Music's Opera Theatre. His photos are also featured in the Quick Reference Guides to the Birds, Trees, and Wildflowers of New York and the Trees and Wildflowers of the Mid-Atlantic Region.

ACKNOWLEDGMENTS

If there's one thing we love about the work we do, it's the collaborative process that culminates in our books with Globe Pequot. We owe many thanks to the production team at GP including our editor, Sarah Parke, and all of the people who work so hard to produce beautiful books about amazing places. Our agent, Regina Ryan, always provides the wise counsel and solid direction that keeps our publishing career on track. We could not ask for a better team.

Finally, to the friends and family who cheer us on in our travels, we can't say enough about the value of your energy and enthusiasm to our work in the field, behind the camera, and in front of the computer screens. To Ken Horowitz, Rose-Anne Moore, Martha and Peter Schermerhorn, Ruth Watson, John King, Cindy Blair, Paula and Rich Landis, Martin Winer, Lisa Jaccoma, Kevin Hyde, Diane and Chris Hardy, Paul and Debbie Trivino, and all of the other people who look forward to our books and encourage us to keep driving, hiking, writing, and taking photos . . . we thank you so much for being there for us, and for being who you are.

Overview Map

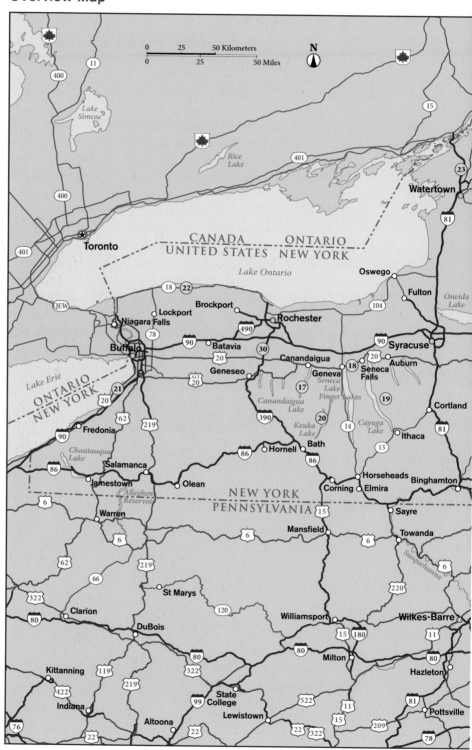

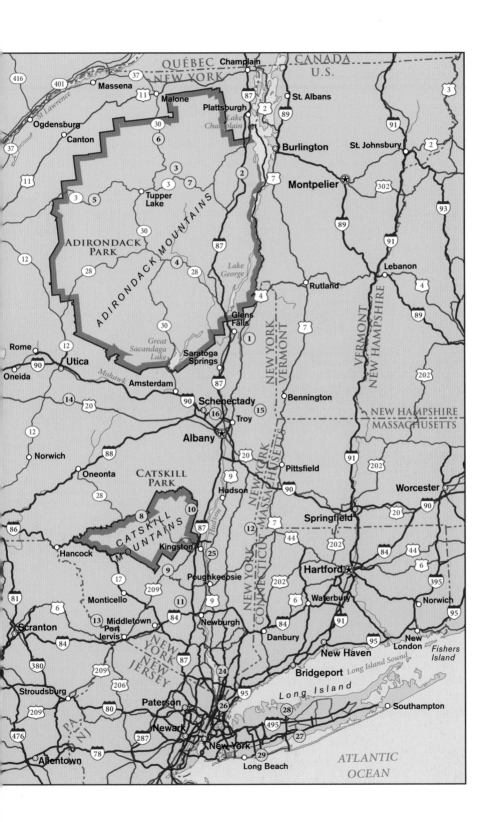

INTRODUCTION

I recently told a friend who lives near me in Rochester that I was working on a book on scenic drives in New York State. With absolute earnestness, she looked me in the eye and replied, "Scenic drives in New York? Are there any?"

So dominant and powerful is New York's reputation as an industrial and commercial center that even lifelong residents discount its natural features or claim ignorance of them altogether. These are the same people who will jump in a car and drive cross-country to see rolling green mountains in the mid-Atlantic states, seashores along the New England coast, or immense canyons out west, never knowing that such riches exist within a 2-hour drive of their own homes.

New York's bounty reaches well beyond the bustling metropolises of New York City, Buffalo, Rochester, Syracuse, and Albany. Scenic New York extends northward all the way to the St. Lawrence Seaway and its bridges to Canada, and southward through luscious forests and undulating mountains along the Hudson River and the Pennsylvania border. Its open farmlands cover 23 percent of the state, producing the second largest apple crop in the country—more than 29 million bushels annually—and 15 billion pounds of milk and dairy products every year, making New York the third largest dairy producer in the US. Even the most passionate wine connoisseurs may not know that New York is the nation's third largest wine producer, with award-winning wines in four prolific grape-growing regions. All of these fields, pastureland, and vineyards make for pastoral views just a few minutes away from the state's largest cities.

A Partner in Preservation

As a state with a history of overharvesting its natural resources, New York makes up for at least some of its past transgressions through its foresight in preserving two of its most spectacular scenic regions. Adirondack Park became a model for states across the country when New York created it in 1892, a move precipitated by 19th-century timber and mining companies' clear-cutting of forests and dumping of waste into waterways. The innovative approach the state took to restoring and preserving this land created the largest publicly protected area in the contiguous 48 states, a mass larger than Yellowstone, Everglades, Glacier, and Grand Canyon

Old churches and historic graveyards are scattered among New York's hillsides.

Extended views of upstate meadows are highlights of western New York.

National Parks combined. Today Adirondack Park's boundaries contain 6 million acres of land, more than 3 million of which is privately owned by individuals, families, and businesses who develop towns and industrial sites in concentrated areas to maintain massive tracts of wild land. The rest of the land—nearly 3 million acres—virtually bursts with natural beauty, offering views of forest-covered mountains, crystal lakes, towering waterfalls, secretive gorges, and seemingly endless rivers.

We have chosen a variety of driving routes through Adirondack Park to provide you with some of the best views in the state, including the 360-degree viewing area atop Whiteface Mountain, the fourth tallest mountain in the Adirondacks. You may find additional viewpoints and visual treasures by leaving the main roads and trolling down county and side roads throughout the park, but the routes we have selected will get your exploration off to a satisfying start.

Catskill Park, several hours south of the Adirondacks, accomplishes much the same task on a smaller scale and in the same way as Adirondack Park. The park protects 700,000 acres of public and private land, just over 287,000 of which are owned by the state as part of Catskill Forest Preserve. Another 5 percent belong to New York City to protect the water supply for the nation's largest metropolitan area, giving us wide views of calm water contained in the preserve's carefully maintained reservoirs.

You may recall that this region was once known as the "Borscht Belt," hosting some of the largest mountain resorts in the country and catering specifically to a Jewish clientele. By the 1970s, national civil rights laws had made it illegal to exclude Jews and other minorities from clubs and organizations, so the need for resorts like these diminished, and the fabulous hotels and restaurants eventually faded and closed their doors. The Catskills remain a favorite vacation area for anglers who seek the area's plentiful fishing, and they attract hikers who enjoy climbing above 3,500 feet on mountain trails—an altitude that does not steal your breath but provides miles of scenery in every direction. Gently winding roads follow the narrow valleys between the peaks, making for some of the loveliest scenic routes in the state.

What About the Interstate Highways?

New York State is blessed with several major cross-state highways that afford sweeping views of mountain ranges, lakes, farmland, and other exquisite areas, and we have driven all of these end to end in compiling the 30 routes in this book.

We chose not to include these in *Scenic Driving New York* for a simple reason: You don't need us to do so. These heavily trafficked roads—specifically I-87, I-81, and I-86 (NY 17)—are on most travelers' way across the state from north to south or across the Southern Tier from west to east. As limited-access roads, they do not provide the opportunity to wander through hamlets or drive up to the entrance of a park without leaving the route altogether.

We chose to introduce you to scenic routes you might not find on your own, from the tips of Long Island to the shores of Lakes Erie and Ontario. If you would prefer a scenic route that you can enjoy at 65 miles per hour, all of the interstate highways mentioned above will provide clear roads and plenty of gorgeous views just about any time of the year.

Wine

No book about New York State can be complete without prominent mention of the Finger Lakes, the long, sculpted crevasses gouged by the receding glaciers thousands of years ago and filled by their icy meltwater. Limned with hills that provide expansive views, often crowded with family cottages along their shorelines, and invariably laden with the fruit of the vine, lakes including Canandaigua, Seneca, Cayuga, and Keuka share their bounty along roads that curve to follow their lengthy banks.

The Adirondack Mountains in spring are a study in shades of green.

Driving along the Finger Lakes, on the shores of Lake Ontario, or on Long Island simply must include some stops to taste New York's extraordinary wines. We have endeavored to help you plan ahead and choose which wineries you will visit on each route. We do not provide reviews of the various wines, but we do offer a little information about what makes each winery unique or special, and which award-winning, don't-miss wines you should sample. Please remember that wine tasting does involve alcoholic beverages, so for heaven's sake, drink responsibly. Naming one person as your designated driver will allow you to enjoy New York's wine country safely.

Weather

Legendary for its winters, New York State enjoys the dubious honor of being one of the snowiest states in the country—and its western region is among the cloudiest. Only a few of the scenic routes in this book will remain passable during a snowstorm—and seriously, if you're going for a scenic drive in a snowstorm, what exactly do you expect to see? Check the weather forecast for the towns along your

Wild turkeys have become a common sight in New York's parks and fields.

planned route, and make your scenic drive on days when the meteorologist does not use words like "lake effect," "wind chill," and "significant accumulation." All of these routes offer the best scenery in spring, summer, and fall, with some of them inducing gasps of awe in autumn when the leaves turn crimson, orange, and gold.

Hurricane season has become a factor in planning a New York drive as well. Over the last several years, major storms in August and October have wiped out entire communities along the coastline, through the Catskills, and all the way up into the Adirondacks, making it even more important to check the forecast before you set out on a route. While Hurricane Irene and Superstorm Sandy were anomalies, climate change certainly sends more volatile weather into New York State more frequently. If high winds and rain will be factors on your planned day out, think about staying in.

How to Use This Book

Scenic Driving New York provides descriptions of 30 state and back road drives throughout the state. Each route description includes a map showing the route,

Weather can change in an instant in New York's mountain regions.

towns along the way, special features, campgrounds, historic sites, recreation areas, and other points of interest.

You also will find information at the beginning of each route description, delineated into the following categories:

General description provides a quick summary of the length, location, and scenic features of the route.

Special attractions are prominent, interesting activities and features found along the route. Additional attractions are included in the description.

Location gives the area of the state in which the route is located.

Route numbers include the specific highway names and numbers you will see as you drive.

Travel season notes whether the specific route is open all year or closed seasonally. Some highways are closed to automobiles in winter due to snow, but are open for snowshoeing, cross-country skiing, and snowmobiling. Always check local conditions before you travel.

Camping includes listings of all state park, state forest, and private campgrounds along the route.

Services lists communities with at least a restaurant, groceries, lodging, phone, and gasoline.

Nearby attractions are major attractions or activities found within 50 miles of the drive.

The route provides detailed traveler information, along with interesting regional history, geology, and natural history. Attractions are presented in the order a traveler encounters them when driving the route in the described direction. If you travel the route in the opposite direction, simply refer to the end of the route description first.

Your ice cream stop gives you a great place to pause for a treat. We have tried to find a provider of homemade or state-made ice cream on every route, though a couple of the back roads stumped us. As you might imagine, the research for this feature contributed to the fun of writing this book . . . and to our waistlines.

At the end of the book, **Appendix A: Sources of More Information** lists names and contact information of organizations that provide detailed information on each area and its attractions.

Appendix B: Guide to Roadside Wildflowers and Plants helps you identify the blossoms you will see along these routes throughout the spring, summer, and early fall.

Map Legend

Interstate Highway/
Featured Interstate Highway

US Highway/
Featured US Highway

Canada Autoroute

State Highway/
Featured State Highway

Paved Road/
Featured Paved Road

Visitor, Interpretive
Center

Bridge

Point of Interest

Mountain, Peak, or Butte

▲ Whiteface Mt.
4,867 ft.

Ferry Route

River, Creek, or Drainage

Reservoir or Lake

State Line/
International Line

UTAH

Small State Park, Wilderness
or Natural Area

Historic Site

Campground

National Park/
State Park

National Forest/
State Forest

Wilderness Area/
Wildlife Management Area

ADIRONDACK PARK
SCENIC DRIVES

Lakes to Locks Passage, Part 1

Waterford to Ticonderoga

General description: Everything you ever wanted to know about the eastern border waterways of New York State can be learned along this 183-mile drive, which we have divided into two parts for your convenience. In the first 85 miles, discover the Erie Canal, the Lake Champlain Canal, the Hudson River, and Lake George as you follow the path of the Great Northeast Journey on this analogous land route.

Special attractions: Erie Canal, Lake Champlain Canal, many canal locks, Peebles Island State Park, Saratoga National Battlefield Park, Fort Ticonderoga, Hancock House, LaChute River

Location: Along the northeast border between New York State and Vermont, from Waterford to Ticonderoga, NY

Route numbers: US 4, NY 22

Travel season: Spring, summer, and fall

Camping: Poke-O-Moonshine State Campground near Baldface Mountain, Ausable Point State Campground in Keesville, Rogers Rock Campground near Ticonderoga

Services: In Waterford, Glens Falls, Hudson Falls, Whitehall, Ticonderoga, Crown Point, Port Henry, Keesville, Plattsburgh

Nearby attractions: Whiteface Mountain, Santa's Workshop at North Pole, Adirondack mountain hiking, Lake George Battleground, Great Escape and Splashwater Kingdom near Glens Falls, Grant Cottage State Historic Site, National Bottle Museum in Ballston Spa, Saratoga Race Course

The Route

From the days of trading between Native American tribes to the era of canals that made New York State a central corridor for commerce, the northeastern state border has figured prominently in New York's history. What began as a handful of settlements soon became the lines of defense in the French and Indian Wars, the Revolutionary War, and the War of 1812—and once these conflicts were resolved, the pivot points became ports along a network of waterways including Lake Champlain, the Champlain Canal, and the Erie Canal.

   The transformation of New York State began with Elkanah Watson, a native of Massachusetts, who first proposed that the state's natural waterways could be connected by canals to create a continuous waterway to the Great Lakes. He brought his ideas to New York State Senator and General Philip Schuyler, and together they worked toward passage of an act to create a pair of canal corporations in 1792. A series of wars and other issues pushed the project back nearly 30 years, but the Champlain Canal finally opened in 1819, and the Erie Canal followed in

Lakes to Locks Passage, Part 1: Waterford to Ticonderoga

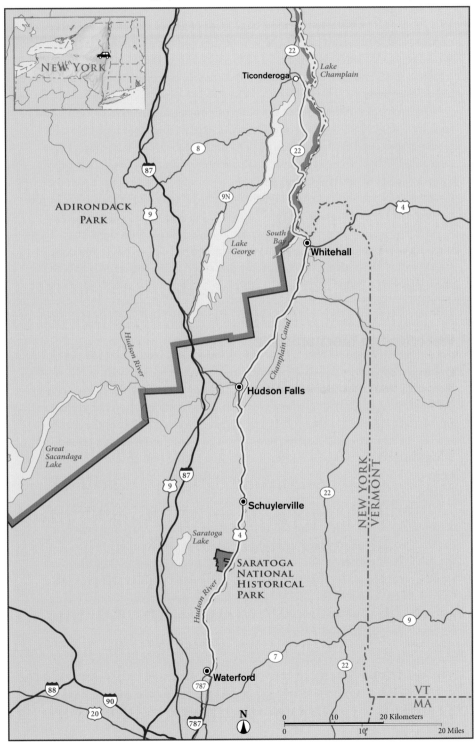

NEW YORK

Ticonderoga

Lake Champlain

22

8

22

87

9N

9

ADIRONDACK
PARK

Lake
George

South
Bay

Whitehall

4

Hudson River

Champlain Canal

Hudson Falls

Great
Sacandaga
Lake

87

9

Saratoga
Lake

22

Schuylerville

NEW YORK
VERMONT

4

SARATOGA
NATIONAL
HISTORICAL
PARK

Hudson River

9

88

90

20

787

7

22

Waterford

VT
MA

N

0   10   20 Kilometers

0   10   20 Miles

1825, making it possible to transport large loads of grains, minerals, and other goods to and from ocean ports in New York City, mines and timber companies in the Adirondacks and New England, and the agricultural fields and mills of central New York. The state became the nation's most prosperous commercial center almost overnight.

Today, thanks to the work of the nonprofit organization Lakes To Locks Passage, Inc., you can follow this scenic byway to explore the panoramic vistas, the hidden history, and the modern attractions of this network of waterways. Beginning at the visitor center in Waterford, this route travels along two-lane roads to towns you may never have heard of, tracing the route of the Hudson River, the Champlain Canal, and Lake Champlain and stretching up all the way to the border between the US and Canada.

We recommend that you plan a weekend for this drive, slowing your pace and stopping overnight in a lovely country town or two as you go. While you certainly can drive this 183-mile route in a day, the low speed limits and many sights will make you want to linger, especially if you're exploring history as well as enjoying the views.

Waterford to Mechanicville

(See more on Waterford in Route 16: Mohawk Towpath Scenic Byway.)
Stop at the **Waterford Harbor Visitor Center,** now shared by the Erie Canalway National Heritage Corridor, where you'll find lots of information about the canal and ways to make the most of your Erie Canal experience. Here at the confluence of the Mohawk and Hudson Rivers, you also will find **Peebles Island State Park,** which provides an excellent 3-mile hiking trail around the island for views of both rivers and the swells and rapids that make this place particularly striking.

The large factory buildings on Peebles Island once housed Cluett, Peabody & Company, at one time the largest manufacturer of men's shirts and collars in the US. Owner Sanford Cluett invented a process for pre-shrinking the cloth with which men's shirts were made, and this "Sanforizing" process made him a very wealthy man. In the 1940s, Cluett, Peabody became the world's largest manufacturer of shirts . . . but in the 1960s, changes in mass production manufacturing processes drove down profits until the company closed in 1972. Peebles Island became a park the following year.

Peebles Island draws outdoor recreation enthusiasts.

As you leave Peebles Island, turn left onto US 4 north. Watch for the **Waterford Public Library** in the old Delaware and Hudson Railroad Depot at 117 3rd St. If you'd like to know more about local history, the **Waterford Historical Museum** in an 1830 homestead at the first intersection of the Cohoes-Waterford Bridge (NY 32) provides permanent exhibitions on a city and its relationship with its two rivers, as well as a Victorian period room and a model of Champlain Canal Lock 4.

Continue up US 4 north and see the **Champlain Canal**—here in the form of the Hudson River—come into view on your right as you enter Saratoga County. Pass the massive Momentive plants, where an assortment of resins and silicones are made for manufacturing use, and watch for Lock 1 of the Champlain Canal. You will see a total of 11 locks on this canal as you drive north, though they are numbered 1–9 and 11–12, with no lock 10—the planned lock turned out to be unnecessary, so it was never constructed.

From here to Fort Edward, eight locks raise boats a total of 126 feet, making it possible to move up the river around the 130-foot drop at Hudson Falls. Locks 9–12 then lower boats 43 feet to meet the level of Lake Champlain. The first six of these locks work as part of a system of features including dams, spillways, and hydroelectric plants, making them distinctly different from the five locks that follow them. If you are thinking of taking a boat up the canal just to see how the locks work, you will have the opportunity to observe this heavy industrial machinery in action.

Mechanicville may seem like a sleepy town today, but it once boomed as a center for paper manufacturing, producing 1.5 million tons of paper and 800,000 tons of pulp every year at the turn of the 20th century. Recovering from the Great Depression to become the largest producer of white paper in the US by 1937, Westvaco (which bought out the local paper company in the early 1900s) survived World War II and a series of union strikes. Eventually, however, the clear-cutting of the Adirondack forests took its toll: The company began to run out of the natural resources it needed to make paper, at the same time that the war in Vietnam and the lure of college education filtered out many of the young men who might have followed their fathers into the plant. Westvaco closed its doors abruptly in 1971.

Stillwater to Schuylerville

If you're a history buff, the name of Stillwater, NY, should be familiar: This is where the Battle of Saratoga took place, turning the tide of the Revolutionary War in the Americans' favor. Here you can learn about 1770s lifestyles at the **Stillwater**

This replica of a Revolutionary War blockhouse was built in 1927.

Blockhouse and Visitor Center, a re-created blockhouse—a single building in which townspeople gathered to shield themselves against the enemy—in which you'll find a small museum. In addition to displays about Stillwater in the time of the Revolution, the blockhouse offers peaceful views of the Hudson River, a walking path, and benches and picnic tables if you've brought your lunch. You may find costumed interpreters demonstrating daily colonial activities on special days throughout the summer, or soldiers in period dress completing military drills. Don't forget to stop at the gift shop, the proceeds from which support the National Park Service.

Once you have a feeling for the role the Revolution played in the lives of 18th-century Stillwater residents, it's time to move on to the main event: **Saratoga National Historical Park.** Here American artillery on Bemis Heights blocked the advance of General John Burgoyne and the British army. Burgoyne had chosen to risk everything on a push to Albany despite one setback after another on his way there. Brilliant engineering of the fortifications at Bemis Heights by Colonel Thaddeus Kosciuszko, a Polish military engineer, made the heights virtually impenetrable. In the battles that ensued on September 19 and October 7, 1777, Burgoyne would lose more than 1,200 men, while the Americans lost fewer than 500. The British attacked and withdrew several times while arriving troops reinforced the American forces. When the British retreated on October 8, the swelled American army followed, surrounding the enemy with nearly 17,000 men. Burgoyne and his 6,000 men finally surrendered on October 17—and with this victory, Americans knew they had begun to win the war.

At this National Park Service site, you can drive through the battlefield and listen to the narration of the battle on your mobile phone (call 518-665-8185, and enter the number of the tour stop you've reached), or you can choose to walk the fields on one of several meticulously maintained trails. Whichever way you select to enjoy the park, make a point of pausing at Stop 9 on the battlefield trail for one of the best views of the Hudson River you will see anywhere along the river's length.

Before you move on, pay a visit to two additional Saratoga battle stops. The first is the **country estate of General Philip Schuyler**—the same Schuyler who became Alexander Hamilton's father-in-law when Hamilton married his daughter, Elizabeth. Schuyler served his country admirably by assisting in the transport of supplies to the troops, though he began the war as the third in command under General George Washington. After the Americans lost Fort Ticonderoga (more on that shortly), Congress relieved Schuyler of command, and he faced further hardship when his home and farm were destroyed in the British retreat from Saratoga. Schuyler rebuilt his much plainer home that fall.

The view of the Hudson River from Saratoga National Battlefield is one of the best in New York.

Gerald B. H. Solomon Saratoga National Cemetery is worth a stop as well. From US 4 in Schuylerville, turn left onto Wilbur Road and continue to Duell Road; turn right onto Duell Road and drive to the cemetery. Dedicated in 2002, this is the resting place of servicemen and women from the northeastern US who served in the wars of the 20th and 21st centuries, most of whom lived out their natural lives. This is a peaceful, beautiful, and strangely empty place, where today's veterans may one day receive their last respects.

When you're ready, continue north on US 4. When you reach the town of Schuylerville, there's one more stop to make: **Saratoga Monument,** on the spot where General Burgoyne actually surrendered to US General Horatio Gates. It's at the Prospect Hill cemetery, where the monument was erected in stages from 1877 through 1912, and finally dedicated on the 135th anniversary of the British surrender. If you visit when the 154-foot-tall monument is open, you can climb 188 steps to the top and enjoy several levels of bas-relief plaques, brass moldings, stained glass, and other tributes to the American victory.

Schuylerville to Kingsbury

Head north on US 4 to Northumberland, then bear right on US 4 toward Greenwich and Hudson Falls. Cross the Hudson River and enter Washington County, and watch for the signs for **Denton Wildlife Sanctuary.** This Nature Conservancy property offers several walking trails through woods and wetland, from which you may see and hear quite a list of nesting and migrating birds. Local wildflowers carpet the ground in spring and early summer, and wet weather can produce a wide variety of fascinating fungi.

Here you can see a section of the original Champlain Canal, to the right (east) of the road, and the Hudson River on the left (west) side. Pull-offs along the road give you the opportunity to get a better view of the canal, which is now a passageway for pleasure boats instead of major freight.

As you approach the town of Fort Edward, **Oliva Vineyards** comes into view, a fairly young winery that shares its land with the owner's other passion: racehorses. The 150-acre property includes stables for Tony Oliva's horses, some of which have won races at Belmont, Aqueduct, Monmouth Park, and Philadelphia Park. The winery produces varietals including its popular Sparkling Hannah, a red wine with bowl-of-fruit flavor. The tasting room, open on weekends, offers a six-wine flight of samples for each guest.

Lock 6 of the Champlain Canal appears in Fort Edward, as does the location of the **Duer House,** the headquarters of the British army for 3 weeks in August and September 1777 during the Revolutionary War. The house is long gone, but a blue and yellow historical marker recognizes its location. The fort that once stood here did not withstand the test of time either, but stories of the war pervade this area and pop up on signs or in street names, barely hinting at the drama and intrigue behind them.

One such story tells a gruesome tale of young Jane McCrea, who was 25 years old and engaged to a soldier in British General John Burgoyne's army when she was captured in Fort Edward by Native Americans serving under Burgoyne. The natives apparently believed they could collect a reward for her capture, perhaps not realizing that she was a Loyalist. Eyewitness accounts differ, but one suggests that later the same day, Miss McCrea's soldier fiancé saw one of the natives carrying her scalp, while another purports that she was killed by an American's bullet during a skirmish. Whatever the truth may be, McCrea's body was interred in the Union Cemetery just north of Fort Edward—though grave robbers exhumed and distributed some of her remains, deeming them somehow holy.

Visit Prospect Hill Cemetery in Schuylerville to see this monument.

US 4 takes you right through Fort Edward, where a marker at the **Anvil Inn,** a former 1840 blacksmith's shop, denotes the site of the northeast bastion of the original fort. To get a sense of the fort's perimeter, turn right onto Old Fort Street and watch for another marker in a resident's yard, noting the location of the old moat. Continue to the dead end on this street to see the site of the fort itself, noted by a plaque on a boulder past a white rail fence. (The adjacent land is privately owned.)

Finally, the **Old Fort House Museum** on US 4 looks at a resident named Patrick Smyth and his family, as they settled into life in the colonies in the 1770s. Built using timbers taken from the ruins of Fort Edward, the house's strategic location made it ripe for takeover, so it became a headquarters for generals from both sides of the Revolutionary War. General George Washington had dinner here twice in 1783. Today five buildings on the property include an 1840s tollhouse from the Plank Road, including the toll collector's living quarters, a one-room schoolhouse, and the Cronkhite Pavilion from the Washington County Fairgrounds, which houses displays on the history of the Fort Edward area.

Back on US 4, you'll spot Lock 8 as you leave the town of Fort Edward and head north through Hudson Falls on your way to Kingsbury. A slender canal running parallel to the Hudson River may catch your eye; this is the **Glens Falls Feeder Canal,** which originates in the city of Glens Falls west of Hudson Falls. Built in 1822 and widened and deepened in 1832, the 7-mile canal transports water from above Glens Falls to the highest point on the Champlain Canal, keeping the canal filled with enough water to transport barges and other boats through the locks. While other forms of transportation eliminated the need for the Champlain Canal as a shipping lane in the early 1900s, the feeder canal still supplies the Finch Paper LLC with water and hydroelectric power for its operations. If you'd like to know more about this canal, make a side trip to Glens Falls to see the massive dam and power plant.

Kingsbury to Whitehall

Pastureland and dairy farms provide wide views of eastern New York State as you continue through Kingsbury and proceed north. Lock 11 appears in the town of Fort Ann, but you won't see any of the forts that stood here during the late 1600s and throughout the 1700s, as each of these was destroyed when it was no longer useful, to keep it from falling into enemy hands. The French established a stronghold here in 1689, and the English colonized this area and held it fast in the 1750s during the French and Indian War. In 1777 the Battle of Fort Anne took place here during the Saratoga Campaign—which ended in American victory, driving the British army out of the area. Today this quiet town hosts the Washington State Correctional Facility.

Cropland, pastures, and views of the distant Adirondack Mountains guide you from Fort Ann along US 4 to Whitehall, where you will bear right to get to the historic waterfront. Don't miss the castle-like **Whitehall Armory,** built in 1899, which now houses the Whitehall Athletic Club. If you're touring the state on its scenic roads, you may recognize the similarities in design and architecture between armories across New York. This is more than coincidence—one designer, Isaac Perry, supervised the construction of 27 armories in New York, using the medieval gothic style made popular in the 1800s in New York City. Not many buildings in the US sport the crenelated parapets, iron portcullises, and molded terra-cotta cartouches you'll see on this grand structure.

Turn left before the bridge on US 4 to reach the waterfront and the **Whitehall State Heritage Area,** where a 19th-century main street and a canal-side park give you the opportunity to take in the northern terminus of the Champlain Canal.

Here at 1 Saunders St., the **Skenesborough Museum and Heritage Area Visitor Center** tells the story of Whitehall's important role in the development of the US military. Whitehall was the official birthplace of the US Navy, where shipbuilders designed and constructed the Valcour Fleet of ships that became the first American vessels to be used in military combat. Racing against time for control of Lake Champlain, the new Americans constructed enough ships to confront the British fleet in the Battle of Valcour in October 1776, off the shore of Valcour Island in the lake. Led by General Benedict Arnold, the American navy lost the battle, but they did enough damage to the British ships that they forced the British to delay their advance by water until 1777.

The museum building itself is a 1917 reinforced concrete canal terminal, which was rescued from demolition by the Historical Society of Whitehall in 1959 and pressed into service as a visitor center. Here you can view artifacts, see a diorama of the shipyard that built the first US Navy fleet, and pick up information about the 20-minute walking tour past historic buildings and monuments. The original hull of the USS *Ticonderoga*, a ship built for the War of 1812, is here outside of the museum.

If you hear a noon whistle from the fire department up the street, it's time to head up Skene Mountain for lunch at **Skene Manor.** The striking stone castle sits atop a crest along the east shoreline of the Hudson River, and it was built in the late 1800s for New York State Supreme Court Judge Joseph H. Potter. Now a restaurant open for lunches and tours, the house was constructed using gray sandstone quarried from Skene Mountain. Its colorful past includes a long string of owners, a bogus legend about a body interred in a basement coffin, an on-again, off-again restaurant business, and a preservation project that landed the building on the National Register of Historic Places. You are welcome to visit to enjoy the Victorian gothic style of the place.

Here the Champlain Canal ends at Lock 12, just north of Whitehall, and it's the end of our tour of US 4 as well. From Whitehall, follow NY 22 north.

Whitehall to Ticonderoga

Cross Lake Champlain and begin to follow its western shore as you head north on NY 22. In a few minutes, you'll see a sign welcoming you into **Adirondack Park,** the largest park and the largest state-protected area in the 48 contiguous.

More than 6 million acres—about the size of the state of Vermont—Adirondack Park contains all or parts of 12 counties, though more than 50 percent of the land within the "Blue Line" is privately owned. When the park was established in 1892, the legislation that created it stated that no more land within the boundary line (shown in blue on most maps) could be sold or leased. State-owned land within the boundaries will be protected in perpetuity, keeping millions of acres of wilderness area from being logged or mined to the point of becoming an eroded wasteland.

Today about 130,000 people actually live within the Blue Line throughout the year, with another 70,000 swelling the population in the summer months. Many of these people own land in the park. The mix of private and public land and the large population of year-round residents make this park more like a national forest, in which residential and commercial use can coexist with protected wilderness and indigenous plants and animals. Adirondack Park was the first state preserve of its kind in the US, and this has earned the entire park the designation of National Historic Landmark, although it has a "Watch" threat level according to National Park Service standards. Acid rain, global climate change, invasive species, and pockets of development throughout the park have drawn federal attention to the park and the factors that may damage its ecological integrity.

None of this dampens the effect of seeing the Adirondacks firsthand, however, and your drive into these mountains—on this and a number of other scenic routes

The original hull of the USS Ticonderoga *is at the Skenesborough Museum.*

in this book—will be filled with spectacular mountain views, winding roads, gorgeous fall foliage, innumerable waterways, and the kind of peace and quiet most New Yorkers consider unobtainable within the state.

From the park boundary to Ticonderoga, it's 25 miles of sheer scenery. Heavily forested mountains turn crimson and gold in fall and offer a monochromatically green spectacle in spring and summer, and glimpses of Lake Champlain come into view to the east, framed by foliage and short bursts of civilization. This continues until the town of Ticonderoga greets you with a wider and more panoramic view of the lake.

Restaurants have been few and far between on this road for some time, so if you're ready for a quick lunch or dinner, we recommend the **Wagon Wheel Diner,** where the french fries are handmade and the post-and-beam dining room reflects the cozy Adirondack atmosphere you will experience as you go farther north. Be sure to leave room for pie, especially if they're serving French silk—a dense chocolate confection with a thick layer of real whipped cream.

If you grew up anywhere in New York State, chances are good that you came to **Fort Ticonderoga** as a child with your parents, your summer camp, or your

Farmland dominates the lowlands east of the Adirondacks.

scout troop. The fort you see here is a reconstruction of the original 18th-century Fort Carillon, built by the French to guard this narrow point in Lake Champlain during the French and Indian War. Fortified to last through the Revolutionary War as well, the renamed Fort Ticonderoga saw action in 1775 when the American militia known as the Green Mountain Boys took it from the British in a surprise attack. Conflict arose again in June 1777, when General John Burgoyne and the British army took the fort back from the Americans. The Americans tried to take it back again in September 1777, but their attack failed—though they didn't have to wait long to seize it at last in October 1777, when Burgoyne and his men abandoned it after their defeat at Saratoga.

In the early 1900s, the Pell family—who bought the fort in 1820—restored it to its 1775 style and created a foundation to care for it and operate it as a tourist attraction. Today the fort has a place on the National Register of Historic Places, and it welcomes visitors from mid-May to mid-October.

While you're in the village of Ticonderoga, don't miss the stunning **Lachute Falls,** just off Montcalm Street on the Lachute River—a falls that played a role in preventing the British from advancing too quickly on the fort. You'll also find the **Hancock House,** a replica of the home of John Hancock's uncle in Boston, constructed specifically to serve as a headquarters and museum for the New York State Historical Association.

Ticonderoga village offers several pleasantly appointed motels, the Sugar & Spice Country Shoppe, and a number of restaurants and shops for your browsing pleasure. This is a good place to get gas, too, as the opportunities become fewer and more expensive as you go north.

2

Lakes to Locks Passage, Part 2

Crown Point to Rouses Point

General description: Continue your adventure along the eastern border waterways of New York State on the remaining 97 miles of the Lakes to Locks Passage. Discover Lake Champlain and seminal moments of the Revolutionary War, the French and Indian War, and the War of 1812.

Special attractions: Crown Point State Historic Site, Lake George, Adsit Log Cabin, Ausable Chasm, Battle of Plattsburgh Interpretive Center, Valcour Island State Park, Point Au Roche State Park, Rouses Point Overlook

Location: Along the northeast border between New York State and Vermont, from Crown Point to Rouses Point, NY

Route numbers: NY 22, US 9, NY 98

Travel season: Spring, summer, and fall

Camping: Crown Point State Campground in Crown Point, Lincoln Pond Campground near Mineville/Wesport (on I-87), Champlain Park State Campground north of Plattsburgh

Services: In Crown Point, Port Henry, Keesville, Plattsburgh

Nearby attractions: High Peaks Scenic Byway, Whiteface Mountain, Santa's Workshop at North Pole, Adirondack mountain hiking, Grant Cottage State Historic Site

The Route

Continue your discovery of the early days of New York State along this border route, following along the sparkling Lake Champlain through small towns that played key roles in the state's and the nation's history.

Crown Point to Willsboro

The hamlet of Crown Point comes up quickly after Ticonderoga, affording you some terrific views of Lake Champlain as you come into town. You will want to head out to the point for your best view yet of this lake and the bridge to Vermont, but there's one stop you should make in town first.

Penfield Homestead sits on 500 acres of farmland and has few neighbors, but it holds an important place in history: The homestead was the first in the US to use electricity in an industrial process, way back in 1831. How this farmhouse in the Ironville neighborhood of upstate New York received this honor is not as big a mystery as it may seem. Ironville was the site of an iron ore separating

Lakes to Locks Passage, Part 2: Crown Point to Rouses Point

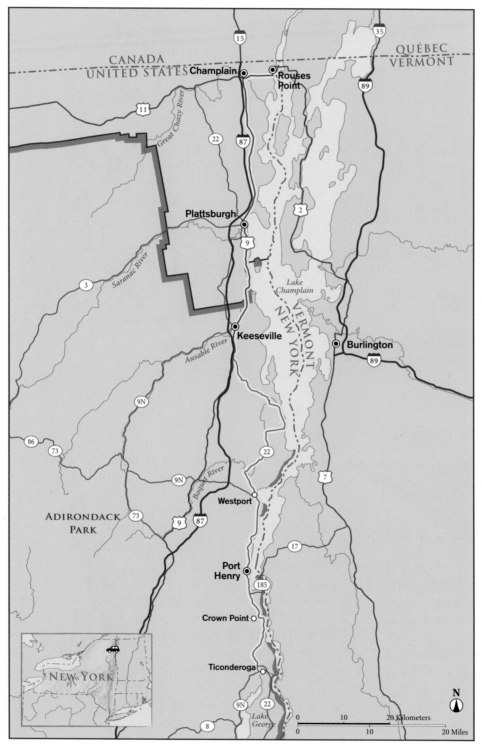

operation, taking the ore mined down the road in Hammondville and separating it from other materials before putting it on the train to Lake Champlain for use in shipbuilding. The ore separation process used heat to make the stone let go of the iron, and then a sluicing process to wash away the rock and gather the iron in the bottom of the trough. This time-consuming, often wasteful process resulted in a lot of iron washing away with the rock and dirt. The Penfield family, who ran the Ironville separating operation, replaced the heat and water with electromagnetism, pulling the iron away from the nonmagnetic dirt using a system of rotating magnetic bars. The Penfields harvested more iron from the dirt in less time than the old process required, earning them a page in history.

Head back to NY 22, which joins NY 9N in Crown Point, and go north until you see the signs for NY 185 and the bridge to Vermont. Take this road to visit **Crown Point State Historic Site** and the **Champlain Monument and Lighthouse,** as well as the **Lake Champlain Bridge to Vermont.** Here at the state historic site, you'll find ruins of French and British forts, as well as a museum that reveals the history of the French, British, and American periods in this lakeside settlement.

On the lakeshore, the Champlain Monument and Lighthouse honors Samuel D. Champlain, who was the first European to find his way to the lake that would eventually bear his name. A French explorer, Champlain is recognized here with a sculpture by French artist Auguste Rodin, a gift to the US from France in celebration of the 300th anniversary of Champlain's accomplishment in 1909. From here, you can enjoy expansive views of the lake from land, or you can walk or drive over the Lake Champlain Bridge to Vermont, where a visitor center offers some interesting information about the lake's geology and history.

The hands-down best way to view the lake is from the middle of the bridge, so I highly recommend that you walk at least halfway across on the bridge's wide pedestrian walkway. The brand-new, 2,184-foot bridge opened in November 2011, replacing the bridge built in 1929. This is one of only two opportunities you will have to cross into Vermont over the lake on foot or by car—there's only one other bridge over Lake Champlain, and it's all the way up at Rouses Point, just before the Canadian border.

When you're ready, return to NY 22/9N and continue north along the lake to Port Henry, where you'll find more information about New York's history as an iron ore mining center. The **Railroad and Mining Heritage Park** features a converted carriage house that serves as a museum, telling the story of iron ore mining and its relationship with the railroad. The development of the Moriah Railroad

Walk or drive across the Lake Champlain Bridge to Vermont.

here dramatically reduced the cost and the time of transporting iron ore to manufacturing operations throughout the region, making iron mining a boom industry for more than a century. The ability to transport more iron more quickly spurred the Moriah iron company to build additional blast furnaces here at Cedar Point, until they could produce 250 tons of pig iron per day.

Take time to enjoy the lovely views of the lakes, farmland, and forests along the road from Port Henry to Westport, where NY 22 and NY 9N split. Stay on NY 22 as you head toward Wadhams, and watch for a waterfall on your left as you cross a bridge there. North of Wadhams, more woods close in around you as the road begins to climb. The next waterway you cross is the **Boquet River,** a signal that you're entering the township of Essex.

Watch for an octagonal stone building with a bell tower in the center of its roof. This **octagonal schoolhouse** was constructed in 1827 and is now listed on the National Register of Historic Places. So is the **Essex Village Historic District,** where 150 different buildings constructed from 1793 to somewhere around 1853 demonstrate the kinds of building materials and styles of the original town center. Most of these buildings are privately owned and not open to the public, but it's worth driving around town to see some of this striking architecture and the progression of styles from oldest to newer.

You'll notice that the homes you pass as you continue north to Willsboro definitely reveal a more upscale residential population, many of them with views of Lake Champlain. The most interesting thing in this town, however, is the **Willsboro Fishway,** a route that fish swimming upstream to spawn can take to get around the man-made dam and waterfall that block their way. You can follow a wooden walkway next to the fish ladder to see the fish leaping upstream in season, or watch through windows as they make their way upriver from lower levels. Nearby, the **Willsboro Heritage Center & Museum** in the former Champlain National Bank building provides a glimpse into life in this lakeside village and the role it has played in area industry and commerce.

Willsboro to Plattsburgh

North of Willsboro, settlement becomes less and less prevalent and you no longer see cropland or pastures; here in the northeastern corner of New York State, the scent of pine fills the air and the dense forests shade your windshield. It's a bit of a shock, then, when the industrial section of the town of Keesville begins. Hold on, however, and cross the Ausable River, and you're back to Adirondack views as **Ausable Chasm,** one of the most popular attractions in the Adirondacks, pops up just a mile down the road.

The Willsboro Fishway helps fish travel upstream to spawn.

Just the name of this place conjures up images of high stone walls, winding trails, narrow passages, 500-million-year-old rock faces, mysterious caves, and gently flowing waters. That's exactly what Irishman William Gilliland discovered in 1765 when he took a boat up the west shore of Lake Champlain and glided into this almost mystical place on the Ausable River. Hearing of his discovery, settlers soon followed to make the most of the dependable waterpower and the abundant Atlantic salmon that swam up the river to spawn within the gorge. Mills, lumber industry operations, iron ore mining and processing, and nail manufacturing moved into the area to take advantage of its bountiful natural resources—all powered by Horseshoe and Rainbow Falls, the two waterfalls you can see from the bridge over the river without going through the entrance gate.

Today it's easy to enjoy all of the wonders of this remarkable gorge. In particular, the Upper Chasm guided hiking tour takes you on the route of the trail that was destroyed on January 18 and 19, 1996, when more than 4.5 inches of rain fell on a 45-inch snowpack and caused massive flooding in Clinton County. (The same trail got walloped again in August 2011, when Hurricane Irene dropped more

The Adirondack Mountains come into view as you drive north.

than 10 inches of rain on the area.) The hike leads you behind the mists of Rainbow Falls and through a number of other landmarks within the chasm, including Devil's Oven Cave and the ruins of the horseshoe nail factory. If you need a break from driving the back roads of New York's North Country, this place provides just the right change of pace.

When you're ready to drive on, leave NY 22 and begin to follow US 9 North. Cross the Little Ausable River and continue north to the **Peru Dock Boat Launch.** Stop here for a moment to view **Valcour Island,** where you can see a lighthouse built in 1874. This is the Valcour Island we discussed earlier, where the very first battle between the fledgling US Navy and the professional British naval force took place in 1776. The Americans lost the battle rather spectacularly against the far better armed British, but General Benedict Arnold managed to sneak his ships past the British fleet under cover of night and start their journey southward. The British caught up, however, and captured or burned several of the American ships.

In the end, the American navy slowed the British fleet's progress southward, gaining some advantage that helped them prepare for the eventual victory at Saratoga.

Continuing north, cross the Salmon River and arrive in Plattsburgh, the largest city on this drive and a great place to stop for a meal, a snack, a walk, or even for the night. The trendy downtown area offers a good selection of restaurants, including our favorite: **Irises Cafe and Wine Bar,** a bistro with cloth napkins, creative specials, and a contemporary take on pasta, seafood, steaks, and poultry dishes. The ample wine list may have just what you're craving after a long day's drive.

Here in the center of town, you'll see a 135-foot-tall, gray obelisk adjacent to a park by the Saranac River. This is the **MacDonough Monument,** commemorating the victory of Commodore Thomas MacDonough—known locally as "the hero of Lake Champlain"—in the August 1814 Battle of Plattsburgh. In his first-ever battle as commander of a sailing vessel under fire, MacDonough pulled off a brilliant maneuver against the HMS *Confiance*, gaining the advantage by swinging his own ship, the USS *Saratoga*, around the British flagship and firing a broadside that caused enough damage to force the opposing captain to surrender. The British navy retreated to Canada, relinquishing any territory they held in that region of the US.

The MacDonough Monument serves as the focal point for a very pleasant little park with paved walkways along the lake. This is part of the **Heritage Trail Riverwalk** that also leads to the **Kent-Delord House,** a 1797 home that now serves as a museum with a magnificent garden; and City Hall, where you'll find the **Battle of Plattsburgh Interpretive Center** on the second floor if you'd like to know more about Commodore MacDonough's impressive 1814 victory.

YOUR ICE CREAM STOP: HARRIGAN'S SOFT ICE CREAM

It really says something about an ice cream parlor when the customers rave about its vanilla flavor, so try this purest of all flavors—maybe with scrumptious hot fudge—at this seasonal stop on NY 3 in Plattsburgh. Creamy soft-serve embellished with a wide variety of toppings, including unusual ones like blackberry and peanut brittle crunch, makes summer visitors return to this store night after night for a frozen treat. Try an extra-thick milk shake or a "hurricane" with your choice of candy mix-ins. If you're watching calories, Harrigan's offers a variety of Dole Whip flavors as well.

Plattsburgh's marina is a key port for Lake Champlain travelers.

Plattsburgh to Rouses Point

The last stretch of Lakes to Lock Passage crosses through more coniferous forest to the farthest reaches of the state. Just north of Plattsburgh, **Elfs Farm Winery & Cider Mill** provides an introduction to Cumberland Head, a peninsula that separates Cumberland Bay from Treadwell Bay in Lake Champlain. A cider mill before it was a winery, Elfs Farm produces apple wines that began winning gold medals in competitions in their first season. Its grape wines and other fruit varieties are turning heads as well.

Continuing north, **Point Au Roche State Park** provides a retreat into nature after a long series of museums and historic sites, offering 6 miles of Lake Champlain shoreline as well as forest, marshland, and lots of habitat for birds and other wildlife. A nature center here can help you choose a trail to walk or an area to explore, or you may want to walk the sandy beach and enjoy the views of the lake away from the roads and bridges you've encountered since you began this adventure.

In the town of Chazy, you'll spot the **Alice T. Miner Museum** right on US 9, a 15-room Colonial home that contains the collection of the wife of William H. Miner, a native of New York's North Country who made his fortune in railroad draft gear in Chicago in the 19th century. Alice Miner collected American artifacts, paintings, furniture, textiles, and much more, and she and William purchased this building to house her collection and share it with the general public. The museum opened in 1924 and includes period rooms and more than 4,000 objects.

Keep an eye out for **Amazing Grace Vineyard & Winery** as you pass through Chazy. Cold-hardy Northern varietal grapes are the specialty here in the North Country, so you'll find a series of crisp, dry, or semisweet white wines, semi-dry reds, and even a semisweet Concord and a bold peach dessert wine.

The last push to Rouses Point follows the Lake Champlain lakeshore to the last bridge from New York to Vermont, where marinas dominate the coastline and one notable landmark stands out: the remains of a fort built on the shoreline in 1816. Through an unfortunate miscalculation on the part of the surveying team, construction of this American fort took place about three-quarters of a mile north of the US-Canadian border. When officials discovered the error, all work on the never-named fort ceased, and locals began to refer to it as **"Fort Blunder."** They scavenged a great deal of the gray stone material used to construct the fort, repurposing the materials in their own homes, so very little went to waste. You can see the remaining two bastions of what is now known as Fort Montgomery, and the remains are listed in the National Register of Historic Places.

When you reach the bridge to Vermont, your Lakes to Locks Passage journey has come to an end. If you're heading across the state to the west from here, consider taking NY 3 from Plattsburgh through the heart of the Adirondacks (Route 3 in this book).

3

New York Route 3

Plattsburgh to Tupper Lake to Blue Mountain Lake

General description: This 71-mile drive through the Alder Brook Mountains and the Saranac Lakes Wild Forest crosses some of the most dramatic country in northern New York.

Special attractions: Saranac Lake, Long Lake, Blue Mountain Lake, Saranac River, Six Nations Indian Museum, shopping in Saranac Lake, Wild Center Natural History Museum of the Adirondacks, Raquette Pond, Tupper Lake, John Dillon Park, Buttermilk Falls in Deerland, Adirondack Experience, Adirondack Lakes Center for the Arts

Location: From Plattsburgh in the northeastern corner of the state through the center of Adirondack Park

Route numbers: NY 3, NY 28N/30

Travel season: Late spring, summer, and early fall

Camping: Plattsburgh and Shady Oaks RV Parks in Plattsburgh, Baker's Acres Campground in Saranac, Little Wolf Campground in Tupper Lake, Saranac Lake Islands and Fish Creek Pond Campgrounds in Saranac Lake, Rollins Ponds State Campground in Saranac Lake, Buck Pond in Saranac Lake, Blue Jay Campground in Tupper Lake, Forked Lakes and Lake Eaton State Campgrounds in Long Lake, International Paper John Dillon Park in Long Lake (fully accessible to the handicapped), Hide-A-Way Campsite on Long Lake, Hoss's Country Campground in Long Lake, Lake Durant State Campground in Blue Mountain Lake

Services: In Plattsburgh, Saranac Lake, Tupper Lake, Long Lake, and Blue Mountain Lake; scattered service stations and convenience stores along the route

Nearby attractions: Ausable Chasm, Loon Lake, Buck Pond, Lake Kushaqua, Whiteface Mountain Ski Center, High Falls Gorge, Santa's Workshop, US Olympic Training Center, John Brown Farm State Historic Site

The Route

Straight through the heart of the Adirondacks and along the edges of the High Peaks Region, this route includes a segment of the Adirondack Scenic Byway as it meets several of the park's most famous and popular lakes. Beginning in Plattsburgh on the outskirts of Adirondack Park (see the details of this city in Route 2), the road traces the ridge of the Alder Brook Mountains in the northeastern Adirondacks, a region with tangy-scented coniferous forests, clear mountain lakes, and merrily burbling rivers.

Plattsburgh to Saranac Lake

From the main mercantile district on the west side of Plattsburgh, take NY 3 west through a residential area and out into a forested corridor beyond the city. This

New York Route 3: Plattsburgh to Tupper Lake to Blue Mountain Lake

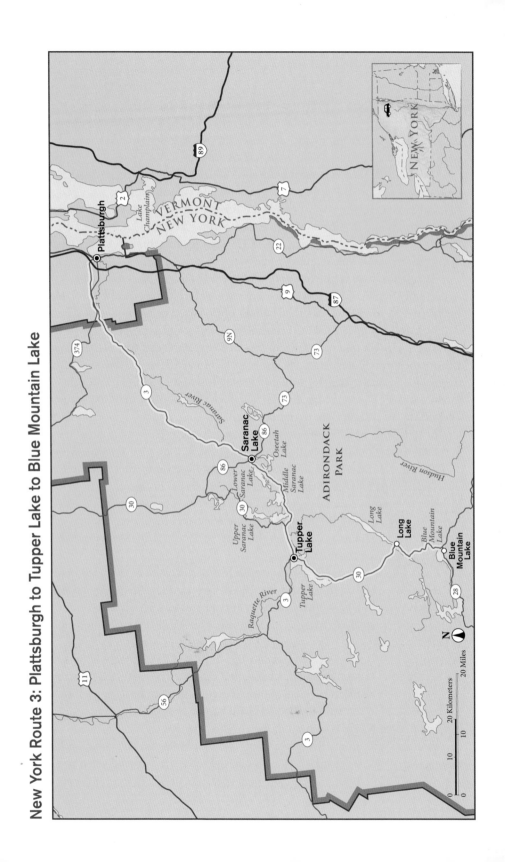

road follows the north branch of the **Saranac River,** which appears on your left. Pass the sign for the "Blue Line," the boundary of the protected lands of Adirondack Park. The rest of your drive will be within this state-stewarded acreage of woods, mountains, rivers, lakes, and small communities.

As you reach the town of Saranac (not Saranac Lake—that's some distance away), the Alder Brook Mountain range comes into view in the distance. Crest a hill into Saranac, where pastures extend to the base of the mountains and fields of wildflowers nod in your direction. Here a country store in a log building offers gas, just in case you didn't fill the tank in Plattsburgh. Pass through Saranac and enjoy the scenery as you approach Moffitsville.

At an old, closed trestle bridge in Moffitsville, you may want to take the opportunity to pull off the road and shoot some photos of the Saranac River. Here interpretive signs tell you about the **hamlet of Russia,** a community that shut its doors in 1892 but once contained an iron forge, mills, and a company store. Forges are used to process iron ore, which miners extracted from the Adirondack Mountains in the form of magnetite. The ore must be heated to remove impurities from the material, using charcoal—made by burning trees from the area's abundant forests—to keep the forges hot enough to liquefy the ore. More than 100 ironworks operated in the Adirondacks in northeastern New York, and this region produced almost 10 percent of the entire nation's iron ore. (You can learn more about this at the Adirondack Museum in Blue Mountain Lake, at the end of this scenic drive.)

Cross the Saranac River and enter the town of **Riverview,** where the mountain views nearly preempt the river's moment in the sun. Here bridges lead you across the river repeatedly, each one affording an excellent look at the Saranac's twists and turns. After these crossings the road begins to climb and rocky outcroppings come into view on the mountainsides. Start watching for moose in the shallow waters and wet areas along the roadside.

Short side trips begin to present themselves after Riverview. Turn left onto Alder Brook Park Road to go to Union Falls, where an impressive dam on **Union Falls Pond** creates a powerful waterfall. The dam and falls generate power for the Canadian company Kruger Energy in Montreal, Quebec, less than 2 hours north of here.

Back on NY 3, head west to Gabriels-Onchiota Road and turn right to reach the **Six Nations Indian Museum,** where more than 3,000 artifacts tell the story of the Iroquois Confederacy—also known as the Haudenosaunee—in a building constructed to resemble an Iroquois bark house. The peaked ceiling and walls hold more Native American historic and contemporary items than you can absorb in one visit, from arrowheads to birch bark canoes, but you will know more about New York's native heritage when you leave than you did when you

Saranac Lake offers many reasons to stop and enjoy the town.

arrived. The gift shop features many contemporary craft items and artwork by members of the Six Nations.

Return to NY 3 and turn right to continue to Saranac Lake. Pass through Vermontville and watch as the mountains begin to get taller, with **Moose Mountain** straight ahead at 3,921 feet. Other peaks appear as you arrive in Saranac Lake.

A town with the confidence to call itself "the Capital of the Adirondacks," Saranac Lake serves as a center of tourist activity from May through leaf-peeping season in October, and then again when skiers arrive in winter. Here you'll find fun shopping in galleries that showcase the work of local artists and in stores like **Adirondack Trading Company** and **The Village Mercantile.** Restaurants feature a number of different ethnicities, from Owl's Nest Pizza to Borracho Taco and Left Bank Cafe, a French bistro that truly is on the left bank of the Saranac River. Stock up on organic provisions at Nori's Village Market or Fusion Market, or try on some natural fiber fashions at Eco Living Alpaca.

So where's the lake? If you want to see it, you'll need to hit the road again. Continue down NY 3 when you're ready.

Saranac Lake to Tupper Lake

The **Lower and Middle Saranac Lakes** come into view as you leave the town of the same name. This stretch of road to Tupper Lake provides some of the most dramatic scenery on this route, with forested mountains and chains of lakes becoming the lead players. Watch for long lines of vehicles on the side of the road; these signify trailheads for Ampersand Mountain and Panther Mountain, two of the most popular hikes in this region.

Much of this route traverses **Saranac Lakes Wild Forest,** a 79,000-acre area protected from development by the New York State Department of Environmental Conservation. The forest contains 142 different bodies of water, including all three Saranac Lakes, Tupper Lake, Lake Placid, and the Raquette and Saranac Rivers, making boating and fishing two of the most popular pastimes in this area. If you come through here in winter, watch out for snowmobiles crossing the road from one trail to the next.

Smack in the middle of all this amazing countryside lies the town of **Tupper Lake,** the hub from which four scenic spokes radiate. You've come in from the east; NY 30 goes north from here to Malone, as you will find detailed in Route 6 (Adirondack Trail Northern Section: Tupper Lake to Malone). To the west, NY 3 continues to Watertown on the Olympic Trail (Route 5). Today you'll take the southern route on NY 28N/30 to Blue Mountain Lake, following the central section of the Adirondack Trail.

Lakes in the Adirondacks are particularly picturesque.

Because of this strategically advantageous position in the midst of the Adirondacks, Tupper Lake became a transportation and freight center in the 1800s as commercial logging operations brought railroads to the area. The Utica-Montreal and Tupper-Ottawa rail lines met here, and for many years the rail yard facilities and roundhouse dominated the center of town. As lumber companies moved westward, the railroad operations eventually faded, and Tupper Lake became the quieter mountain town we see today.

Town officials had to get creative to bring new jobs and opportunities to their village, so in the 1920s they rallied the residents around a new cause: care of its World War I veterans. You can't miss the complex of white buildings in the center of town, currently the site of the **Sunmount Developmental Center** for people with developmental disabilities. Sunmount began its life as a veterans' hospital after World War I, attracted here by an extraordinary show of patriotic spirit from a town affected—like just about every other community in America—by the casualties of a long and bloody war. Townspeople raised $20,000 to buy this land from a local farmer, and then "sold" it to the US government for a single dollar to convince the Veterans' Administration that a hospital for former servicemen would be welcome here. The government took the bait, and the hospital opened in August 1924. It served its country's veterans for many years before being repurposed in its current form.

You may be tempted to drive on to enjoy more of the fabulous views in and around town, but first, plan to spend a few hours at the **Wild Center Natural History Museum of the Adirondacks.** This massive indoor-outdoor science museum and nature center makes excellent use of the 31 acres of forest, wetland, and waterway that surround it, building marked trails that bring you into the wilderness to discover all the things promised in the exhibit halls inside. Live exhibits give you an opportunity to visit with a porcupine or get a close look at a river otter—two animals you may struggle to see in the wild—while indoor activities include a number of multimedia show choices in the panoramic Flammer Theatre. Open 7 days a week, 362 days a year, the Wild Center can be a great rainy day destination or the perfect stop for a snowshoe hike on a sunny winter day. Here's the biggest surprise: Ticket prices are a fraction of what you would pay for a similar venue in a large city.

As you leave Tupper Lake, take NY 30 south toward Blue Mountain Lake.

Tupper Lake to Blue Mountain Lake

Just as you turn south, you will see a parking area with a viewing platform that provides a panoramic view of Tupper Lake. Here you may see great blue herons fishing, hawks flying, otters or muskrats swimming, or loons crossing the water

Tupper Lake in spring.

with their young close behind (or riding astride). Interpretive signs here supply information about the **Tupper Lake/Raquette Pond/Simon Pond ecosystem,** the intricately interdependent wetland that thrives here because of careful protection. Across the water, northern hardwood forest covers the mountains with a strikingly uniform blanket of green, changing to yellows and oranges in fall.

More parking areas appear along the lake as you drive south, several with gasp-out-loud views of the lake, ponds, and peaks beyond. Pass a junction with NY 421 and look ahead to **Fishing Brook Mountain,** the tallest peak in the area at 3,550 feet.

Of all the trails and wilderness areas that whiz past along this route, **John Dillon Park** stands out as one to note. The park is named for the former chairman and chief executive officer of International Paper, who dreamed of a park made completely accessible to people with disabilities to allow them to interact with the Adirondacks. When Dillon retired from the company, International Paper designed and constructed this park in his honor. In addition to 3 miles of wheelchair-manageable trails, the park offers accessible camping lean-tos, each equipped with a fold-down bed platform, a fireplace, and a picnic table.

The Adirondack Experience is in Blue Mountain Lake.

Boardwalks and a canoe/kayak dock make it easy to get around this park no matter what your mobility level may be.

After you see Lake Eaton Campground, enter the hamlet of Long Lake by crossing the lake itself on a trestle bridge. Motels, inns, and rental cottages line the roads, but one merchant stands out: **Hoss's Country Corner,** a two-story landmark now in its fourth decade and chock-a-block with locally produced wares and practical items for your cabin in the woods. You'll find maple syrup, handmade items created by local craftspeople, all kinds of books on the Adirondacks, and housewares and clothing to take home with you. Hoss's also dips Perry's brand ice cream and serves hot dogs and burgers at its stand next door—and if you've got a hankering for a handful of night crawlers, you can get live bait here, too.

Watch out for deer as you leave Long Lake on Deerland Road (NY 28N/30), as they tend to be numerous in this area. Next, keep an eye out for a turnoff for **Buttermilk Falls,** one of the area's most popular waterfalls and easy to reach from North Point Road/County Route 3 (a right turn from NY 30). Drive 2.1 miles down CR 3 to the parking area, and walk in about 50 feet to see the falls. Forty feet tall and equally wide, this creamy cascade slides down a series of metamorphic ledges to end as a foamy churn directly in front of you. It's worth walking out on some of the huge slabs of rock here for a better view.

Once you've returned to NY 28N/30 and continued south, the **Adirondack Experience** comes into view fairly quickly. Here in the shadow of Blue Mountain and just outside the hamlet of Blue Mountain Lake, this largely open-air museum features 22 exhibition galleries, as well as historic buildings including a 1907 schoolhouse and camp cottages built from the 1870s to the 1960s. Top off your visit with the view of Blue Mountain Lake from a deck that rises 200 feet above the water.

You may want to stay overnight in this remote but well-appointed area, so here are a couple of things to keep in mind: If having cable television, WiFi connectivity, or radio reception in your room is a priority, ask about these things when you make your hotel room reservation. Many guests come to this area to get away from the constant prattle of these modern conveniences, and some of the inns and rental cottages in this area pride themselves on excluding TV, radio, and even telephone service from their rooms. Mobile phone service can be entirely absent as well. You may want to head south for Old Forge (see Route 4) if you need to stay connected during your time in the 'Dacks.

4

Central Adirondack Trail
Warrensburg to Old Forge

General description: If you love mountain lakes, this 83-mile route through the center of the Adirondacks provides crystal-blue water surrounded by forests of maple, beech, aspen, spruce, and cedar. Roll down your windows and enjoy all the sights, smells, and sounds of New York's most beautiful and rugged landscapes.

Special attractions: Antiquing in Warrensburg, Hudson River, Millington Brook, Gore Mountain Ski Resort, Garnet Mine Tours, Siamese Ponds Wilderness Area, OK Slip Falls Trail, Lake Abanakee, Lake Adirondack, Byron Park, Cedar River, Lake Durant, Blue Mountain Lake, Grassy Pond, Golden Beach Park, Raquette Lake, Train Wreck Point, Utowana Lake, Eighth Lake, Seventh Lake, Sixth Lake, Fifth Lake, Fourth Lake, Sis Lake, Bubb Lake, View Center for Arts and Culture, Enchanted Forest Water Safari, Calypso Cove Family Fun Park, Old Forge Hardware

Location: Across the middle of northern New York State from east to west, through the Adirondack Mountains

Route number: NY 28

Travel season: Spring, summer, and fall

Camping: Lake Durant Public Campground near Blue Mountain Lake, Golden Beach and Tioga Point Parks and Public Campgrounds in Raquette Lake, Limekiln Lake Campground near Inlet, Nicks Lake Campground near Old Forge/Thendara

Services: In Warrensburg, Indian Lake, Blue Mountain Lake, Inlet, and Old Forge

Nearby attractions: Natural Stone Bridge and Caves, Adirondack Experience in Blue Mountain Lake, McCauley Mountain Ski Area, hiking trails to Sawyer Mountain, Rock River, Rock Lake

The Route

We've chosen a substantial segment of the official Central Adirondack Trail to maximize your exposure to magnificent scenery. Between Warrensburg and Old Forge, the trail—actually NY 28—winds past no fewer than 14 lakes and ponds, over three creeks and the Schroon River, and along the Hudson River, creating a landscape filled with rippling lake surfaces and babbling waterways. In between, the Adirondack Mountains rise to fill the horizon, and thousands of acres of forest provide shady cover for much of your drive.

Warrensburg to North River

The route begins in the town of Warrensburg, the birthplace of Congressional Medal of Honor recipient Floyd Bennett. In 1926, Bennett—who served as a military pilot in World War I—became the first pilot to attempt to fly a plane over the

Central Adirondack Trail: Warrensburg to Old Forge

North Pole, in the company of explorer Richard E. Byrd. While there's some speculation that Bennett and Byrd did not quite reach the pole during their flight, New York City's first municipal airport, Floyd Bennett Field, is named for this pilot, as is the memorial airport in Queensbury, not far from Warrensburg.

No doubt the town would love this distinguished history to be its claim to fame, but instead, the town's renown stems from its production of the **World's Largest Garage Sale,** a miles-long array of vendors from all over the country who come in the first weekend of October to sell antiques, used items, new merchandise, crafts, and much more. So massive is this event that it attracts dozens of food vendors as well, so you can walk, eat, and shop all day once you've found parking. Check the town's website at warrensburggaragesale.com for the dates of this annual event.

From Warrensburg, head north on US 9 to its junction with NY 28 just north of town. Bear left on NY 28 as the Adirondack Mountains begin to come into view. You're now officially on the Central Adirondacks Scenic Byway. Thick forest lines the roadsides as you cross **Millington Brook** and head northwest, with the **Hudson River** beginning to parallel the road. Soon the Hudson flows under the road, giving you a nice opportunity to get a good look at the mighty river's comparatively shallow, wild state this far north.

Cross **Mill Creek** and pass through a small section of the town of Wevertown at the junction with NY 8. The forest crowds in again just after this corner, and the view opens up to reveal mountains ahead. In about 5 miles, reach **North Creek,** where the mountains become dominant and you can see some distance to the north, while the Hudson River slices through town and parallels the road ahead. You'll find a parking area outside of town with a picnic table, where you can stop and enjoy the view of the river as it gambols across the rocky landscape.

American history buffs will know the name of North Creek because of the role it played in 1901, when Vice President Theodore Roosevelt learned at the **North Creek railroad depot** that President William McKinley had died of complications caused by the gunshot wound he received in Buffalo, New York, at the Pan-American Exposition eight days earlier. On vacation with his family at the Tahawus Club near Mount Marcy, Roosevelt had already departed for the railway station in North Creek—35 miles away—because of a telegram he'd received warning him that the president appeared to be dying. By the time he arrived in North Creek, McKinley was dead, and a special train awaited Roosevelt to take him directly to Buffalo. He was sworn in as the 26th President of the United States that afternoon.

If you're a New York State resident, you may have wondered in passing how the garnet became the state's official gemstone. You'll find the answer in North River, where the **Barton Garnet Mines** at Gore Mountain provide tours and an opportunity to hunt for your own gemstones in the largest garnet reserve in the US. The mine started back in 1878 when Henry Hudson Barton, a resident of North River, used chisels and picks to bring garnets out of a field of feldspar and hornsblend on his own land. Once jewelers got wind of his discovery, Barton quickly created a garnet mining company and began supplying these gems for public consumption. When the demand grew beyond his ability to supply garnets, he used dynamite to blast away the mountainside . . . but he hit the water line and created three new lakes, blocking his access to the quarry. Barton moved his commercial operation to nearby Ruby Mountain, and his original mines have become a tourist attraction. Today Bonnie Barton, a descendant of the founder, keeps the mine open to tourists from the end of June through Labor Day, so you can pick along the ground to find gems and bring them to the mine's gift shop to be weighed and identified. In addition to the admission fee, any rocks and gemstones you collect are yours for a dollar per pound.

North River to Indian Lake

A new trail begins about 4 miles west of North River and 8 miles east of Indian Lake. The Finch Pruyn timber company owned the 2,800-acre tract in the Indian Lake area until the Adirondack Chapter of The Nature Conservancy bought it in 2007, but the land remained closed to the public until 2014, when New York State purchased it with the goal of opening it for hiking and other recreational uses. This new trail provided the first-ever public access to **OK Slip Falls,** the tallest waterfall in the Adirondacks, raining straight down for 250 feet from the top of the gorge that bears its name. The falls thunders in spring and early summer and maintains a steady pace through the late summer months, refueling during fall rains for another impressive season.

Add to this spectacle another natural phenomenon in the same area: the **Blue Ledges,** outcroppings of Grenville marble that mark their age in the billions of years. Top it all off with one of the finest views of the Hudson River Gorge to be found anywhere along the length of the river's northern transit, and you have a very fine North Country wilderness experience. Watch for this road and trailhead on your drive between North River and Indian Lake.

Back on NY 28, **Lake Abanakee** comes into view on both sides of the road, viewable in between stands of conifers until you cross it by bridge. In another mile or so, **Adirondack Lake** appears to the north of the road, just before you reach the town of Indian Lake. If you'd like to enjoy this lake before you enter town, there's a pull-off to the right at Byron Park, just over the bridge.

Indian Lake to Old Forge

With its more than 300 miles of hiking trails, three lakes, and the Hudson and Cedar Rivers all passing through the same concentrated area, Indian Lake becomes the Adirondack midpoint for all manner of treks and sports. Peaceful canoeing, kayaking, or riding the Hudson's whitewater can all begin here, while the river, creek, lakes, and adjacent wetlands draw anglers of many different stripes. If you're passing through in winter, Indian Lake offers many cross-country ski adventures or wilderness snowshoe hikes, and the lakes provide smooth, hard surfaces for ice skaters.

Even if you prefer to view the outdoors from the comfort of your car, you'll find plenty of vivid sights to enjoy here—sparkling mountainsides in winter, brilliant fall colors, wildflowers blanketing hillsides and crowding along roadsides in spring and summer, and lakes shimmering under expansive blue skies. Stop here for lunch and sit outside on one of several restaurant or deli patios and give yourself time to take in all of this wild, wide scenery.

When you're ready, continue west on NY 28 (which joins with NY 30 in Indian Lake), crossing the **Cedar River** and heading deep into mountain country. Pass the Sawyer Mountain trailhead and watch for **Rock Lake** to your right, some distance back from the road. In a few minutes, **Rock River** passes under the road just as you reach **Lake Durant** on your left. You may want to stop at this one for photos; there's a parking area on the right to allow you to do this safely.

Just before you enter Blue Mountain Lake (you'll find a description of the town and its offerings in Route 3), cross the **official divide between the St. Lawrence River and Hudson River watersheds,** marked by a sign with a cutout lavender moose. You'll find a large pull-off area just south of the sign, where you can get great photos of the sign and of Lake Durant.

Stay on NY 28 as you leave the town of Blue Mountain Lake, and watch as the lake of the same name spreads north from the road. Over the next several miles, water views dominate the landscape as **Blue Mountain Lake** joins with **Eagle Lake,** a much small water body, and then with **Utowana Lake.** In between, watch

The heart of the Adirondacks is all about lakes and forests.

for a short trail to **Grassy Pond**—definitely worth the brief hike—and for the **Eagle Nest Seaplane Base** between Eagle and Utowana Lakes. If you're lucky, you might see a seaplane landing or taking off.

Golden Beach Park is the next major landmark, with a day-use area (fee required) that features plenty of lakefront along the **South Bay of Raquette Lake.** If you just want to enjoy the lake views and you're not looking for a place to camp, picnic, or dip your toes in the lake, keep going on NY 28 as it follows along the lakeshore for several miles. Half a mile after the entrance to Golden Beach, there's a pull-off area just before a bridge over a narrow tributary. Park on the right, apply plenty of bug spray, cross the road, and take the easy, sandy trail to the water's edge for the kind of quintessential Adirondack view you just can't get from the car: clear mountain waters, steep hills rising in the background, an inlet edged with cattails and grasses, and if you're very fortunate, the eerie call of a loon.

Back in your car, head west on NY 28 again and pass Burke's Marina. Here comes the best view of Raquette Lake from the road as you reach **Otter Bay,** just before you enter the hamlet named for the lake. The tiny community of Raquette Lake goes by in a flash, and it would be little more than a place to rent a cabin or pitch a tent were it not for the most famous of all the Adirondack "great camps," one of the last vestiges of the days when wealthy families departed from the stifling, crowded cities for entire summers and escaped to the mountains for months of rest and recreation.

Built by William West Durant between 1895 and 1897, **Great Camp Sagamore** served as a getaway for the richest families in America, who engaged in the fashionable practice of "rustication," returning to the undisturbed lands of the natural world without actually leaving any of their civilized luxuries behind. When Durant could no longer support the property, he sold it to the Vanderbilt family in 1901, and they made improvements that reduced the property's primitive state even further, adding flush toilets, running water, and a hydroelectric plant. A. G. Vanderbilt died on the *Lusitania* when it sank in 1915, but his wife, Margaret Emerson, continued to enjoy the camp until she gave it to Syracuse University in 1954, and it served as a conference center until the university transferred it to the not-for-profit Preservation League of New York (now the Sagamore Institute of the Adirondacks). Today the Sagamore Institute continues to operate the property—now a National Historic Landmark—as a rustic inn and conference center, and opens many of its 27 historic buildings to the general public for guided tours from Memorial Day to mid-October.

After Raquette Lake, the Adirondacks' famous **Fulton Chain of Lakes** comes into view. Part of a river system dammed in Old Forge in 1798, the Fulton Chain meets the **Middle Branch of the Moose River** in Old Forge, and the dam built at this meeting point currently holds back 6.8 billion gallons of water in a reservoir.

Rivers and streams flow into Raquette Lake as you travel NY 28.

The dam resulted in a massive expansion of the size of the lakes, from about 2,700 acres to nearly 3,500 acres, a level the Hudson River-Black River Regulating District continues to maintain because of an agreement made with the cottage owners around these lakes back in the late 1800s. Thanks to this foresight, the chain of lakes provides some of the best recreational waters in the Adirondacks, allowing boaters to motor from one lake to the next with a short portage between Fifth and Sixth Lakes. Fish including northern pike, lake and brook trout, large-mouth and smallmouth bass, and landlocked salmon keep anglers busy throughout the fishing season.

Glimpse **Eighth Lake** through the trees as you pass, and enjoy a wider view of **Seventh Lake** from a bridge. Shortly a concentration of cottages, a cluster of bed-and-breakfast establishments, and a number of small camping areas bring you into Inlet, which is on **Sixth and Fifth Lakes** as you continue down the chain.

If you've been keeping an eye out for the cutest Adirondack-style town, Inlet is the one, featuring a district of shopping and services built almost entirely in the distinctly Adirondack mode. Rough-sawn wood covers the few buildings that are not made of logs, Adirondack chairs stand on every porch, and the indoor furnishings in every building consist of log tables and chairs, shelves of unfinished wood, and polished wood countertops. Most restaurants here are open year-round, so you'll have no trouble finding a meal, and stores like the Crazy Moose Quilt Shop and Adironstix will give you some hints about what people do here when they're not out on the water.

YOUR ICE CREAM STOP: NORTHERN LIGHTS CREAMERY

More than a dozen flavors of homemade gelato make Northern Lights a busy place on warm summer days. Flavors like salted caramel, danutella (chocolate and hazelnut), and cannoli—a miraculous concoction of marscapone, ricotta, and chocolate chips—keep visitors coming back to try something different every day. Sundaes, floats, and shakes round out the bountiful menu. If you prefer something simpler, the vanilla ice cream dipped in chocolate is a much-lauded treat.

Past Inlet, Eagle Bay appears slightly less rustic-gone-trendy and more down-home than Inlet, which may mean that this little village is just the mountain getaway you hoped to find. The restored **Big Moose Inn,** a wilderness lodge that dates back to the early 1900s, sits on the shores of **Big Moose Lake** and offers 16 rooms, each of them decorated differently; there's a restaurant right at the inn with a "casual fine dining" menu, so you needn't go far to find a good dinner.

Sis and Bubb Lakes come up quickly as you continue west on NY 28. In a moment, you're sure to spot a sign for the ominously named **Train Wreck Point,** close to the railroad tracks between Eagle Bay and Old Forge. Here the Raquette Lake Railway passed through from 1899 to 1933, running along the edge of NY 28 to reach the Eagle Bay Station (which you can still see in town). On November 9, 1913, a train hit a log here and jumped the track spectacularly, tumbling over the cliff and killing the three crew members aboard. The date coincides with the Great Lakes Storm of 1913, a blizzard with hurricane-force winds that ravaged the lakes for 16 hours before moving eastward; this may have caused the blowdown that tossed a log across the tracks.

Trailheads to **Bald Mountain** (not the one in the Mussorgsky musical work, but an impressive peak regardless) and the **Rondaxe Fire Tower** often draw crowds in good weather, so you may see many cars parked along the roadside as you approach Old Forge. **Fourth Lake** comes into view on your right and **Little Moose Lake** on your left . . . and then the **Enchanted Forest Water Safari**

Seventh Lake is the second of the numbered lakes as you approach Old Forge.

dominates the landscape, and you're in one of the most-visited hamlets in Adirondack State Park.

Old Forge

The center of recreation and entertainment on the western Adirondacks, Old Forge blends commercial attractions with outdoor activities and tops it all with a dollop of mountainside charm. The jumping-off point for hikers, boaters, canoeists and kayakers, anglers, skiers, birders, and leaf-peepers, Old Forge provides modern accommodations as well as rustic cabins and cottages, and plenty of restaurants and diners to keep you fueled for whatever activity you choose. The Old Mill Restaurant is a local landmark and a favorite for a "nice" dinner out, while Keyes Pancake House jams up on weekend mornings with breakfast seekers longing for homemade pancakes doused in local butter and maple syrup.

If you're looking for a uniquely Adirondack shopping experience, **Old Forge Hardware** may be the single best store in the park. The store dates back to 1900 when Moses Cohen moved here and bought land on this street corner, finding immediate success with a store that brought much-needed supplies and hardware to people living in this remote area. The original store burned down in a town-wide fire in 1923, but Cohen rebuilt the store and continued to serve the people who had made his enterprise such a success. Today the store is in the hands of the Wilcox family, who have been associated with the Cohens for decades, and it retains all of the diversity of offerings on which it built its reputation as a destination store. You can certainly find hardware here if you need it, but you'll also find a bookstore loaded with local titles, fishing and camping gear, a fascinating array of housewares and locally made ceramic items, plenty of jams, syrups, and other yummy local delicacies, clothing from many of the top outdoor outfitters, yarn kits for making your own hats and scarves, and a great deal more. Take home a bumper sticker with the store's logo graphic of Henry the Hardware Store Bear, and look like you're "in the know" about what's fun in the Adirondacks.

The Central Adirondack Scenic Byway continues from Old Forge to Otter Creek and out of Adirondack Park, but we chose to end here at Old Forge, surrounded by mountain peaks, clear lakes, crackling leaves, and a wide range of amenities and recreational choices. Should you continue down NY 28, the park's magnificent scenery ends just past Otter Lake, giving way to farmland and open fields as you approach the city of Utica.

Olympic Trail

NY 3 from Great Bend to Lake Placid

General description: For 114 miles from the Black River to the site of the 1932 and 1980 Winter Olympics, take in the views of rolling mountains, bubbling rivers, and deep emerald forests.

Special attractions: Black River Recreation Area, Oswegatchie River, Lake Bonaparte, Star Lake, Twin Lakes, Cranberry Lake, Raquette River, The Wild Center, Olympic Center and Lake Placid Olympic Museum

Location: Across the northern third of the Adirondack Mountains, ending where the High Peaks Scenic Byway begins in Lake Placid

Route numbers: NY 3, NY 3A, NY 86

Travel season: Spring through fall

Camping: Bud's Campsite in Carthage, Adirondack/Thousand Islands Campground in Natural Bridge, Cranberry Lake State Campground

Services: In Watertown before the route begins, Natural Bridge, Tupper Lake, Saranac Lake, and Lake Placid; limited services in small towns between these towns

Nearby attractions: High Peaks Scenic Byway, Whiteface Veterans Memorial Highway, Whiteface Mountain Ski Resort, John Brown Farm Historic Site, Santa's Workshop at North Pole, High Falls Gorge

The Route

Just about any road you choose to drive through Adirondack Park offers sprawling mountain views, multiple river crossings, and glimmering highland lakes, but this route provides access to some of the areas you might not discover on your own—especially if you, like most travelers, are focused on the High Peaks Region. The summits may not be quite as high on this end of the Adirondacks, but they are just as beautiful, and the hamlets along this route offer an easy North Country charm that makes you want to set the cruise control a few miles an hour slower than normal.

The entire Olympic Scenic Byway stretches across the state for 170 miles, but we chose this especially scenic section of the official byway as a manageable route for a sunny afternoon. We covered much of the rest of the byway as part of other routes in this book: Lake Placid to Wilmington is part of the High Peaks Scenic Byway (Route 7), and Watertown to Sackett's Harbor is part of the Great Lakes Seaway Trail, Section III (Route 23).

Olympic Trail: NY 3 from Great Bend to Lake Placid

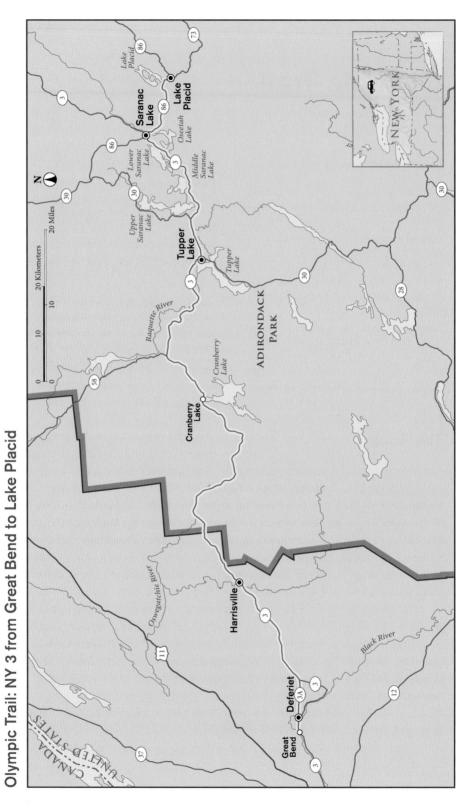

Great Bend to Pitcairn

Your drive begins at the junction of NY 3 and NY 3A just east of Great Bend, about 11 miles east of Watertown. If you follow the Olympic Scenic Byway signs from here, you'll take a short route across the "great bend" in the **Black River** through a corner of land protected by **Fort Drum,** home of the 10th Mountain Division of the US Army. If you prefer to follow the river a little longer and enjoy some pleasant views, continue on NY 3 as it bends southeast and then northwest.

At the junction with NY 3 and NY 126 in Carthage, turn left on NY 3. In a couple of miles you'll see NY 3A join NY 3 from the left. Stay on NY 3 and head east.

Soon you will reach the hamlet of **Natural Bridge.** If the name of this town raises your expectations for the kinds of formations you see in national parks in southern Utah, I gently suggest that you dial it back a bit. The bridge itself is a limestone arch that was probably well known to Native Americans living in the region, discovered by a European descendant, a hunter named Aleaser Carr, in the early 1800s. The Indian River channel and its load of cedar tannin wore away this culvert, creating a simple arch. A town grew up around the bridge area, much of it planned by its most famous 19th-century resident: Joseph Bonaparte, the elder brother of Napoleon Bonaparte. Joseph became king of Spain for 5 years (as José I), abdicated after a defeat by the British, and moved to upstate New York when the Bonapartes were exiled from France in Napoleon's downfall. He used the Spanish crown jewels to purchase more than 150,000 acres near Natural Bridge, including the lake that immediately became known locally as **Lake Bonaparte.** Legend has it that Joseph dug a tunnel under his home from his basement to the natural caverns at the river, just in case his enemies came after him and he had to make a hasty escape. Local residents picked the house apart for scrap after Joseph left the area, and eyewitnesses who explored the empty foundation found no evidence of a tunnel . . . but the story lives on.

Today you can visit Lake Bonaparte by taking South Bonaparte Road or Hermitage Road to the left from the village of Lake Bonaparte. The land around the lake is largely privately owned, but you can view the lake from the ends of several roads.

The sizeable town of Harrisville comes up next, where you'll find a parking area to the left (take Maple Street to Elm Street) for a short walk to **Grand View Park.** This little scenic stop lives up to its name, providing a close look at the **Oswegatchie River** from a paved walkway and gazebo. Continue down Maple Street to visit the **Town of Diana Historical Museum** in a former railroad depot, where you can learn more about the somewhat less royal folks who settled this area and made it their home. The museum is only open by appointment, but in an

extraordinary demonstration of hospitality, the members of the historical society graciously list their names and phone numbers on a sign on the front door, with the note that they will be happy to come over and open the building for you if you would like to visit.

Shortly after Harrisville and the small town of Pitcairn, the road begins to climb as you enter Adirondack Park. Now all the road signs are brown with yellow type, the easiest way to tell if you are within the "Blue Line," the boundary of the 6-million-acre park. Conifers line the roadway on either side for many miles, with breaks that reveal views of hidden lakes, winding rivers, and the occasional home—some of them luxurious with wide windows overlooking expansive views, some the kind of back-to-nature, rustic-looking log homes you might expect to see in a mountain resort area, and some manufactured homes on otherwise untouched natural land. The take-away from this is clear: If we want to live in a scenic paradise, some of us may need to make some compromises.

Oswegatchie to Tupper Lake

Cross the **Little River** as you approach Oswegatchie, a town so tiny that it has no town center on the main road, and continue through dense woods to the town of Fine and its hamlets, Star Lake and Wanekena. Here you'll find services including a grocery store, pharmacy, ATM, gas station, a diner, and several motels, as well as two landmarks with historical significance.

First, the **Griffin Memorial Forest** may be the only town forest in the US, donated to the town of Fine by John P. Griffin in 1914. Griffin wanted the town to have its own forest, so he gave the town his land—a 40-acre parcel to be used "for a perpetual town forest," according to the plaque dedicating the forest in his memory.

The **Wanakena Footbridge** across the Oswegatchie River has been a local landmark since the Rich Lumber Company built it back in 1902 to give workers at the local mill a way to get to their jobs and back home at the end of the day. In 1999 the bridge was placed on the National Register of Historic Places, and it continued to welcome people across the river until January 13, 2014, when an ice jam in the river caused significant damage to the century-old structure. The Wanakena Historical Association raised money to rebuild the bridge, and on November 11, 2016, the reconstructed suspension bridge reopened.

Just after the junction with County Route 61 (the turn for Wanakena), the **Adirondack Mountains** come into full view. By now your vehicle has climbed to

Travel from lowlands to mountains on the road to Lake Placid.

The South Branch of the Grass River flows through Piercefield.

1,450 feet, and you're coming into the **James F. Dubuar Memorial Forest,** the property of the State University of New York campus of Environmental Science and Forestry (SUNY ESF). Here the college conducts its forestry technology program and its undergraduate summer program in resources management and environmental and forest biology. The 2,800-acre forest provides the SUNY program with a living laboratory in which students at every level can learn the university's teamwork approach to resource science and management. If this all sounds a little dry, consider that students of this program tend to be nicknamed "stumpies" by other students at Syracuse University, where the main ESF campus is located.

The Dubuar forest blends smoothly into the **Cranberry Lake Wild Forest,** and soon you can see **Cranberry Lake** to your right and the much smaller **Silver Lake** to your left. Forest continues to edge the road as you reach the **Grass River,** where you'll find a parking area for fishing access that also offers long views of the river and the grassy areas on either side.

The Raquette River provides scenic views any time of year, but it's at its best in fall.

As you pass **Camp Masswepie,** the famous Boy Scouts of America camp, mountain views begin to dominate the landscape. Pass through the towns of Gale and Piercefield and watch for views of **Raquette Pond** to your right, just after you cross the **Raquette River.**

After 8 miles of spectacular views, pine-scented air, and flashing waterways, Tupper Lake emerges from the mountains and provides all of the services you have not seen in quantity since Harrisville.

Your drive continues from here to Lake Placid, passing through Saranac Lake on the way. For details on the town of Tupper Lake and the road to Saranac Lake, see Route 3 (Plattsburgh to Blue Mountain Lake) earlier in this book. The road from Saranac Lake to Lake Placid is part of the High Peaks Scenic Byway, described in Route 7.

6

Adirondack Trail, Northern Section

Tupper Lake to Malone

General description: Chains of lakes, northern hardwood forests, and mountain slopes make this 59-mile drive a particularly delightful way to sample Adirondack Park.

Special attractions: The Wild Center, Adirondack Sky Center and Observatory, Paul Smith's College of the Adirondacks Visitor Interpretive Center (VIC) and trails, Raquette River, Upper Saranac Lake, Fish Creek Ponds, Clear Pond, New York State DEC Fish Hatchery, Lake Clear, St. Regis River, Barnum Pond, Meacham Lake State Park, Deer River, Titus Mountain Family Ski Center, Almanzo Wilder Homestead

Location: In the northern third of Adirondack Park, in St. Lawrence and Franklin Counties

Route numbers: NY 3, NY 30

Travel season: Spring through fall

Camping: Donaldson's Campgrounds and Fish Creek Public Campground in Santa Clara, Meacham Lake State Campground and Deer River Campsite in Duane

Services: In Tupper Lake and Malone

Nearby attractions: US Olympic Training Center, John Brown's Farm State Historic Site, Adirondack Experience, hiking and fishing in the Adirondack Mountains

The Route

The northern Adirondacks may not draw as many visitors as the High Peaks region and other hiking and fishing centers in the middle of the park, but that's what makes a drive northward such a delight. Less traffic—even on a fall foliage weekend—means that you'll have lots of places to pull over and enjoy the view alongside the area's myriad lakes and ponds, without the crush of other tourists walking in front of your camera. This route takes you along a network of lakes, through several state forests, and along the outskirts of a number of towns, enveloping you in wilderness until you're out of Adirondack Park and back in New York's rich agricultural cropland.

Tupper Lake to Paul Smith's College

Like so many scenic drives in the Adirondacks, this route begins in Tupper Lake. If you have not found your way here via another of the routes in this book, take a look at all this appealing town has to offer in the descriptions of Route 3

Adirondack Trail, Northern Section: Tupper Lake to Malone

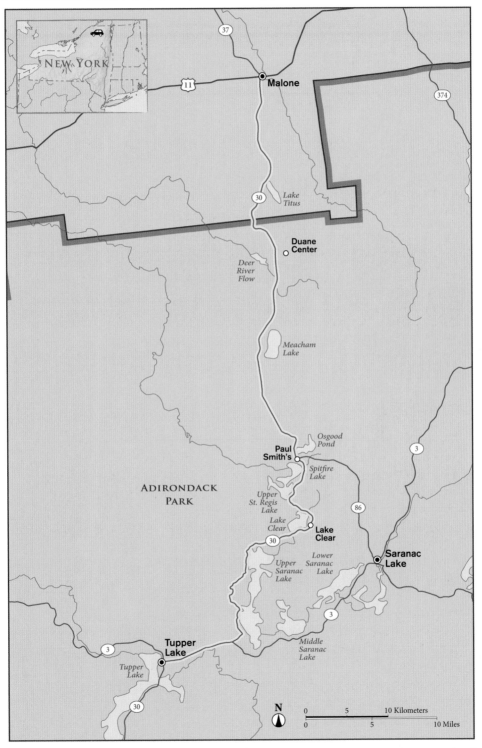

(Adirondack Trail, Central Section) and Route 7 (High Peaks Scenic Byway). Even with all of the activities recommended on these two routes, however, Tupper Lake has one more unusual attraction: the **Adirondack Sky Center and Observatory,** where the mountain range's dark skies create the perfect environment for observing the stars, planets, and other celestial bodies in the dead of night. As of this writing, the observatory is largely an outreach organization, but it holds stargazing sessions on alternate Fridays in winter and every Friday night in summer, at its Roll Off Roof Observatory at 178 Big Wolf Rd. north of town. If you're staying the weekend in Tupper Lake and you're looking for a great way to spend a Friday evening after dark, check out the observatory's website at adirondackskycenter.org for the session schedule.

Take NY 3/NY 30 east (past the Paul Bunyan statue) from Tupper Lake, and cross the Raquette River. Turn left when NY 30 North splits from NY 3, following the signs for the Adirondack Trail on NY 30 North.

Upper Saranac Lake becomes visible briefly to the right as you enter the town of Santa Clara. Watch for a bare spot on the roadside where you can stop to take photos and get a good look at this lake and the mountains beyond the far shore. In another mile, **Fish Creek Ponds** appear to the left. Cross a bridge over the ponds, and more views of Upper Saranac Lake open up to the right.

From here, one water view after another reveals itself between the densely packed hardwood trees, so take it easy on the gas pedal to give yourself time to see all the lakes, ponds, and creeks. **Follensby Clear Pond** comes up on the left, while Upper Saranac Lake widens to your right, large enough to create its own bays east and west of the main body.

A sign on your right for **Saranac Inn** alerts you to the approaching country club and golf course on your right, while **Green Pond** appears to the left. The famous Saranac Inn burned to the ground in a 7-hour fire in 1978, but in its heyday it served as a mountain retreat for US Presidents Grover Cleveland and Chester A. Arthur, as well as for many wealthy industrialists and others who came up to the mountains on the Mohawk and Malone Railway. When the Great Depression sapped the resources of most of America's wealthiest people, the hotel ceased to be profitable and finally closed its doors in 1962. The golf course you see here belonged to the inn at one time, as did the cottages and other outbuildings.

At the end of the hamlet of Saranac Inn, the New York State Department of Environmental Conservation maintains a **fish hatchery** that specializes in raising landlocked Atlantic salmon for distribution to lakes and rivers statewide. The hatchery produces an average of 30,000 pounds of salmon every year, sending

White birch provide stunning contrast in the fall forest.

Maple leaves turn flaming red in fall.

them out for stocking as 6-inch long smolts. You are welcome to visit from Apr 1 to Nov 30 and see the salmon in a pool at the visitor center, and to learn about the process of fish stocking and its positive effects on the species and the environment.

YOUR ICE CREAM STOP: DONNELLY'S ICE CREAM STAND

If it's Tuesday, then it's red or black raspberry ice cream day at Donnelly's, an ice cream stand in front of the family dairy at 1556 SR 86 in Lake Clear. Since the 1950s, Donnelly's has twisted one flavor per day with its luscious vanilla soft-serve, and area residents know exactly which day to come for their favorite flavor—Wednesday and weekends for chocolate, Monday for a surprise nut flavor, Thursday for something fruity, and Friday for strawberry. Just choose your size and whether you want a cone or a dish, and the machine the Donnellys bought in the 1930s does the rest. It's been open from Memorial Day to Labor Day for three generations. Tell Pete that we sent you.

As you enter the town of **Lake Clear,** turn left at the junction with NY 186 to stay on NY 30 North. The actual lake is on your left, and it barely has time to fade into the distance in your rearview mirror before the chain of St. Regis lakes comes into view ahead. Pass **Upper St. Regis Lake** on your left, followed by **Spitfire Lake; Lower St. Regis Lake** is third in the chain. The road crosses a small tributary of the lake just before you reach Paul Smith's College, also known as the College of the Adirondacks.

Best known for its School of Natural Resource Management and Ecology, **Paul Smith's College** trains people to become "stewards of the Earth," as the college calls its graduates. Offering degrees in environmental sciences, fisheries and wildlife sciences, forestry, natural resources management and sustainability, and parks and recreation management, the college prepares students for careers in a wide range of environmental fields. It also provides a way for members of the community and visitors to appreciate the outdoors through its **Visitor Interpretive Center (the VIC),** the gateway to a network of trails through 3,000 acres of diverse habitat on the college campus. The VIC provides an interpretive room with information on all of the Adirondacks' various ecosystems, a number of which you can then explore on the trails. Learn about successional forest, climax forests, the difference between pinelands and mixed woods, and the makeup of the northern hardwood forest that dominates so many of the mountainsides you've seen in your travels through this region.

When you're ready to move on, continue north on NY 30.

Paul Smith's College to Malone

From here, there are no town centers on NY 30 until you reach Malone, so this stretch of road provides one pond, lake, and sigh-inducing view after another.

Barnum Pond comes up quickly on your left as you leave the VIC, with lots of open shoreline for good views. In another minute or two, **Mountain Pond** comes into view, followed by an open wetland as you approach **Meacham Lake,** the next major body of water on your right. You will see signs for Meacham Lake Campground as NY 30 bears east and north. **Clear Pond** appears next; then the forest closes in until **Deer River Flow** passes under the road and extends back to campsites on your left.

The mountains that have provided beautiful views around the edges of lakes and ponds for the last 30 miles now pop into the foreground as you pass Duane Center. Adirondack Park ends fairly abruptly in a few minutes, though the mountains and forest continue all the way up to the outskirts of Malone.

The town of Malone is one of the largest in the entire Adirondack area, with a population of more than 15,000 and a thriving mercantile center. Here you'll find

Every bend in the road on the way to Malone reveals another lake.

Titus Mountain Ski Area, as well as the Upstate and Bare Hill Correctional Facilities, a maximum- and medium-security state prison.

Much of Malone's Main Street, a series of stone and brick edifices, dates back as far as the 1850s when railroads first arrived in this isolated North Country town. With more visitors and increased commerce in this area, many of the commercial buildings received fashionable face-lifts to impress the influx of new people and encourage them to return. Residences were modernized in grand 1890s style with porches, front columns, and stylish entryways. You can see the echoes of this boom time on Malone's main streets today.

Because of its proximity to the Canadian border, Malone became a pivotal stop on the **Underground Railroad** as abolitionists from Virginia to Canada worked to help African-American slaves escape to freedom. Malone's Anti-Slavery Society employed the **First Congregational Church** at the corner of Clay and Main Streets and the **home of retired Major John Dimmick** on NY 37 as hiding places for runaway slaves, quietly smuggling these people across the Canadian border in hay or lumber wagons. The church earned a place on the National Register of Historic Places in 1999.

In 2012 the village of Malone received approval from the New York State Secretary of State to proceed with a local waterfront revitalization program along the Salmon River. The plan includes protection for a scenic corridor along the river and its tributaries, the creation of parks and pathways, improvements to existing parks, amphitheater, skating rink, and an indoor pool. Keep an eye out for evidence of this plan going forward when you visit the village.

Before you bid adieu to the northernmost of the New York North Country, make a side trip to the **Wilder Homestead, the boyhood home of Almanzo Wilder**—husband to *Little House on the Prairie* series author Laura Ingalls Wilder. If you haven't read *Farmer Boy*, Laura's retelling of Almanzo's life as a young lad in the wilds of northern New York, you can pick up a copy in Malone or at the gift shop at the Wilder Homestead—but you may want to read it before you visit to enjoy the full impact of actually seeing the locations mentioned in the book. Your tour includes Almanzo's boyhood home, the reconstructed barns at the homestead, and a museum with model replicas of the homestead and antique tools used when the Wilders lived here on their farm. There's a general store and gift shop here as well, if you need to take a Wilder-themed item home to your favorite *Little House* fan. To reach the homestead, take US 11 for about 2.5 miles to County Road 23 (Burke City Road), and bear right on CR 23. Turn right onto Donahue Road, and right again onto Stacy Road. The Wilder Homestead is on your left.

7

High Peaks Scenic Byway & Whiteface Veterans Memorial Highway

General description: The single most beautiful drive in New York State takes you through the heart of the Adirondacks on a 24.2-mile route, with a bonus trip to Wilmington (an additional 12.4 miles) and a 5-mile meander up the fifth highest mountain in the region.

Special attractions: Clifford Pettis Memorial Forest, Saranac Lake, Lake Placid, 1980 Olympics Ski Jump, John Brown Farm State Historic Site, Olympic Recreation Center, Cascade Lakes, Roaring Brook Falls, Chapel Pond, North Pole and Santa's Workshop, High Falls Gorge, Monument Falls, The Flume, Wilmington Notch

Location: In the middle of Adirondack State Park in Essex and Hamilton Counties

Route numbers: NY 86, NY 73, Whiteface Veterans Memorial Highway

Travel season: Spring through fall; Whiteface Veterans Memorial Highway is open from mid-May to mid-October

Camping: Wilmington Notch Campground on NY 86, North Pole 100 Acre Woods Campground, backcountry camping on many of the high peaks' trails

Services: In Saranac Lake, Lake Placid, Wilmington, Keene, Jay and Upper Jay

Nearby attractions: Wilderness hikes to the summits of many of the Adirondacks' 46 High Peaks, Ausable Chasm, Adirondack Scenic Railroad, Wild Center, Adirondack Experience, The Great Adirondack Corn Maze, Paul Smith's College Visitor Interpretive Center (VIC)

The Route

If you want to impress your out-of-state friends with the splendor of New York State's most extraordinary wilderness areas, take them for a ride on the High Peaks Scenic Byway with a side trip to Whiteface Mountain. A unicolor riot of greens in spring, a spectacular display of wildflowers and verdant mountainsides in summer, and an artist's palette of warm, rich autumn tones in late September, this drive will make even the skeptics from the Rocky Mountain region gaze in wonder—and it's a treat for those of us who live nearby to experience it all again and again.

So special is this drive that we're suggesting you do it twice, once from west to east, and then back again with a side trip up NY 86 to Wilmington, North Pole, and Whiteface Mountain. The reverse perspective on the return trip ensures that you won't miss a nuance of this gorgeous ride, and it gives you the opportunity to stop more than once at your favorite spots.

High Peaks Scenic Byway & Whiteface Veterans Memorial Highway

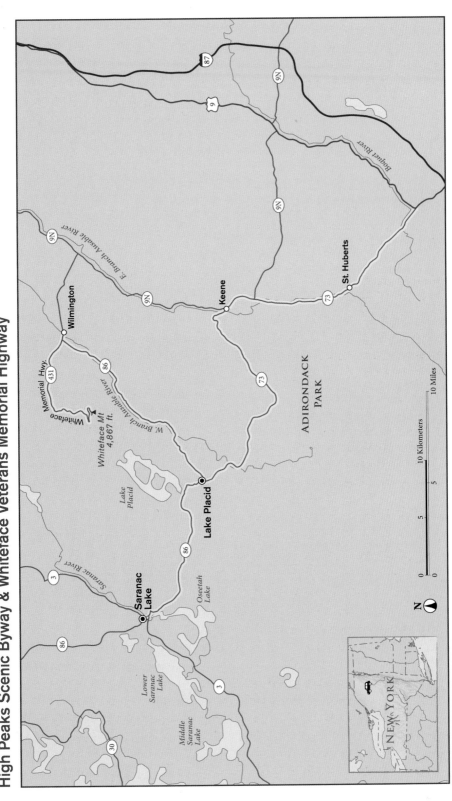

Stopping can be tricky, especially in fall during leaf-peeping season (which is in the last two weeks of September at this elevation) when this road becomes one of the most well-traveled in northern New York. Expect traffic, though nothing like what you might be used to in New York City or the Long Island area. "Traffic" in the Adirondacks means that there might be a bit of a backup behind slow-moving cars as the passengers take in the view. You may see lots of vehicles parked at popular trailheads (we counted more than 200 cars at the two Giant Mountain trailheads on our last visit), but you're not likely to sit in a stagnant line at any point on the road.

Saranac Lake to Lake Placid

Does some distant memory of medicine jangle in the back of your mind when you read the words "Saranac Lake"? That's not a coincidence—this town once housed the first laboratory in the US for research of tuberculosis. The process began in 1873 when Dr. Edward Livingston Trudeau came to Saranac Lake for relief from his own case of tuberculosis. He found the mountain air restorative, but each time he tried to return to his home in New York City, the disease relapsed. When he learned that a scientist in Germany had isolated the organism that caused the disease, Trudeau made it his life's work to advance the world's understanding of tuberculosis so a cure could one day be found. (Tuberculosis is now curable with antibiotics.) His laboratory closed in 1954 and the original building eventually was donated to Paul Smith's College north of Saranac Lake, but the local historical society—known as **Historic Saranac Lake**—restored the building to the last detail and opened it as a museum in 2009. You can visit **Trudeau's laboratory** year-round from Tues through Fri, and on Sat in summer.

From Saranac Lake, take NY 86 east on the Olympic Scenic Byway. **Turtle Pond** appears on your right, a nice place for a short, level walk around the pond to get a sense of the understory of greenery that carpets this area. Ferns and creeping plants create a lush, soft bed on either side of the trail, which starts at the second parking area after you leave Saranac Lake. The walk is less than a mile round-trip, giving you the opportunity to inhale plenty of spruce-scented air before you begin your car trip.

Once you're back on the road, it doesn't take long before the views are dominated by mountains ahead and to the right, and forest to your left. The town of **Ray Brook** sneaks up on you while you're admiring the scenery. This is the home of the regional office of the New York State Department of Environmental Conservation,

Impress your out-of-state friends by taking them for a ride on the High Peaks Scenic Byway.

the organization that oversees all of the remarkable vistas along this route. You can't miss **Tail O' the Pup Barbecue** on your right, with its rentable cabins, gift shop, and lobster pound as well as some very respectable ribs. Across the road, **The Pine Cone** furnishes upstate New York's Perry's Ice Cream for dessert.

YOUR ICE CREAM STOP: WHITEBROOK DAIRY BAR

Come for a burger or a hot dog, but stay for the luscious soft-serve—chocolate, vanilla, or twist—or hard flavors like honey-roasted peanut butter, blueberry cheesecake, and salted caramel truffle. Choose one of the yummy sprinkle options to top off your cone—in addition to rainbow and chocolate, try mint or cotton candy—or dress up a dish with a variety of sundae toppings. You can even choose mix-ins for a "tornado" of whipped soft serve and your favorite candy treats. Whitebrook will be the perfect end to your trip up Whiteface Mountain, or an energy boost before you start your drive to the top.

As you leave Ray Brook, enter the **Clifford R. Pettis Memorial Forest.** Pettis distinguished himself when he served as assistant to the head of the New York State Forest, Fish and Game Commission, by establishing the first forest tree nursery in the Adirondacks at Wawbeek. Later, in his capacity as superintendent of state forests, he championed a bill in the state legislature to provide nursery stock to private owners, increasing the number of trees planted in the Adirondacks from 25,000 annually to more than 20 million. Pettis established the state's forest fire control system, led the successful battle against the invasive gypsy moth, and wrote the *Bulletin of Forest Nursery Practices* that became the handbook of the US Forest Service. It's only fitting that a forest now stands as a memorial to this man and his work.

Traffic will pick up as you approach Lake Placid, home of the 1932 and 1980 Winter Olympics—and the **Herb Brooks Arena,** in which the "Miracle on Ice," the victory of the US hockey team over the Soviet Union's team, took place on February 22. The arena now bears the name of the coach who trained his team of American college students for a year and led them to this startling victory over the USSR's team, who had led the international hockey world for two straight decades. Remarkably, this game was not the gold-medal match: The United States went on to beat Finland for the gold on February 24.

The most striking landmarks of Lake Placid's Olympic heritage are the **two Olympic ski jumps,** which tower over the town and the surrounding landscape at

Abolitionist John Brown's farm is just outside of Lake Placid.

90 and 120 meters (roughly 295 and 394 feet). In snowless seasons, you can buy a ticket and take an elevator to the top of the taller jump to see through the eyes of Olympic athletes before they race down this slope at breakneck speed. The view of the Adirondacks is worth the price of the ticket, though you will be much higher up at the top of Whiteface Mountain.

In the town of Lake Placid, you'll find plenty of shops and restaurants, both unusual and well-known (such as Izod, Eastern Mountain Sports, and Van Heusen), and a number of hotels—including some with brand names. If you need a caramel macchiato, there's a Starbucks here as well. The streets of Lake Placid become crowded by late morning as sightseers and morning hikers return for lunch, so plan your day accordingly if you want to stop here and browse the galleries and gift shops.

Just outside of town and in the shadow of the ski jumps, **John Brown Farm State Historic Site** provides a startling contrast to the ski resort atmosphere in Lake Placid. Solitary and contemplative, this little farm once belonged to the fierce abolitionist who organized a raid on the US military arsenal at Harpers Ferry, West

Virginia, on October 16, 1859, before the Civil War began. Brown had the noblest of goals: He intended to arm the African-American slaves in the South so that they could battle their way to freedom. The US government did not see his point of view, however, and sent the US Marines (led by Colonel Robert E. Lee) to defeat Brown and his raiding party of 20 men. Brown was wounded in the Marines' attack, captured, tried, and convicted of treason in the courthouse in Charles Town, Virginia, and hanged on December 2, 1859. His body lies in a grave on his own land, beneath a tombstone he himself moved from his grandfather's grave several years earlier. Twelve of his fellow raiders are buried here as well.

Lake Placid to Keene

For the next 14 miles, sit back and enjoy the view. **Porter Mountain** looms ahead of you at 4,070 feet as you pass the **Olympic Recreation Center at the Mt. Van Hoevenberg Recreation Area.** Bobsledding and biathlon training take place here in winter as Olympic hopefuls prepare for the coming competitions.

The road weaves through the valleys between high peaks, with plenty of pull-off areas for viewing and taking photos. The narrow **Cascade Lakes** appear on your right—watch for a place to pull off on a narrow strip of land between the two lakes. Stop here and look up high on the mountainside to see **Cascade Mountain Falls,** a ribbon of shimmering water that pours down through the slot its flow has created in the rock face.

Mountains stand high on either side of the road as you reach Keene, a town geared toward rugged hiking and paddling in the High Peaks Wilderness. The only community of any size in the midst of the Adirondacks' 46 high peaks, Keene caters to lovers of the outdoors, supplying everything from rustic furniture for residents to energy-producing provisions for backpackers. Its hamlets of Keene Valley and St. Hubert's exist almost entirely to accommodate people planning or returning from long wilderness hikes up mountains that rise above 5,000 feet, so if you stop here for a meal, no one expects you to dress for dinner.

Cross **John's Brook** and you're back in the wilderness, heading south and east on NY 73.

The Cascade Lakes are a highlight of the High Peaks Byway.

Keene Valley to US 9

The route follows the course of the **Ausable River,** which you will cross repeatedly in your drive. Anglers know this river well as a legendary waterway for eastern trout, and hikers recognize it as a route for some of the finest waterfall hikes in the Adirondacks. You will glimpse a few of these falls along the route, but most of these are deep in the mountains and accessible only by hiking for several miles in one direction. We'll get a good look at the river's West Branch when we return on this route and detour up NY 86.

Watch for the ever-crowded **Giant Mountain trailheads** on your left. You will see one parking area labeled Giant Mountain/Roaring Brook; if there's room to stop on the roadside or in the parking area, pause here to look up at the rock face. Even in fall, water pours down from the mountaintop here, especially if it's been a particularly wet season. This is **Roaring Brook Falls,** and it's a sight to behold (though it rarely roars, as its name would suggest it should).

Just past Roaring Brook, you'll see a parking area for **Chapel Pond.** It's worth stopping here to take a short, easy walk down to this glasslike pond, just the sort of water feature you would expect to find in a mountain wilderness. Bring your binoculars and look across the road to the rocky mountaintop where peregrine falcons nest in spring. You can see these birds returning to this cliff face throughout the summer as a resting spot from their hunting adventures—and if you're lucky, you may see one catch a bird or bat overhead in midair.

As you drive south from here on NY 73, watch for impromptu waterfalls pouring down the rock faces along the roadside, especially in spring snowmelt season or after a heavy rain.

The scenic byway ends when you reach New Hudson and the junction with I-87, but we recommend turning around here and heading north on NY 73 to see the high peaks from the opposite side. New sights make themselves apparent as you drive, from mountains you did not see the first time to lakes and waterfalls that were obscured as you drove south.

NY 86 to Wilmington

When you reach NY 86 just before Lake Placid on your return trip, turn right. New mountains come into view, and soon you will see the Ausable River to your left along the road. Watch for **Monument Falls,** a small falls with big visual

Plan to stop and see High Falls Gorge, one of the most impressive waterfalls in the Adirondacks.

impact, where New York State has placed two plaques commemorating the 50th and 100th anniversaries of the creation of the New York State Forest Preserve. This lovely spot provides a fitting tribute to the state's astute accomplishment in preserving these lands in their natural state.

Pass Shadow Rock Pool as the road winds along the river, and keep an eye out for **High Falls Gorge.** You *must* stop here. Like you, we were dubious about stopping at an "attraction" in the middle of a natural area, but Roanka Attractions Corp. has done a real public service in making this place extraordinarily accessible to viewers. The gorge contains 700 feet of waterfalls—three major falls in all—with a network of brilliantly engineered bridges, stairs, and walkways that seem to defy gravity. Visitors have the pleasure of standing directly opposite one of the most spectacular natural wonders in the Adirondacks and watching the river plummet downward through the gorge. There's a reasonable admission fee and a very nice gift shop.

Wilmington Notch campground follows High Falls Gorge on NY 86, a state-run campsite along the Ausable River gorge with access to views of more waterfalls, if you're willing to clamber down (and back up) a steep hill to see them. Just past the Notch, the famous **Whiteface Mountain Ski Center** offers gondola rides up the mountainside in summer and fall, and some of the area's best skiing in winter.

Just before you reach the town of Wilmington, pull off at the parking area for **The Flume.** Here you can see the river rushing through a narrow channel with great force, creating this flume effect that fascinates visitors. A number of fairly easy hiking trails begin here if you fancy a walk; check the map at the information kiosk in the parking area.

The town of Wilmington exists to accommodate anglers, hikers, and skiing enthusiasts, so you'll find plenty of hotels, inns, bed-and-breakfasts, restaurants, and other amenities in this concentrated area. Here you can enchant your children and grandchildren with a trip to **Santa's Workshop at the North Pole,** a theme park established in 1949. Visit Santa Claus in his home, see his toy and candy makers at work, meet some reindeer, ride in Santa's sleigh (actually a roller coaster), enjoy a meal at Mother Hubbard's restaurant, and see a children's show in one of the park's theaters. There's even a nativity pageant, if you want to remind your young ones of the true meaning of Christmas. The hamlet of North Pole, New York, has a real US Post Office at the park, so you can send holiday letters and cards from here and have them postmarked from the North Pole. At the gift shop, you can purchase a letter from Santa and have it sent to the child of your choice at Christmastime.

Whiteface Veterans Memorial Highway

At the north end of Wilmington, you'll find a turn to the west that leads to Whiteface Veterans Memorial Highway, the only route in the Adirondacks that leads

The views from the top of Whiteface are unparalleled on New York's scenic routes.

to the top of one of the high peaks. Climbing 2,500 feet in 5 miles, this winding mountain road ends at a corridor to an elevator in the heart of the mountain, where you can ride easily to the summit at 4,867 feet, the fifth-highest peak in New York. From here, you can enjoy a 360-degree view of the entire mountain range—one of the most astonishing vantage points in the northeastern US.

President Franklin Roosevelt attended the opening of this highway personally in 1936, seven years after construction began while he was governor of New York State. It's a toll road, so you will pay a fee at the alpine-style tollhouse as you enter the highway—and if you're here on a weekend during peak fall foliage season, you may wait in line for an hour or more at the tollhouse until parking spaces open up at the top of the mountain. We highly recommend visiting on a weekday or in the summer if idling at an entrance gate will put a damper on your day. The road is open from late May to mid-October.

Once you're on the highway, you will want to maintain the speed limit or even drive more slowly, giving yourself and your passengers the opportunity to enjoy the view. You will find plenty of places to pull off for a bit, including a prime viewpoint for **Lake Placid**—the only place you can reach by car to see the entire

horseshoe-shaped lake at once. When you get out of the car, the strong evergreen scent you're inhaling is balsam, the predominant fir tree at this elevation in New York. Sometimes this scent is mixed with the acrid odor of burning brakes, a good reminder to shift into low gear on your way down the mountain.

At the top, follow the instructions of the parking area attendants and circle through the stone castle. Built with the mountain's own granite excavated during the road construction project, **Whiteface Castle** stands at an elevation of 4,610 feet and contains a restaurant with a surprisingly healthy, casual menu as well as a gift shop, clothing store, and restrooms. The road winds through the castle to provide a turnaround point for cars, making it easy to park along the road once you've completed the loop. From here, you have the option of climbing stone stairs to the summit (another 276 feet up) or walking down a 426-foot-long corridor through the mountain itself to an elevator that will take you to the top.

On a clear day, your view from the summit extends all the way to **Lake Champlain** and the **Green Mountains** of Vermont to the east, and includes all 45 of the other high peaks, including **Mount Marcy,** the tallest point in the state. Maps on interpretive signs at the top help you find major landmarks. You'll also notice the University at Albany's three-story **Atmospheric Sciences Research Center,** where you are welcome to visit the extensive laboratory and observatory. Here researchers measure chemicals including carbon monoxide, nitrogen oxide, hydrogen peroxide, and formaldehyde in cloud, fog, and rainwater, while maintaining measurements of one of the longest continuous records of surface ozone in the world—a critical factor in air quality studies. If you have an interest in climate change, you may pick up some useful facts here.

When you are ready, return to your car by taking the stairs or elevator back to the castle area. Enjoy the return trip down the mountain (again, use low gear) and into the town of Wilmington.

Lake Placid, seen from a pull-off on the way to the top of Whiteface Mountain.

CATSKILL MOUNTAINS
SCENIC DRIVES

New York Routes 28 & 30

Kingston to East Branch

General description: An 87-mile drive through the Catskill Mountains and along the Pepacton Reservoir in eastern New York

Special attractions: Pepacton Reservoir, The Emerson Resort and Spa, the Kaleidoscraper (world's largest kaleidoscope) at Emerson Country Store, Catskill Mountain Railroad, Panther Mountain, Rip Van Winkle Flyer scenic train rides, Downsville Dam, Downsville covered bridge

Location: The drive begins at the junction of US 209 and NY 28 just west of Kingston, off I-87, and ends in East Branch at the junction of NY 30 and NY17.

Route numbers: NY 28, NY 30

Travel season: Year-round. Snow and ice can limit visibility and make these roads slippery in winter.

Camping: Kenneth L. Wilson Campground in Mt. Tremper; Woodland Valley Campground, Phonecia Black Bear Campground and RV Park, Romer Mountain Park, Hide-A-Way Campsite and Sleepy Hollow Campsite, all in Phonecia

Services: In Kingston, West Hurley, Olive, Ashokan, Boiceville, Mt. Tremper, Mt. Pleasant, Phonecia, Arkville, Margaretville, and Downsville

Nearby attractions: Woodstock Colony of the Arts; downhill skiing at Sawkill in Kingston, Bobcat in Andes, Plattekill Mountain Resort in Roxbury, and Bellayre near Highmount; Delaware and Ulster Rail Ride; Bailiwick Animal Park and Riding Stables in Catskill; Hudson River Cruises in Kingston

The Route

Welcome to Catskill Park, one of two massive preserves in New York State that contain both private and public land. About 100 miles north of New York City and 40 miles south of Albany, the park forms the northeastern end of the Allegheny Plateau, a mountain range that extends all the way to Kentucky and as far west as Ohio. The mountains begin dramatically on the shores of the Hudson River, where they rise sharply, and they roll gradually through the southeastern part of the state until their height begins to decline as they join the plateau to the west and blend into the Poconos to the south.

Modeled after European parks in which highly valued natural land areas coexist with the people who live within their borders, Catskill Park became a protected area in 1885 in an effort to save the area's natural beauty from destruction. Logging, bluestone quarrying, and other unregulated harvesting threatened

It's worth the hike to see Kaaterskill Falls, the tallest waterfall in New York State.

New York Routes 28 & 30: Kingston to East Branch

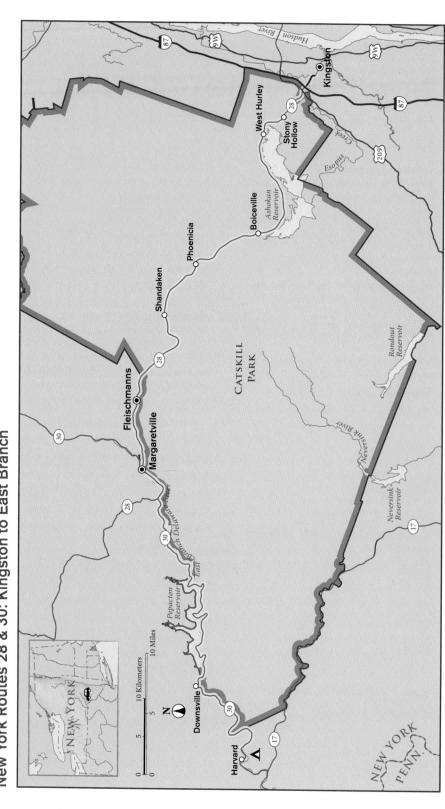

to strip and clear-cut the 98 peaks' forests and mountainsides, leaving a denuded landscape in place of the heavily forested mountainsides we enjoy today. The effort has not only paid off, but it has saved nearly ten times the originally protected land mass: While the Catskill Forest Preserve began with 34,000 acres, it now shelters nearly 300,000 pristine acres that will "be forever kept as wild forest lands," as the New York State Constitution states. "They shall not be leased, sold or exchanged, or be taken by any corporation, public or private, nor shall the timber thereon be sold, removed, or destroyed."

Just about any drive through Catskill Park leads through classic views of the beech, birch, and maple forests that blanket these emerald mountains, but the drive we've chosen provides some of the finest highland views with the added attraction of the placidly shimmering Pepacton Reservoir. The largest of the upstate bodies that provide water to New York City, Pepacton presents a number of opportunities to pull into a parking area and enjoy expansive views of the startlingly clear water, the surrounding green peaks, and a protected shoreline with none of the cottages and trailers that surround most of New York's lakes.

The route we've selected winds through some of the Catskills' highest peaks, including **Slide Mountain**—the highest mountain in the region—and **Panther Mountain,** a peak with its own curious story. Visible from NY 28 near the towns of Highmount and Shandaken, the 3,720-foot peak forms a ridge in the center of a circle created by Esopus and Woodland Creeks. This configuration of the mountain and the two waterways caught the attention of a New York State Geological Survey (NYSGS) scientist, Yngvar Isachsen, back in the 1970s. Isachsen hypothesized that the mountain rose from an impact crater created by a falling meteorite some 375 million years ago—a ridge formed by landslides that were triggered when the meteor hit the ground, piling up dirt and rock in the middle of the crater. He examined cuttings taken from the area by the NYSGS, finding evidence of minerals that could only come from the impact of a meteorite.

The Catskills are among the oldest mountains on the North American continent, the result of the erosion of the Acadian Mountains to the north around 395 million years ago. Streams and glaciers carried off much of the sediments that settled on these mountains since their original formation, so the Catskills do not present the kinds of high peaks we find in the younger Rocky Mountains—but the beauty of the landscape here rivals just about anything you will find in other parts of the country. For endless green forests stretching beyond the horizon and turning crimson and gold in fall, the Catskills provide the refreshing change city dwellers seek when they head away from congested highways and into the open air.

The Catskill Mountains provide spectacular views along this road.

Kingston to Mt. Tremper

The drive begins at the junction of US 209 and NY 28 just west of **Kingston,** where the road is also known as Onteora Trail. The seat of Ulster County, Kingston briefly served as the capital of New York State during the Revolutionary War in 1777, when Albany—which had just been named the capital of the free State of New York—was under threat of British attack. Relocating the seat of government to Kingston seemed like a prudent move, but like so many precautionary measures, this one ended ironically: The Continental Army stopped the British at the Battle of Saratoga, so the enemy never made it to Albany . . . but they did burn Kingston on October 16, 1777, by coming up the Hudson River and entering the city near Rondout Creek. The joke was on the British, however, because the residents of Kingston knew the British were coming and evacuated the area, fleeing down the road to Hurley. If you happen to

Pepacton Reservoir provides water to New York City residents.

be passing through the area in October of an odd-numbered year, you can see a dramatic, town-wide reenactment of this historic event.

Pass the Tibetan Center—where you may want to visit the fascinating Tibetan Gift Store—on your way out of town, and watch as the mountains come into view as you approach West Hurley. To your left beyond the trees is the **Ashokan Reservoir,** one of six that supplies water from the Catskills to New York City. The reservoir rarely becomes fully visible on this road, but you will glimpse it repeatedly until it tapers down into Esopus Creek after you pass through Olive.

As you pass NY 375, you'll see signs for the town of **Woodstock.** The town itself is worth a stop to explore more than a dozen galleries and shops that showcase the work of local and nationally recognized artists. If you're looking for the famous farmer's fields that became the site of the Woodstock Music Festival on August 15–18, 1969, however, you may be surprised to discover that the festival actually took place at the farm owned by Max Yasgur in Bethel, 43 miles southwest of the town of Woodstock.

As you pass Boulevard Road, **Kenozia Lake** comes into view. Water lilies often cover this lake in summer, creating an unusually picturesque spot surrounded by reeds and other tall grasses. In a moment you're in the town of **Olive,** a town for which life changed in 1905 when New York City's demand for clean water required the Board of Water Supply to go well outside of the five boroughs to access the state's natural resources. The Board targeted the Catskills in general and **Esopus Creek**—which runs parallel to NY 28—in particular, building the dams that formed the Ashokan Reservoir and the Catskill Aqueduct. New York City got its clean water, but at the expense of the livelihoods of farmers who tilled the Esopus Valley. As the reservoirs flooded the valley and the farmland disappeared, these people moved into the foothills and changed their way of life. You can see a sign that marks the former site of Olive to your left as you drive into the town of Shokan.

The **Olive and Hurley Old School Baptist Church** has stood in this spot along NY 28 since 1857, and while its congregation has long since moved on, it still hosts an annual service every fall. In 1998 the building and grounds were listed on the National Register of Historic Places, making them ripe for renovation—so the building you see today has undergone a significant restoration that began in 1999. The roof replacement, rebuilding of the belfry, porch reinforcement, and locally procured bluestone front porch saved the building from the ravages of nearly two centuries of weather.

Mountain views become more impressive as you continue down the road toward Mt. Tremper. Don't miss whatever bizarre sculpture may be standing in front of **Fabulous Furniture** in Boiceville; when we last passed it, a makeshift rocket capsule labeled "Roswell or Bust" stood in the front yard beside a wide range of curiosities.

Mt. Tremper to Margaretville

As Esopus Creek comes into view on your left and the Migliorelli Farm stand appears, the view of the Catskills opens up to the right and ahead of you. In a moment, keep an eye out for **The Emerson Resort and Spa** on your right, where you'll find upscale boutique shopping, high-quality antiques, and the **Kaleido-store**—a shop dedicated almost entirely to kaleidoscopes. The resort is a fairly new addition to the area's hospitality scene, and it features a fine restoration of a number of older buildings, as well as some new construction to accommodate guests in 53 rooms and suites. The Catamount Restaurant and the Emerson Spa add to the complete package, making this a highly rated getaway spot for a weekend or longer.

As if luxury pedicures and rustic-chic guest rooms weren't enough, The Emerson features a one-of-a-kind attraction: the World's Largest Kaleidoscope, built within the large silo on The Emerson's grounds. Not surprisingly, the nearly 60-foot-tall kaleidoscope has a multidimensional past: Built in 1996, the scope was designed by Charles Karadimos (a name you will recognize if you're a kaleidoscope aficionado), and the video used to create the scope's imagery came from the psychotropic brain of 1960s artist Isaac Abrams and his son, computer artist Raphael Abrams. For $5 per person, you can enjoy a 10-minute show by stepping into the silo, lying on the ground or leaning on a support platform designed for this purpose, and looking up. A 37-foot-tall, 2.5-ton assembly of mirrored surfaces reflects Abrams's artwork and makes the prismatic images.

YOUR ICE CREAM STOP: JANE'S HOMEMADE ICE CREAM

Served at Migliorelli Farm as well as in Kingston, this rich confection—developed by two sisters in nearby Phoenicia—delivers some of the most intense flavors we've found in New York State. Killer Chocolate serves up as much cocoa flavor as a high-end candy bar, while the White Pistachio bursts with the aroma and essence of freshly picked and ground nuts. Visit the store at 307 Wall St. in Kingston if you want to try out a wider selection of flavors.

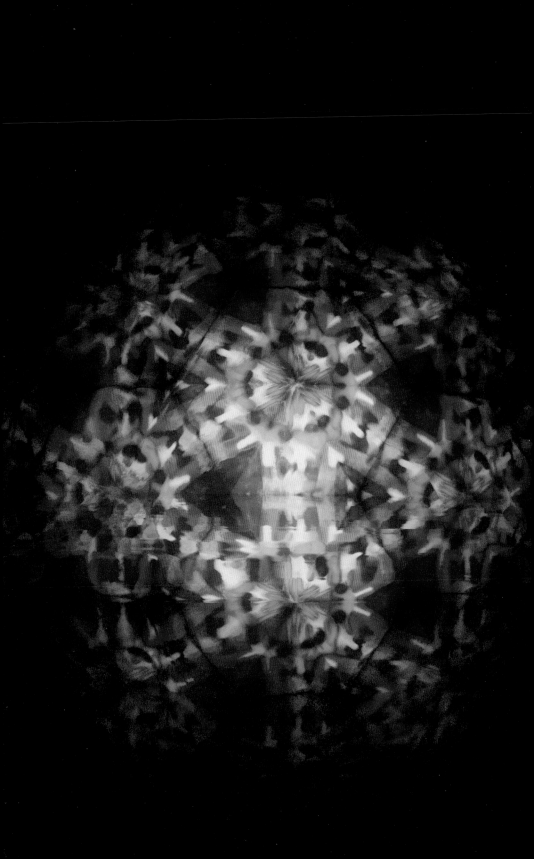

From Mt. Tremper to Arkville, relax with sweeping views of the mountains, and consider a side trip into **Phoenicia** when you see the signs for it to your right (up NY 214). Recently named "one of the 10 coolest small towns in America" by *Budget Travel*, Phoenicia offers a remarkable assortment of galleries, shops, restaurants, and services for a town of its size, with just enough quirkiness to make visitors smile—like a library that allows you to check out ukuleles and fishing gear.

As you cross Dry Brook in Arkville, you officially enter Catskill Park and follow its border for the rest of this drive. Watch for the junction with NY 30, and turn south on NY 30 to continue into Margaretville.

The tiny village of Margaretville took a beating in 2011 during Hurricane Irene, losing its CVS Pharmacy and a number of other buildings. The village recovered admirably, however, and you will find interesting places to shop and explore along its Main Street, from **Catskill Mountain Artisans Guild Shop** to **Barbara Alyn Artwear**, both filled with the work of local painters, sculptors, and potters.

Margaretville to East Branch

As you leave Margaretville, the road crosses the **East Branch of the Delaware River,** and some of the best mountain vistas on your route so far come into view. Here you can begin to see the **Pepacton Reservoir,** which you will follow all the way to East Branch. Towns are few and far between along this section of the road, as most of the small villages were relocated when the New York City Board of Water chose this location for the largest of its six Catskill reservoirs. Keep an eye out for signs that note the former locations of these towns: Arena, Pepacton, Union, and parts of Middletown, Andes, and Colchester, all of which were displaced when reservoir construction began in 1947. You can enjoy excellent views of this reservoir from several parking areas along its length, the best of which comes up just after you cross a bridge over the reservoir and see the Andes town sign. In another few miles you'll reach the Downsville Dam and East Branch Release Chamber, where you can pull over briefly for a photo—but this is heavily posted New York City Department of Environmental Protection land, so walking out onto the dam is not permitted.

When the reservoir begins to fade from view, watch for the town of Downsville, and turn left onto Bridge Street from NY 30 when you see the sign for the **Downsville Covered Bridge.** The bridge is just off the main road, adjacent to a

Stop at The Emerson to see the world's largest kaleidoscope.

park and picnic area where you can leave your car and walk out onto the bridge. Built in 1854 and restored in 1998, the 174-foot bridge was added to the National Register of Historic Places in 1999. It's a one-lane bridge, but you are welcome to drive across it.

From here, NY 30 winds through the tiny towns of Colchester, Shinhopple, and Harvard, with stunning views of the mountains to the west and south before you reach East Branch and the junction with NY 17.

Downsville's covered bridge was built in 1854 and restored in 1998.

9

Watson Hollow & Peekamoose Roads

General description: If you're looking to escape the perpetual din of New York State's cities and really hear yourself think, Peekamoose Road is far enough off the beaten path to provide peace and quiet. This 18-mile rural byway through the Catskill Mountain reaches as many as 8 waterfalls—or as few as 3, depending on the season and the annual rainfall.

Special attractions: Waterfalls, Bush Kill, Rondout Creek, Rondout Reservoir, possible sightings of black bears, white-tailed deer, and other wildlife

Location: The route begins at the junction of NY 28A and County Route 42 in Ulster County, north of Ellenville and west of Woodstock on the far western edge of the Ashokan Reservoir.

Route numbers: Ulster County Route 42, County Route 153, NY 55A, NY 55

Travel season: Spring, summer, and fall; while the road is maintained in winter, it can be narrow and slippery

Camping: Woodland Valley Campground is west of the route.

Services: In Kingston and Hurley to the east, and in Woodbourne and Fallsburg to the southwest

Nearby attractions: Stone Arch Bridge Historical Park, Upper Delaware Scenic and Recreational River, Ashokan Reservoir, Holiday Mountain Ski Area, Sam's Point Preserve, High Mountain, Peekamoose Mountain

The Route

One of the best-kept secrets in the Catskills, Watson Hollow and Peekamoose Roads follow along the edges of two creeks—**Bush Kill and Rondout Creek**— while providing access to tiny tributaries that descend from the surrounding mountains. The fairly short drive winds through a valley in the **Balsam Lake Mountain Wild Forest,** a protected part of Catskill Park and a sparsely populated neighborhood. There are no services along this route, but this lends charm to a rustic area where black bears cross the road to drink from the streams, and white-tailed deer stand along the roadside and blink at you as you pass.

Most interesting here are the number and variety of waterfalls revealed every time you drive across a bridge. Brooks and streams tumble down the nearby mountainsides and under Peekamoose Road, and the rocky hillsides become ledges from which this water can fall in particularly attractive ways. How many waterfalls you see will depend on the weather in the season you drive this route: If the Catskills have experienced heavy rainfall, or if the winter delivered a significant amount of snow, you may see as many as eight waterfalls during the spring thaw and into the

Watson Hollow & Peekamoose Roads

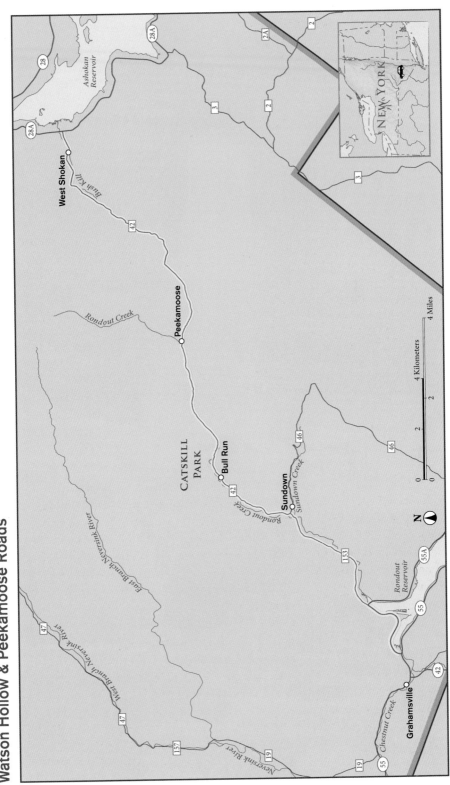

summer. A dry season, however, may replenish only three or four of the waterfalls. Either way, you will have the opportunity to see falling water, and there's a good chance you'll spot some of the creatures that come to drink from the falls.

Watson Hollow Road

The drive begins at the junction of NY 28A and County Route 42 in the town of Olive. Drive west on Watson Hollow Road (CR 42), and cross **Bush Kill** after you pass High Point Mountain Road. **High Point Mountain** rises in front of you, a 3,080-foot peak that stands as the 83rd highest mountain in the Catskills. Hikers highly recommend the 8-mile hike to the summit and back that begins at the Kanape Brook parking area ahead of you, but the 1,980-foot elevation gain may seem daunting to those of us who choose to see these mountains from the car.

Bush Kill continues to the left of the road as you drive through open meadows that end at thickly wooded slopes. **Misty Hollow Brook** comes in from the right to meet Bush Kill, flowing under a bridge as you pass. In another moment, **South Hollow Brook** comes down a mountain to your left.

The view opens up as you reach the top of the road's first major climb, giving you a pleasantly winding descent as you approach Bush Kill's junction with Rondout Creek. **Peekamoose Lake** comes into view on your right—a body of water created by the dam you see here. There's an electric gate and no guardrail or shoulder along the road, so you may want to content yourself with a quick look from the comfort of your vehicle. From here, Watson Hollow Road has become Peekamoose Road.

Peekamoose Road

Follow Peekamoose Road as it traces the path of Rondout Creek, and watch for the first bridge. When you cross the bridge, look right to see the waterfall. This is **Bear Hole Brook,** and you can use the pull-off areas on either side of the bridge if you'd like to get out for a closer look. The surrounding land is posted against trespassers, but you are welcome to explore the brook and the falls.

Return to your car and continue to the next bridge over **Stone Cabin Brook.** There's a waterfall here in wet weather, and you can stop in the gravel pull-off area if you like. **High Falls Brook** is the next waterway to come in on your right—the

Waterfalls come and go throughout the year on Peekamoose Road, but you can depend on seeing at least a few.

falls here drops from a high ledge, just as its name would suggest. Continue to watch for additional falls each time you cross a bridge.

Sundown Creek meets Rondout Creek on the left side of the road at **Sundown Wild Forest,** where you will find trailheads, a campground, and other amenities in season. As you come into the town of Sundown, homes begin to appear along the road. This is the end of the waterfall portion of this drive, but you can continue on County Route 46 as it becomes NY 55A, and turn left on NY 55A for a very pleasant drive along **Rondout Reservoir.**

Built from 1937 to 1954, Rondout Reservoir provides water to New York City—in fact, it's one of six reservoirs in the Catskills constructed for this purpose. For Manhattanites to get this water, however, three Catskill villages had to be sacrificed. As you drive along the reservoir, watch for signs that note the previous locations of Lackawack, Montela, and Eureka, all of which were condemned and flooded to create this 6.5-mile-long lake. Today Rondout Reservoir contains 49.6 billion gallons of water, which reaches New York City through the 85-mile-long Delaware Aqueduct—the world's longest continuous underground tunnel.

Merriman Dam marks the southeastern end of Rondout Reservoir, and NY 55A soon joins NY 55 as it follows the southern end of Rondout Creek all the way down to **Honk Lake.** Here the road enters the town of Ellenville and US 209, ending the scenic drive.

Rondout Creek provides the waterfalls along Peekamoose Road.

10

Hudson River School Art Trail

General description: A different kind of scenic drive, this 25-mile tour takes you to eight of the places where Thomas Cole, Frederic Church, and other artists of the Hudson River School found the scenic views that inspired their paintings. Once you've completed this route, we recommend adding a 25-mile drive west on NY 23A as far as Prattsville to take in some of the region's most impressive views of the Catskill Mountains.

Special attractions: Thomas Cole National Historic Site, Olana State Historic Site, Kaaterskill Clove, Kaaterskill Falls, Bastion Falls, North-South Lake

Location: Catskill, Palenville, and Haines Falls, NY

Route numbers: US 9W, NY 23A, County Route 18

Travel season: Spring, summer, and fall

Camping: North-South Lake Campground in Haines Falls, Devils Tombstone Campground in Hunter, Kenneth Wilson Campground near Woodstock

Services: In Catskill and Palenville

Nearby attractions: Catskill Mountains

The Route

It's one thing to drive through the Catskill Mountains and take in all the lovely views from your car, but it's quite another to walk in the footsteps of the painters who created the first uniquely American style of artistic expression: the **Hudson River School.** Back in the mid-1800s, a young artist named Thomas Cole became the founder of an art movement that interpreted the natural landscape, long before photography allowed every traveler to document each pretty view in the blink of an eye. Transplanted from England by his parents in 1818, Cole discovered the Catskill wilderness in 1825 and made it his home beginning in 1832, renting a small studio at the Cedar Grove home that is now a National Historic Landmark. With the goal of creating a legacy to help Americans, in his words, "know better how to appreciate the treasures of their own country," Cole created paintings of wild, unspoiled scenery, with gnarled trees, sweeping clouds, dense forests, and tumbling waters—all the elements that artists had smoothed out of their paintings in favor of pristine landscapes for many generations. Cole's work inspired other painters of his era to join in this new American style of art, and their paintings continue to persuade others to seek personal renewal through the beauty of the nation's landscapes.

The Thomas Cole National Historic Site put together this driving and hiking tour of eight sites at which Cole and his contemporaries found the scenes they

Hudson River School Art Trail

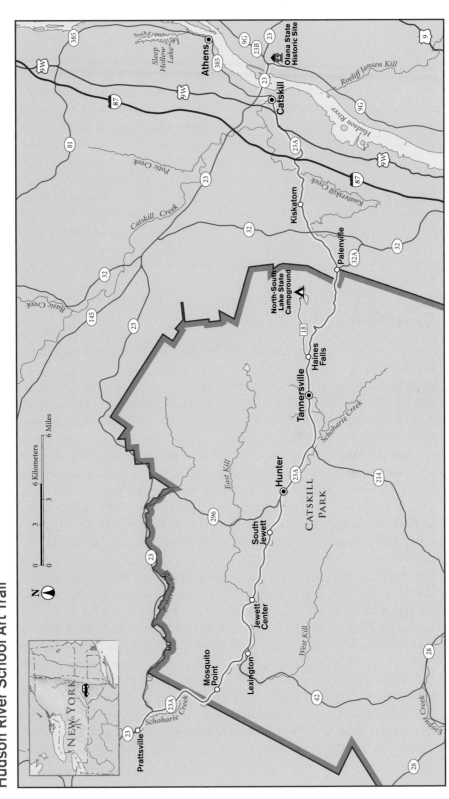

made famous. Now you can stand in the same places and see mountains, lakes, trees, and waterfalls that appear markedly similar to the way they were more than 150 years ago, perhaps in tribute to the artists who showed us that these places had value just as they were when they captured them in watercolor or oils.

To see some of these iconic places, you will need to do some walking. The trail to Kaaterskill Falls requires a 0.5-mile uphill hike, though the Adirondack Mountain Club maintains and stabilizes the path to make it passable for any healthy person with good hiking shoes. Likewise, the Sunset Rock viewpoint appears at the end of a gentle 1-mile hike with some uphill slopes. The one promise we can make is that the scenes at the end of these hikes are oh-so-worth the effort—and if you think about what it took for Cole and his compatriots to reach these points in the 1820s and 1830s, the energy you expel will seem almost trivial in comparison.

Cedar Grove

The journey begins at **Cedar Grove, the Thomas Cole National Historic Site,** at 218 Spring St. in the town of Catskill. When you see the view of the Hudson River from the front yard and the upstairs windows of this hillside mansion, you will know exactly why Cole chose to make this place his home. At the time, Cedar Grove's property extended all the way to the river, an advantage that his descendants continued to enjoy for many decades after his death.

Four years after renting the studio (which stood where Temple Israel is now) and shortly after he completed some of his best-known paintings in a series he titled, "The Course of Empire," Cole married Maria Bartow and the Coles moved into the big house. Years later he designed the ultimate studio and had this New Studio built in 1846, a marvelous Italianate structure that the National Historic Landmark has reconstructed based on photos and drawings of the original building.

It's free to walk the grounds here at Cedar Grove, and you are welcome to enjoy the view for as long as you like. The site charges a nominal fee for tours of the house. Here you will find the first of eight interpretive signs that will appear at each of the stops on the art trail. Look also for the **Hudson River Skywalk,** a new walkway that connects the homes of Thomas Cole and Frederic Church (more on Church in a moment) with a pedestrian route across the Hudson River via the Rip Van Winkle Bridge. The views from this walkway are some of the best you will find in the Hudson River Valley.

From the parking area at Cedar Grove, turn right onto Spring Street and cross the **Hudson River** on the **Rip Van Winkle Bridge.** Bear right on NY 9G south. Your goal is **Olana State Historic Site,** 1 mile south of the bridge on the left.

This view from the grounds at Olana inspired Frederic Edwin Church's landscape paintings.

Olana and Its Landscape

Thomas Cole inspired a number of painters to capture the Catskill landscape, including Frederic Edwin Church, who became one of the most famous of the Hudson River School artists. In many ways, his glorious Olana became another of his many masterpieces, a Persian-style mansion created not only to take best advantage of the landscapes and views around it, but to contribute to and become one with these natural wonders.

Tour the home, walk through the lush gardens as they take full advantage of each season, and stop on your way out as you wind down the carriage road at the Hudson River view (you'll see the interpretive sign there). Today's view from here sports more foliage than it did in Church's day, and the three radio towers have been provided as a courtesy of modern progress, but you can still appreciate the splendid panorama of the Hudson River and surrounding hills.

Olana is open for tours Apr through Nov and is closed on Mon, but the grounds are open just about any day you'd like to visit.

As you leave Olana, turn right and continue to the Rip Van Winkle Bridge. Cross the bridge and continue straight on NY 23 west for 0.5 mile. Turn left onto US 9W south, and drive about 1,000 feet past the ramp to Jefferson Heights. Continue to the bridge across **Catskill Creek.** Just before you reach the bridge, pull into the parking area at 601 Main Street. You'll see the next stop just past the building (a former restaurant) alongside the creek, where there's a gazebo and an interpretive sign.

View on Catskill Creek

Both Thomas Cole and Frederic Church painted this scene a number of times, capturing it in different seasons and at both sunrise and sunset. The historic site has done us a courtesy by putting up a white wooden frame to let us know just where to stand to see the famous view the way the artists saw it. The view faces west, so Church in particular worked to reproduce the "magic hour" that so fascinates artists and photographers with the quality of the glow in the sky just before twilight.

Note the sharply pointed mountain in the painting, and stand where you can position this mountain in the right place in the wooden frame. This is the best way to see today's landscape as it compares with the way Cole and Church saw it. It's particularly interesting to note, however, that Cole's first painting of this scene had little to do with its actual appearance—the painting was commissioned by Jonathan Sturges, who specifically asked Cole to paint Catskill Creek as he wished it looked. At the time, the area had become an industrial center crowded with gristmills, sawmills, carding machines, factories, ironworks, and tanneries. Knowing this, we can be even more impressed with the skill of these artists to create such a fancifully natural landscape out of this chaos of manufacturing.

From here, continue south on NY 9W to pick up NY 23A south of Catskill. Begin traveling west on NY 23A.

Catskill Creek drew Thomas Cole to its banks again and again.

YOUR ICE CREAM STOP: CONE E ISLAND

What better way to top off tours of two historic sites than with an ice cream cone? Cone E Island at 8 West Bridge St. in Catskill offers home-made hard ice cream and the richest, creamiest vanilla/chocolate twist soft-serve we've had anywhere—with that velvety finish that wine connoisseurs talk about when they sample a fine Cabernet. It's almost a shame to dip such a thing into a chocolate, cherry, or blue raspberry topping, but these may be too hard to resist. The Strawberry Extreme ice cream, another clas-sic flavor, brings out the bold sweetness of the fruit without overpowering it with sugar. If you want something really special, try a slice of the brownie pie—a dense chocolate cake crust covered in a thick layer of chocolate ice cream, with real whipped cream and sprinkles. You just might decide to skip lunch and go straight to dessert.

Kaaterskill Clove and Kaaterskill Falls

About a mile after you leave Catskill, the mountains begin to rise up on the horizon, the clusters of homes thin out and disappear, and suddenly you're viewing the **Blackhead Mountains**—the northeastern Catskills—over a pumpkin field. Take a moment to find the peak with the sharp point that was in the Catskill Creek painting you saw a little while ago.

The town of **Palenville**—a gas station, a general store, and a sign for Hunter Mountain—comes up quickly, and it's likely that one thing will catch your eye here: Palenville considers itself the home of fictional character Rip Van Winkle. If you read the short story Washington Irving wrote in 1819, or if you've seen any of the film adaptations dating back to 1905 or the episodes of animated television shows that parody the story, you know the tale—but here's a quick refresher: A mild-mannered man falls asleep in the Catskill Mountains and wakes up 20 years later, unaware that he slept for a generation. Based on Irving's vivid description of the town and its surroundings, Palenville chose to adopt the character and take his village's identity. As Irving had never actually been to the Catskill Mountains when he wrote the story, he could not possibly have had a particular town in mind, so no village is slighted by Palenville's adoption of the story as its own. Likewise, NY 23A became the modern designation for what was known as Rip Van Winkle Trail.

Shortly after passing through Palenville, you will cross the "Blue Line" and enter Catskill Park. The road begins to wind through the mountains at this point, signaling that you're in for a treat—this scenic route offers unsurpassed natural beauty, rivaled in New York State only by the Adirondacks' High Peaks Scenic Byway.

Pass **Fawn's Leap,** a narrow waterfall in **Kaaterskill Creek,** and begin watching for **Bastion Falls.** This massive waterfall appears on your right at a 90-degree bend in the road. Drive on by and into the parking area on the left side of the road about a third of a mile past Bastion Falls. You won't miss it; on any nice day, the parking area will be crowded with visitors from all over the world who have come to enjoy the view of **Kaaterskill Clove** and to hike to New York State's tallest waterfall, **Kaaterskill Falls** (see photo on section opener, page 78).

As many of the people parking here have stopped just to see the view and grab a quick photo, a spot probably will open up for you in a few minutes. Once you're parked, take a good look at the view. The deep valley called Kaaterskill Clove, created by a network of creeks and streams winding between mountains, dives downward from here for as much as 2,500 feet. Whatever the weather, this view has the power to thrill visitors with its startlingly majestic mountain slopes and its enchanting hues, but fall really turns the clove into a cavalcade of color, light, and shadow.

Not surprisingly, Kaaterskill Clove inspired a number of artists of the Hudson River School to immortalize it. In addition to Thomas Cole, artists Asher Brown

Kaaterskill Clove inspires artists to this day.

Durand and Sanford Gifford painted this landscape, and artist Jennie Augusta Brownscombe had a studio nearby.

From here, walk east on NY 23A to Bastion Falls, following the road carefully along the left side and stepping over guardrails to stay away from traffic as much as you can. Oncoming cars zip around this bend, making caution a good idea. When you reach the falls, there's plenty of room to step away from the road and admire the 30-foot cascade to your heart's content. Bastion serves as a sort of aquatic appetizer to the main course farther up: Kaaterskill Falls, a 264-foot, two-part drop at the end of a rocky but well-constructed 0.5-mile trail.

If you choose to make the trek up to the big falls—and I did it, which means that any healthy person can do it—you will see one of the most painted sights in the entire Catskill region. The falls splits into two distinct sections, the first a stunning, sheer drop from a notch at the top of the gorge, and the second pouring in half a dozen torrents from a hanging valley to a boulder-clogged pool below. From here, Lake Creek (a tributary of Kaaterskill Creek) flits and frills down the mountain, creating shallow rapids and whitecaps as it trips along to Bastion Falls. You can linger in front of Kaaterskill Falls, sitting on large, flat slabs of rock to observe the hypnotizing glitter of water in the sun, or you can do what some folks enjoy and take the trail next to the falls to get to the hanging valley and stand behind the cascade. Some people climb to the top of the falls, but I can't see any good reason for doing that, ever. If you must see the falls from the top, there's a far less risky trail to it in nearby North-South Lake Campground and Day Use Area.

The trail to Kaaterskill Falls involves climbing a series of stone and/or wooden stairs up the mountainside, with some short, level walks between them. We completed the trek up in about 15 minutes, and took more time going down—the rock steps can be slippery if it's rained in the last few days. All in all, plan an hour of your day to reach and enjoy Kaaterskill Falls. We think you'll be glad you did.

When you've left the falls, walked along the roadside, and returned to your vehicle, continue west on NY 23A.

Haines Falls and North-South Lake State Campground

When you reach County Route 18 in the town of Haines Falls, turn right and drive 2 miles to the **North-South Lake State Campground.** Pay the day-use fee at the campground entrance and get a map from the ranger, as getting around the park can be a little confusing. Once you're in the campground, bear left toward North Lake Beach, and turn right at the stop sign. Drive down the hill and park in the small parking area near the Recreation Center. You'll see a short, level path directly across the parking area from the Recreation Center; take this path about 250 feet. Look across South Lake for the head of Round Top, the mountain rising above South Mountain. This is just about where Cole stood when he sketched the area for his painting *Lake With Dead Trees*. The dead trees themselves are long gone, replaced by successional forest as the area regained its mantle of deciduous trees, so the view may seem even more attractive than Cole's painting had already led us to believe.

From here, your next view is at **Sunset Rock,** reachable with a walk through pine trees and flat rocks for 0.9 mile. Many consider this view to be the single best panorama in the Catskill Mountains, so if you're willing to put in the effort (it's not nearly as challenging as the hike to Kaaterskill Falls), you will be rewarded at the end. Starting from the North-South Lake beach parking area, begin the hike at the bulletin board just before the North Lake Beach parking lot. Follow the short trail with yellow markers into the pine forest, and join the Escarpment Trail in 0.1 mile. Begin to follow the blue trail markers to the left. Scramble up a ledge to the trail register, and walk over some flat slabs of rock from one viewpoint to the next until you reach Artist's Rock (you've gone 0.3 mile at this point). The trail levels out here until you reach another short uphill stretch at 0.7 mile. Turn right at the trail junction and follow the yellow markers to Sunset Rock. Enjoy the magnificent

Here's the spot where Thomas Cole sketched Lake With Dead Trees.

view of North and South Lakes, the Hudson River, and the surrounding peaks and valleys, just as Thomas Cole, Sanford Gifford, and fellow artist Jasper Cropsey did when they paced this trail to capture this sight.

You have one more spot to explore before leaving this most excellent park. Return to the Escarpment Trail (the one with blue markers) and walk east to the grassy, open area where you'll see interpretive signs about **Catskill Mountain House.** This exquisite mansion once served thousands of guests during "season," as wealthy city dwellers made the journey to the mountains to escape the heat and odors of summer in Manhattan. The hotel operated here until 1941, when World War II and the growing popularity of the Adirondacks finally eclipsed the Mountain House's supremacy. The building fell into disrepair and eventually was demolished in a controlled burn by the state conservation department in the winter of 1963, but while the hotel no longer drew guests here, the view of the mountains, lakes, and Hudson River from this spot never ceased to attract admirers.

Perhaps it goes without saying that such a view would also attract artists. The Catskill Mountain House became a favorite resort for painters of the Hudson River School, who came here to make the most of the amazing scenery and the genteel clientele. Thomas Cole himself came here often and produced many great works

From the former site of Catskill Mountain House, this view captured many a Hudson River School artist's imagination.

from this spot, not the least of which was his *A View of Two Lakes and Mountain House, Catskill Mountains, Morning,* which now resides in the Brooklyn Museum. Jasper Cropsey, William Henry Bartlett, and Frederic Church all painted this view from a number of different angles, some of which they sold to hotel guests as expensive keepsakes of their visit. Both James Fenimore Cooper and Washington Irving wrote of this place in their novels and stories. Even 18th-century botanist and explorer John Bartram, considered the father of American botany, purportedly collected specimens and wrote about this area.

The Catskill Mountain House is the last stop on your tour of the Hudson River School Art Trail. It's a lovely place to end the day, but if it's still early and you'd like to see more of the area and its sweeping vistas, we recommend that you continue your drive by returning to NY 23A and heading west once again.

Haines Falls to Prattsville

You'll find gas and other services in Haines Falls, but you may want to wait to stop again until you reach **Tannersville,** a sweet little village with hotels, restaurants,

The Shawangunk Ridge is one of the most distinctive natural landmarks in New York State.

Conservancy—and because of this and the preserve's protection of nearly 40 rare plant and animal species, the conservancy has made this place one of its highest priorities for conservation in the US.

It may not surprise you that artists have found inspiration from these spectacular mountain views and the diversity of plant and animal life here for centuries. Nearby, the **Cragsmoor Historic District** once housed an artists' colony that included the popular rural nostalgia painter Edward Lamson Henry, as well as figure and landscape artist George Inness Jr. The entire district was named to the National Register of Historic Places in 1996. A short drive or a stroll through the 19th-century cottages will give you a sense of what it must have been like to live among those who shared a passion for capturing this natural landscape on canvas.

As you continue along the ridgeline on this winding road, the town of Shawangunk offers its only stunning views from its hamlets, Walkill, Pine Bush, and Walker Valley. Here you'll find that locals pronounce the town's name SHON-gunk, and that the name comes from the Lenape Indian word for "in the smoky air," transliterated into Dutch. Some say the name references the mountains on a

misty morning, while historians suggest that it might refer to the smoke from the burning of a Munsee Indian fort by the Dutch in 1663. Whichever meaning you prefer, the views from this town continue to impress, and the Walkill River running through the area adds another dimension to the local colors.

As you come into Pine Bush, watch for the left turn onto County Route 7. This is the road to **Brimstone Hill Vineyard & Winery,** one of the area's oldest wineries—founded in 1969—with about 13 acres of grapevines and a robust selection of wines from its own grapes. Particularly notable is the Noiret, an unusual grape developed in New York State that produces a solid red table wine. The Noiret is one of Brimstone's most celebrated wines, winning a bronze medal in 2011.

YOUR ICE CREAM STOP: THORNDALE DAIRY BAR

Don't miss this delicious stop on the corner of NY 52 and NY 302 in Pine Bush, where you can order from nearly two dozen flavors made on the premises. The Banana Cream Pie ice cream bursts with fruit flavor even as it provides satisfying crunchiness with chunks of graham cracker crust, and the Brownie Chocolate Chip Cookie Dough would actually be too chocolaty if such a thing were possible. Birthday Cake ice cream has become a staple at a lot of creameries, but here it's loaded with swirls of frosting and chunks of actual cake. Order mix-ins, sundaes, shakes, or any of your other favorite treats here as well, and enjoy them at outdoor picnic tables while you take in the remarkable Shawangunk area views.

Pine Bush to New Paltz

As you continue east on NY 52, descend into the valley and leave the mountains behind you as cropland and pastures spread out in the foreground. Turn left onto Albany Post Road (County Route 14, which soon becomes County Route 9) and continue through pastures with interesting livestock: cattle, horses, the occasional goat, chickens, and sheep grazing on the hillside. Walkill River burbles to the east as the 'Gunks reappear to the north and west.

The approach to the Shawangunk Mountains offers expansive views.

Soon you come to the junction with US 44/NY 55 again, and you begin to see signs for the Shawangunk Wine Trail. As if to prove the point, **Robibero Family Vineyards** comes into view almost immediately as you continue straight on Albany Post Road. This 42-acre winery produces artisan wines in limited amounts—sometimes no more than 40 cases—and sells them only at the vineyard or online, so a visit here is an opportunity to try some fairly rare vintages.

Stay on Albany Post Road as it becomes County Route 7, passing the Ulster County Fairgrounds. Soon you reach NY 299 once again; turn right to head back to New Paltz.

12

New York Route 22

Austerlitz to Amenia

General description: Follow the edge of the Taconic Mountains for 41 miles from the New York State Thruway to US 44, along the Massachusetts and Connecticut borders.

Special attractions: Taconic State Park, Edna St. Vincent Millay Society at Steepletop, Spencertown Historic Sites, Circle Museum, Hillsdale General Store, Mount Washington House Inn

Location: Along the Massachusetts-Connecticut borders with New York State, from the B3 exit on I-90 (north end) to US 44 (south end)

Route number: NY 22

Travel season: Spring through fall

Camping: Woodland Hills Campground in Austerlitz, Taconic State Park—Copake Falls Area and Rudd Pond Area, Copake KOA, Waubeeka Family Campground in Copake

Services: In Austerlitz, Hillsdale, Copake

Nearby attractions: Catamount ski area, Innisfree Garden, Lake Taghkanic State Park

The Route

If you're headed downstate and you'd like to try a leisurely scenic drive instead of the usual trek down I-87, this route is sure to please. Here on New York's border with New England, foliage-covered mountains rise to the east while small towns loaded with country charm cluster to the west. Towns along this route hold fairs and community events for every holiday, country stores and farm markets offer wares that grew on vines and stalks hours before, and carefully preserved homes, churches, and storefronts harken back to times we remember as simpler.

I-90 to Hillsdale

Leave I-90 at exit B3 (Austerlitz/New Lebanon), and head south on NY 22. The Berkshire Mountains become visible to the west before the woods closes in, and soon the road becomes shady as maple and beech boughs cool the road.

A sign alerts you that **Steepletop,** the home of Pulitzer Prize-winning lyrical poet and playwright Edna St. Vincent Millay, is just down the road in Austerlitz. Millay and her husband, Jan Boissevain, lived here from 1925 until their deaths a year apart in 1949 and 1950. Steepletop began as a 635-acre blueberry farm, and the couple added a writing cabin, a vegetable garden, a barn they built from a

New York Route 22: Austerlitz to Amenia

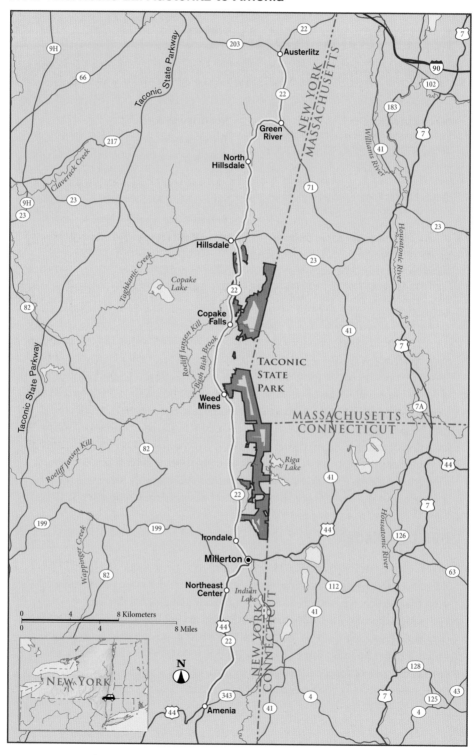

Sears Roebuck kit, and a tennis court. The property became a museum in 2010, along with 230 acres of land that includes Millay's gardens.

The town of Austerlitz contains a number of buildings that date back to the early to mid-1800s, most of them in the **Spencertown Historic Site.** According to local 19th-century historians, Austerlitz itself almost was named for the dozen Spencer families who settled in this area in 1818, but State Senator Martin Van Buren (who would later become the nation's eighth president) demanded an amendment to the bill naming the town for the express purpose of exacting revenge on a colleague who had managed to get a town in upstate New York named for Napoleon Bonaparte's last battleground in Waterloo. Van Buren insisted that the new town be named Austerlitz, after Napoleon's 1805 victory near the Austrian Empire town of that name. If nothing else, this tale serves as an excellent reminder that politics have been petty for hundreds—perhaps thousands—of years.

The Spencertown historic area includes a little red schoolhouse, circa 1852; the former Spencertown Academy, which once served as a school for training teachers; and St. Peter's Presbyterian Church, constructed in 1771. The cemetery across the road from the church dates back to 1760.

The mountains dominate the view as you leave Austerlitz on NY 22, but don't let the scenery distract you from checking out the strange sculpture garden at the **Circle Museum.** Here at the home and studio of artist Bijan Mahmoodi, you can view more than 100 different large-scale works of art installed on the lawn, apparently created from whatever materials the sculptor happened to find. At the very least, these works of art are enough to make visitors wonder about the workings of the mind who saw art in scrap metal; at best, many of them reveal imagination and vision that deserve a place in a finer gallery. Inside the garage/studio, Mahmoodi shares a selection of his oil paintings as well.

From here, the way slopes downhill, opening up views of hills, pasture, and cropland as you navigate the road's many curves.

Hillsdale General Store in the historic town of Hillsdale provides a stroll through antiques, china, household items, old-fashioned toys and games, items selected by local interior designers, and local food products including maple syrup. This building has been a retail store since the late 19th century, serving as a central part of Hillsdale life as a grocery store, sports shop, and even a video store until it became this nicely appointed general store in 2009. Next door, the **CrossRoads Food Shop** is a farm-to-table restaurant with a menu that changes seasonally depending on what's fresh from local fields.

The Austerlitz Historical Society resides in the Spencertown Historic Area.

YOUR ICE CREAM STOP: VILLAGE SCOOP

If Almond Joy, Pumpkin Spice, and Apple Spice ice cream all sound like heaven to you, schedule a stop at Village Scoop, next to Hillsdale General Store at the town square in Hillsdale. Not only can you put together the sundae of your dreams here, featuring Jane's Homemade Ice Cream—one of the best brands in the Hudson River Valley—but you can top it off with a downstate favorite, Sweet Sam's Baking Company cupcakes, cookies, and brownies. Here's an idea: a Sweet Sam's chocolate chunk brownie with Jane's Killer Chocolate ice cream, whipped cream, and a cherry. That's mine; get your own.

While a large part of downtown Hillsdale is now listed on the National Register of Historic Places as part of **Hillsdale Hamlet Historic District, Mount Washington House historic tavern** stands out for its striking architectural character.

Built in 1881, the imposing Victorian mansion once hosted guests throughout the summer. The house has undergone a meticulous renovation, and it now serves as a well-reviewed casual restaurant.

As you leave Hillsdale, the mountainous skyline blooms beyond the roadside and Taconic State Park comes into view.

Copake to Millerton

Signs direct you to the left at Copake Falls, sending you toward one of the entrances to **Taconic State Park.** The Copake Falls area of the 16-mile-long park provides campgrounds, picnic areas, access to the Harlem Valley Rail Trail, and the trail to **Bash Bish Falls,** a series of cascades that create a 200-foot waterfall just over the New York state border in Massachusetts. The falls tumbles through a gorge on Mount Washington, and it can be viewed from Falls Road—the continuation of NY 344 in Massachusetts—so if you're not up for hiking, you can still enjoy this impressive cascade and its dramatic gorge.

This is a great time to visit the Copake Falls unit of the park, because the state recently opened a museum in the park on the site of the old **Copake Iron Works,** just east of the campground on NY 344. What began in 1845 as an opportunity to maximize local resources—water power from Bash Bish Brook, charcoal made from the area's abundant forests, and limestone from the mountains—became one of 40 sources of pig iron in what was known as the Salisbury district. Ironworks from southern Vermont to northwestern Connecticut provided the material for cannonballs, rifle barrels, and wheels for railroad cars throughout the Civil War and well beyond.

Returning to NY 22, head south through pastureland edged with woods, where Holstein and Jersey cattle graze and farm markets sell produce, baked goods, and local milk and cheese. Watch for small farm stands in front of houses or on the edges of fields for opportunities to buy local fruits and vegetables or pies, with the selection changing as crops become available. Sheep are also plentiful along this road, somehow making an already idyllic setting even more pastoral.

As you cross into Dutchess County, Taconic State Park's **Rudd Pond** unit stretches to the east. The pond itself spans 64 acres and is open for swimming, canoeing, and kayaking, but no motorized watercraft are permitted, so you have a real chance at peaceful viewing.

The town of **Millerton** signals the south end of Taconic State Park. Once named one of the "10 coolest small towns in America" by *Budget Travel* magazine, Millerton has a classic, old-style Main Street where you can browse through artworks at Battle Hill Forge, Little Red Bird Studio or meta44, search for the perfect

lamp or table in several antiques stores, or step back into the 1920s at Terni's general store.

In Millerton, **McEnroe's Organic Farm Market** has the good sense to be entirely enclosed, making it possible to stay open even when winter comes early. Farming more than 1,000 acres here in the Harlem Valley, the farm provides fruits, vegetables, poultry, beef, lamb, and pork for sale, as well as soups, prepared foods, fresh baked goods, sandwiches, and ice cream from its kitchen. At any time of year, you'll find eggs, honey, dairy products (including goat cheese from local goats), breads, cookies, pies, doughnuts, and a wide selection of regional and specialty products in the country store.

After Millerton, take the big, checker-painted curve to the right and join US 44 as you continue south. You'll see **Silamar Farm,** where you can pick your own strawberries in June or find the perfect fresh Christmas tree in December. Continue on US 44 through Northeast Center, past a burying ground marked with a blue and yellow New York State waymarking sign, in which the oldest grave dates back to 1801.

If you continue on this road through cropland and pastures, you will reach the Taconic State Parkway shortly after US 44 joins NY 343. This limited-access highway, considered by many to be the prettiest highway in New York State, will take you north all the way to I-90 at exit B2, just one exit west of your starting point on this scenic drive.

Colliers once made charcoal in kilns like this one in the Taconic State Park area.

13

Upper Delaware Scenic Byway

General description: This 75-mile meander along the Upper Delaware National Scenic and Recreational River reveals tiny towns with big personalities, stunning views of luscious valleys and rolling emerald mountains, and ribbons of road along high cliffs that rival the ledges in the Rocky Mountains.

Special attractions: Upper Delaware River, Fort Delaware Museum of Colonial History, Delaware Valley Arts Alliance and Signature art/gift shop, Ten Mile River, Towpath Trail, Minisink Battlefield, Staircase Rapids, Hawk's Nest, Erie Depot Historic Site, Park Avenue Observatory, National Park Service headquarters in Narrowsburg, Roebling Bridge, Eagle Institute

Location: On the New York–Pennsylvania border at the eastern end of New York State

Route number: NY 97

Travel season: Spring through fall; passable in winter, but at a much slower pace

Camping: Upper Delaware National Scenic and Recreational River (National Park Service sites), Barryville Base and Kittatinny Campgrounds in Barryville, Jerry's Three River Campground in Pond Eddy, Mountaindale Park Campground in Mountaindale, Tri-State RV Park in Matamoras, PA

Services: In Hancock, Fremont, Cochecton, Tusten, Highland, Lumberland, Deerpark, and Port Jervis

Nearby attractions: Delaware Museum of Colonial History, Zane Grey Museum, Bethel Woods Center for the Arts

The Route

Where the east and west branches of the Delaware River meet in Hancock, New York, begins an unsullied blue band of water that traverses the state border, winding delicately through the Appalachian Mountains south of the Catskill range and north of the Poconos. Renowned for its fishing and boating opportunities and a favorite for float trips along its 73.4-mile length, the Upper Delaware Scenic and Recreational River remains pristine because of the protection it receives as part of the National Wild and Scenic Rivers System, a branch of the National Park Service. No dams can be erected to divert the river's waters, allowing it to remain the longest and one of the cleanest free-flowing rivers in the eastern US.

While most people driving through this southern portion of New York State zoom through on NY 17/I-86 in a rush to reach New York City or its environs, your drive down NY 97 follows the river through a number of small towns, each with its own kernel of history and its own unusual architecture, impressive bridge,

Upper Delaware Scenic Byway

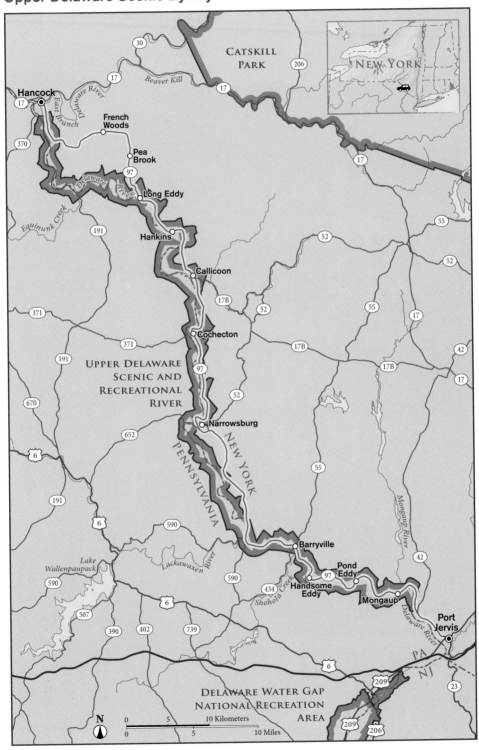

natural wonder, or amazing river view. Side by side with these fascinating finds are galleries, restaurants, antiques shops, and retail stores filled with curiosities. This delightful route will keep you occupied and entertained much longer than its 70 miles would have you guess.

Hancock to Cochecton

You'll come into Hancock to begin your tour from the Hancock exit on NY 17. Begin to follow NY 97 right away as it turns right onto Old Bridge Road, after the Hancock House Hotel and Fanny's Cafe. Stop at the scenic overlook to take in your first expansive view of the **Upper Delaware River,** at the confluence of the Delaware's east and west branches.

As you stand at the overlook, **Point Mountain** is to your left. To your right, the bridge over the river was built in 1929, to replace a covered bridge that had spanned the river here since 1848.

As idyllic as this scene is today, it doesn't even hint at the fact that Hancock made the most of its position at the beginning of the Upper Delaware by using the river for industry, starting as far back as the early 19th century. The local lumber turned out to be exactly what shipbuilders needed for the masts of their oceangoing vessels, so timber industry workers floated virgin pine spars down the river on buoyant rafts to Philadelphia. In the late 1800s, the discovery of bluestone—a bluish sandstone much prized as a paving material—in the surrounding mountains launched a quarrying boom, earning Hancock the nickname of "Bluestone Capital of the World." Stone from this town can be found in the construction of the base of the Statue of Liberty and the Empire State Building, as well as in curbs and sidewalks in many cities in the eastern US.

Return to NY 97 south and take the next right, and cross the Delaware River as you leave Hancock. The road climbs through a thickly wooded area, with occasional homes slipping into view for a moment or two before they disappear behind leafy trees. As you crest a hill and admire the wider view, enter Sullivan County and the town of Long Eddy. If you stop here for a moment at the **Basket Historical Society Museum,** you'll find interpretive signs that provide more information about the bluestone industry and the area's role in providing this valuable material to all manner of developers. The museum itself—a red barn right on NY 97 as you enter Long Eddy—houses a collection of local artifacts with the goal of preserving historical facts and folkways of the area's earlier populations.

NY 97 follows the Delaware River along New York's border with Pennsylvania.

Callicoon appears as the next sizable town along this route, after you pass several signs announcing the towns of Basket, Hankins, and Delaware with no real evidence of municipal activity. In Callicoon, a remarkable castle-like building will pique your interest as soon as you enter the town: This is the former site of St. Joseph's Seraphic Seminary, constructed in 1909 and long since repurposed as **Delaware Valley Job Corps Center.** Today young people between the ages of 16 and 24 find new direction on this campus, where they receive free training in academic and technical subjects in a residential workforce-like environment. Visitors are not allowed here, but you can see the structure and grounds from several vantage points in town.

Named Kollikoonkill in the 1600s by Dutch hunters who found an unusual number of wild turkeys—or "kollikoon"—along the river (or "kill" in Dutch), this town became a center of Catskill region activity in the 1840s when the Erie Railroad laid its tracks and erected a depot here. The station and surrounding hamlet became known as **Callicoon Depot,** a name that remained long after the railroad days ended. The original depot and most other buildings of that area were destroyed in a town-wide fire in 1888, so most of the construction on Main Street is comparatively new.

If you suddenly encounter inclement weather and you'd like to go inside for a spell, the 380-seat **Callicoon Theater** offers a 1940s-style movie-going experience in a post-Art Deco hall. Renovations in the 1990s brought more comfortable seating, air conditioning, and state-of-the-art sound and projection systems, but the original waterfall curtain still hangs above the screen, and the light fixtures and water fountain hearken back to the theater's 1948 origin. Find out what's playing at thecallicoontheater.com.

The railroad history continues in Cochecton, where you will find **Cochecton Railroad Station,** the oldest surviving railroad station in New York State. Built around 1850, the station served passengers of the Great New York and Erie Railway Company for decades until the 1970s, when the railroad—now the Norfolk Southern—determined it no longer required a station at Cochecton. A local company bought the old building and used it for storage, but in 1992 the firm announced plans to tear it down to create a parking area for its trucks. That's when a group of local residents decided to move it to a new location on the tracks and restore it to its original condition. The move has been completed, and as of this writing, the restoration of the building's interior is still in progress.

The Upper Delaware Scenic Byway begins at this overlook in Hancock.

Tusten and Narrowsburg

As you drive through many small towns, villages, and hamlets throughout New York State, it's easy to be confused by the classifications of these communities and the ways they seem to intertwine. Narrowsburg, for example, is a hamlet within the town of Tusten. Officially, a hamlet is a small settlement in a rural area, and it's always part of a larger town or city.

In the case of these two communities, **Narrowsburg**—at the narrowest point in the Upper Delaware River—definitely lends the area a great deal of character and identity. Turn right from NY 97 onto County Route 652 to visit the hidden hamlet, tucked along the banks of the Delaware River at the waterway's largest eddy. A lovely bridge provides wide-open views of the river and a quick walk to Pennsylvania, while a patio with benches on the New York side of the river may be inviting enough to keep you from leaving the state just yet.

YOUR ICE CREAM STOP: NORA'S LUVIN' SPOONFUL

With 24 flavors of soft-serve ice cream—each one mixed to order—Nora's makes the most of the creamy custard she buys from Upstate Farms Niagara Cooperative. This association of western New York State dairy farms provides locally produced milk products to grocery stores and creameries across the state, and Luvin' Spoonful proprietor Nora Manzolillo had the good sense to choose this as the basis for her intense soft-serve flavors. She dishes up lots of friendly chat and personal recommendations along with flavors like crème de menthe, pistachio nut, strawberry cheesecake, and amaretto. Chances are you'll want to try more than one.

Narrowsburg provides the cultural center on this drive, with its upscale shopping, multiple opportunities to see and purchase the work of area artists, and a number of excellent restaurants. **The Heron** received accolades from the *New York Times* for its commitment to fresh local ingredients and its creative menu. Across the street, **The Tusten Cup** serves a diverse menu of salads, wraps, sandwiches, and pastries, as well as coffee, bottled drinks, snacks, and groceries while **Gerard's River Grill** features second-story patio seating overlooking the eddy and the bridge to Pennsylvania.

Narrowsburg provides restaurants, galleries, theater, and events throughout the summer season.

Cross the Upper Delaware in Narrowsburg to get to Pennsylvania.

The hamlet provides a home to the Delaware Valley Arts Alliance, an organization that unites artists in the visual, performing, and literary arts with the general public through galleries, festivals, and programs. Don't miss the **Signature gallery and gift shop** adjacent to the Arts Alliance's offices in the former Arlington Hotel, the best place on this drive to find the work of local artists in pottery, glass, fiber, and a number of other media. Depending on the weekend you visit Narrowsburg, you may have the opportunity to attend a performance by the **Delaware Valley Opera** at the Tusten Theatre, a film festival, a pig roast, or the annual Riverfest at the end of July. (The hotel itself is on the National Registry of Historic Places, making it an interesting stop in its own right.)

Back on NY 97, **Fort Delaware Museum of Colonial History** depicts a different side of life in New York State from the perspective of the people who settled its rural areas and made their living from the land. This living history experience details the lives of the first European descendants who settled on the Upper Delaware, creating a town called Cushetunk and surviving both the French and Indian War and the Revolutionary War. You can see demonstrations of blacksmithing, candlemaking, cooking, weaving, and other chores of everyday life in the 1700s, and tour replicas of settlers' cabins.

Current and former Boy Scouts may find a visit to the **Ten Mile River Scout Museum** a real treat. Memorabilia and photos from nearly 100 years of history of the scout camps along this river—four of which still operate today—line the walls and fill display cases in this jam-packed, unassuming pole barn.

Before you leave Narrowsburg, be sure to look up and over the river to see if you can spot any of the many bald eagles that populate this area. Narrowsburg is famous among birders and other visitors for attracting eagles that glide over the river looking for fish, rise up over the hills on a wind thermal, and nest high in dead snags along the river.

Highland and Lumberland

Views of the river open up to your right as you come into Highland, and soon the **Roebling Bridge** dominates the landscape. Named for its designer, engineer John A. Roebling (who would go on to design and supervise the construction of the Brooklyn Bridge), the bridge is the oldest existing wire cable suspension bridge in the US. Roebling designed it as an aqueduct, a key element in the Delaware and Hudson Canal and Gravity Railroad, which transported anthracite coal from northeastern Pennsylvania to the Hudson River, where it was sold to heat homes and businesses in New York City.

The bridge, an impressive piece of workmanship, replaced a rope ferry crossing that had slowed traffic at the Delaware River. It opened in 1848 and alleviated the bottleneck, making the D&H Canal competitive with railroads and other canals and sustaining its operation until the canal's closure in 1898. When the National Park Service bought the aqueduct in 1980, it had become a driving bridge and had fallen into disrepair. The park service supervised a restoration that included reconstruction of the superstructure according to Roebling's original plans, returning the bridge to its original design and making it an enduring—and useful—landmark. For a full experience of the bridge and a way to stretch your legs, walk the 1-mile Towpath Trail that begins at the parking area near the bridge.

Only one battle of the Revolutionary War took place in the northern Delaware Valley, and it happened here at **Minisink Ford** on July 22, 1779. A sign just before you reach Roebling's bridge marks the place where Joseph Brant, a captain in the British Regulars and a Mohawk chief with knowledge of this land, forded the Delaware with his corps of volunteers once the British had won the battle here. **Minisink Battlefield County Park** is about 2 miles up County Route 68, a left turn just as you reach the Roebling Bridge.

Brant and his men had routed villagers along the river over the course of several days, so local residents rode to the town of Goshen to warn patriots of the potential for an upcoming attack. The Americans threw together a militia led by Benjamin

The Roebling Bridge has historical significance.

Tusten and planned a surprise ambush, and their hopes for victory increased when they met up with Colonel John Hathorn of the Continental Army and part of the Fourth Orange County Regiment. When one of their number fired at an Indian scout from Brant's corps passing through the woods, he gave away the patriots' hiding place. Brant and his men surrounded them and trounced the militia.

Popular restaurants and intriguing antiques stores pop up along the route from Highland to Lumberland. Watch the river for the **Shohola Rapids** just before the National Park Service office in Barryville. Rapids on this river reach Class I and Class II levels, but the gentle current and the lack of any major obstructions keep the rapids from becoming treacherous. You may see canoes, kayaks, and other small pleasure craft on the river, as well as rafts and inner tubes.

Deerpark, Hawk's Nest & Port Jervis

There's a strange little piece of history tucked into Deerpark, one that's easy to miss if you don't know where to look. The **New York–New Jersey Line War** never made it into our 10th grade social studies books, but it erupted periodically over the course of 68 years, from 1701 to 1769, as landowners on either side of the Delaware River railed at one another over which province could claim what patches of farmland. The last "battle"—more of a fistfight—came in 1765, when the New Jersey faction attempted to kidnap and hold hostage the leader of the New York farmers involved in the dispute—the auspiciously named Cadwallader Colden. You might expect significant bloodshed in such a daring move . . . but as the nabbing happened on a Sunday, neither side used weapons in observance of the Sabbath. The hand-to-hand combat quelled the kidnapping but did nothing to resolve the land dispute. Finally in 1769, King George of Great Britain appointed commissioners to determine the permanent border between the two provinces, ending decades of burning cropland, angry words and deeds, and the occasional night in jail. Today nothing but a little blue and yellow sign marks the site of this conflict, so keep an eye out for it as you pass through Deerpark.

Once you reach Pond Eddy, you'll see some of the best views of the river that you can enjoy from your car. Watch for **Staircase Rapids and Mongaup Rapids,** neither of which measure up as whitewater—but both of which add visual interest to the already beautiful views.

An accident of land ownership resulted in one of the most fun two-lane blacktop roads in New York State, located between Lumberland and Port Jervis: a run of curvy, cliff-hugging twists and turns known as the **Hawk's Nest.** A single lane of dirt road existed along the cliffs here since 1859, as this harrowing but speedy route provided the fastest access between the villages and hamlets along the river and the more densely populated areas to the southeast. When the state planned a new highway through here in the 1930s, however, engineers selected a new route along the river's edge, eliminating the need for a road that followed a precarious cliff ledge. Despite widespread agreement that the new route would be better, the consensus did not reach as far as the Erie Railroad, the owner of this riverside land. The railroad refused to sell, and the engineers had no choice but to design as safe a route as possible high on the cliff face.

The result is Hawk's Nest, a delight to drive and a legend among sports car enthusiasts, motorcycle riders, and bicyclists who love the thrill of curvaceous speed. A low stone wall lines the road, the only barrier between you and a drop of several hundred feet to the riverbed. The posted speed limit here is 55 miles per hour with caution signs that lower this to 25, but few drivers seem to pay any attention to this—so keep your eyes open for drivers taking this route much faster than safety would suggest. Pull-offs allow you to stop and enjoy the magnificent view of the Pennsylvania hills from this lofty perch.

Hawk's Nest ends at Sparrowbush, and from here it's a short drive to Port Jervis and the end of the scenic byway. Look for the **Erie Railroad Station** in Port Jervis, a nicely renovated red building that once acted as the hub for passenger

The road known as Hawk's Nest creates the sensation of a tricky mountain pass.

travel from here into the Catskills and along the river. Metro North now provides passenger service from here to New York City, and it chose not to use the old station—but the building was added to the National Register of Historic Places in 1970, saving it from possible demolition. Today you'll find a number of shops in the station.

End your scenic drive at the **Park Avenue Observatory,** a 1933 Civilian Conservation Corps project created to give area residents and visitors the best possible access to one of the state's most appealing panoramic views. From this platform on a ridge above the river, you can see mountains in both Pennsylvania and New Jersey, as well as the Upper Delaware River as it winds southward. Look straight out to identify High Point in New Jersey's Skylands region, which at 1,803 feet is the highest peak in the state.

New York's dominance as a dairy state becomes clear along US 20.

CENTRAL NEW YORK
SCENIC DRIVES

14

Cherry Valley Turnpike

Cazenovia to Cooperstown

General description: This 61-mile drive, winding through central New York's farmlands and hill country, follows the route established in 1927 to reach the state's capital by car.

Special attractions: Lorenzo State Historic Site, Chittenango Falls State Park, Stone Quarry Hill Art Park, Hyde Hall covered bridge, Canadarago Lake, Dyn's Cider Mill, Old Blacksmith's Shop Gallery, Glimmerglass Historic District, Otsego Lake, National Baseball Hall of Fame, Sand Lot Kid statue, Doubleday Field, Heroes of Baseball Wax Museum, Farmers' Museum, Fenimore Art Museum

Location: Central New York State southeast of Syracuse

Route numbers: US 20, NY 28, NY 80

Travel season: Year-round

Camping: Glimmerglass State Park on Otsego Lake, Chittenango Falls State Park north of Cazenovia, Good Sam RV Park in Bouckville, Cedar Valley Campsite in Morrisville, Cooperstown Shadow Brook Campground, Cooperstown Family Campground in Cooperstown

Services: In Cazenovia, Morrisville, Richfield Springs, and Cooperstown

Nearby attractions: Glimmerglass Opera Festival, Glimmerglass State Park, Hyde Hall State Historic Site, Howe Caverns

The Route

Now that the New York State Thruway serves as the main east-west artery for upstate New York, it's hard to imagine that US 20 once bore the bulk of the traffic through the state's industrial centers. At one time, however, this route directed drivers to the state capital in Albany from all parts west, funneling them along this corridor past the mills, service stations, and hotels in Cazenovia, Morrisville, and Bouckville, and bringing commercial success to smart service owners who went into business along the two-lane blacktop.

Today the route still provides a direct road to Albany with many services along the way, but it also supplies us with a perfectly lovely alternative to the high-speed traffic on the New York State Thruway. Here on US 20, you have the opportunity to slow down and admire the scenery, explore some central New York history that may be entirely new to you, and eventually land in Cooperstown, one of the most delightful towns in the entire state.

Cherry Valley Turnpike: Cazenovia to Cooperstown

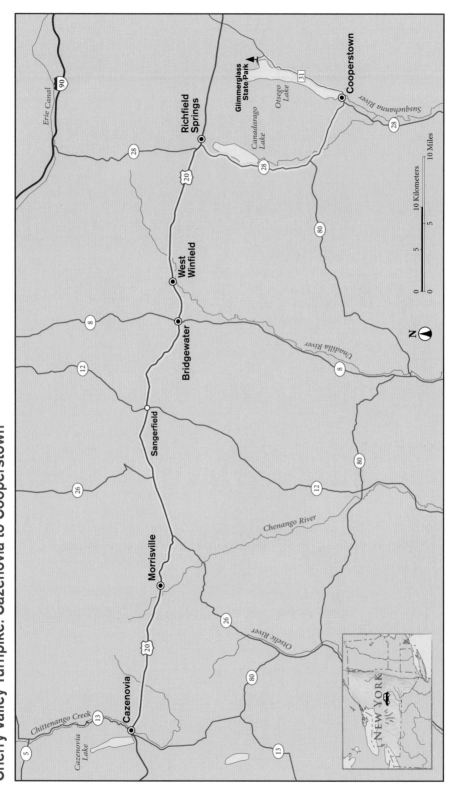

Cazenovia to Morrisville

Begin your drive in town at the southern tip of Cazenovia Lake, across from the **Lorenzo State Historic Site.** One of the only early-19th-century homes in town saved from demolition or conversion into a gas station after the Cherry Valley Turnpike opened, this mansion tells a story of five generations of one wealthy family—while revealing their apparent obsession with boldly patterned wallpaper. Land agent John Lincklaen had the house built for his family in 1807–08, but when the Erie Canal opened and prospects for cheap land ownership encouraged farmers and merchants to move west, Lincklaen found himself in tremendous debt. After his death in 1822, the mansion changed hands within the family repeatedly and underwent a series of renovations, but by the 1950s, maintenance had become unwieldy and the family agreed to donate the building, all of its contents, and the grounds to the New York State Historic Trust. The trust now runs the home as a museum. This rare property contains all of the owners' original furnishings, belongings, and records, making it the kind of gem that historical societies dream of owning. You can tour the mansion Wed through Sun, year-round.

Follow US 20 east past the Cazenovia Lake beach and a city park, and note the architecturally interesting homes along this road as you head into the town center. The **Brae Loch Inn** stands out with its beautiful setting and nice repurposing of the former William Burr estate as an inn and restaurant. Burr himself had the colonnaded Federal-style home remodeled in 1872, bringing it up to date for the period in Gothic Revival style.

A sign points you toward **Chittenango Falls State Park** to the left, an excellent side trip for head-on views of a magnificent waterfall. Chittenango Falls tumbles an impressive 167 feet over a series of ridges in the north-flowing Chittenango Creek. Whether it's a leisurely trickle in the heat of summer or a rushing torrent in early May, this waterfall reveals more than 400 million years of geologic history behind its descending waters. You can see the layers of dolomite and sandstone in the stratified sedimentary wall behind the falls. When you reach the bottom of the stone and wooden staircases that lead into the gorge, you'll stand on a pedestrian bridge that places the falls front and center—a perfect place for photos.

Back on US 20, Stone Quarry Road goes off to the right after you leave the center of Cazenovia. This road leads to another central New York treat: **Stone Quarry Hill Art Park,** a quirky little 104-acre park with an intriguing collection of permanent outdoor art installations. The art comes from emerging and established

While you're in Cooperstown, see a baseball game played where the game first began.

Stop to see the marvelous waterfall in Chittenango Falls State Park.

artists from all over the country, and new works arrive here every year. Walking trails give you up-close-and-personal access to the art, as well as to the forest, open meadow, and fine views of the hills to the south.

Now that you've left Cazenovia behind, the view from the road opens up on both sides and you have a wide perspective on pastureland, rolling hills, cropland, and patches of woods. Holstein dairy cattle are the most prevalent livestock along this route, though horses, chickens, and the occasional goat are likely as well. In fact, keep an eye out as you pass the newly opened **SUNY Morrisville Equine Rehabilitation Center,** and you may see horses arriving for physical therapy.

You will see more of SUNY Morrisville as you arrive in the town of Morrisville, including the **SUNY Morrisville Agricultural College,** one of the main focus areas of the college's School of Agriculture, Sustainability, Business, and Entrepreneurship. Here students study agricultural engineering, dairy science, equine racing management, and a number of business and technology subjects in preparation for careers they can begin right after college.

Morrisville to Sangerfield

No doubt you've spotted the 20 white windmills on the hills outside of Morrisville. The **Fenner Wind Farm** has operated since 2001, and it hosts the **Fenner Renewable Energy Education Center,** a grassroots organization that offers tours of the site from mid-Apr to mid-Nov. The center plans to have a visitor education center building and a walking trail with interpretive kiosks; at the time of this writing, fund-raising for this project is in progress. If you'd like to learn more about wind energy in central New York, contact the center to see if tours are available.

Pass through the small towns of Pine Woods and approach Bouckville, home since 1969 of the massive **Madison-Bouckville Antique Week** in the second week of August. Hundreds of antiques dealers come from all over the country to participate in this show, so visitors have an excellent chance of making some exciting finds.

As you approach the town of Madison, watch for the **Chenango Canal Cottage Museum,** on Canal Road alongside the revitalized **Chenango Canal Trail.** The trail continues from here north and south for a total of 5 miles, from Woodman's Pond at the south end to the north end at Oriskany Creek toward Solsville. Dug from 1834 to 1837, the canal provided a way to transport goods and materials southward once they arrived in the area on the Erie Canal.

In Sangerfield, take note of the stone houses along this route. Using local stone and cobblestone left behind by the glaciers that covered this area thousands of years ago, 18th- and 19th-century settlers were able to reduce the cost of constructing a house or outbuilding by making the materials on their own property serve as natural resources. You will see many of such homes throughout upstate New York, some of them quite striking in the quality of the workmanship.

Bridgewater to Richfield Springs

As you approach Bridgewater, watch on your right for Doe Road and make a quick right. **Roydhouse Bridge,** a covered bridge over Beaver Creek, comes into view quickly. The bridge is 58 feet long and was constructed in 1979. Just for reference, you are now in Oneida County and not Madison County, so if you're looking to connect your stop here with some romantic references from Robert James Waller's 1982 novel, you're pretty much out of luck. Further, while you are welcome to take a photo of this privately owned span, a sign states clearly that if you pass through the bridge, you will be detained until legal authorities arrive.

In a moment, you will pass a point at which three counties meet, so signs indicate that you are passing through Otsego, Herkimer, and Oneida Counties in quick succession. This madness ends in West Winfield, which is in Herkimer County.

YOUR ICE CREAM STOP:
RED DOOR DAIRY STORE

All those Holstein cows grazing in the surrounding dairy country will make you want ice cream—at least, that's what happens to us. Thank goodness for the Red Door, a big, shiny red barn right on US 20 in West Winfield, where Mercer's Ice Cream from Boonville, New York, gets scooped from Apr through the end of fall. You're on the Cherry Valley Turnpike, so maybe Burgundy Cherry is the right flavor—or maybe you'd prefer one of a number of ripples, from chocolate to black raspberry. Soft ice cream, sherbet, and frozen yogurt are also on the menu. You can even get lunch here first.

If you had any doubt before you took this drive that New York was a dairy state, this stretch of US 20 will convince you. According to *Dairy Farming Today*, New York State is the largest producer of yogurt, cottage cheese, and sour cream in the country, and the fourth largest producer of milk. The New York State Department of Agriculture reports that in 2019, 626,000 cows in New York each produced 23,888 pounds of milk, for a total of 14,953,888,000 pounds of milk. Herkimer County's nationally famous cheeses are celebrated each year in July at the Little Falls Cheese Festival; you can keep an eye on upcoming dates at littlefallscheesefestival.com. Let's note that if you've rolled up your windows while you drive through this area, dairy farmers all around you are smiling. As one such farmer said to me recently with a big grin, "That smells like money to me."

Watch for the junction with NY 28 south as you approach Richfield Springs. Turn right at this junction and leave US 20 behind as you head toward Cooperstown.

Richfield Springs to Cooperstown

As you turn onto NY 28 south, make a stop in Richfield Springs at **Dyn's Cider Mill,** a family-owned operation where you can find fresh cider and apples in season, and local cheese and maple syrup throughout most of the year.

Pastures, livestock, and wooded hills pass by as you head down NY 28 until you reach the north end of **Canadarago Lake,** where Baker's Beach gives you the opportunity to pull off and get a nice look at the lake. You'll follow along the west side of Canadarago Lake for 5 miles until you reach the town of Schuyler Lake, but like so many of the lakes in this part of New York, the shoreline hosts a consistent line of summer cottages and permanent homes. Your next good view comes at the lake's southern end.

In Schuyler Lake, the hills start to become mountains as you proceed toward the town of Otsego. Here NY 28 joins with NY 80; keep following them both south and cross **Oaks Creek.** The woods closes in on both sides as you continue toward Fly Creek.

If you're up for sampling a wide range of locally produced foods, **Fly Creek Cider Mill and Orchard** offers a daily tasting of more than 40 specialties, including fudge made at the mill, cheddar cheese, salsa, apple wines, and hard ciders. Here you can enjoy a treat you can only find in apple country: a cider float, which just begs to be paired with a pot roast sandwich, a fresh-baked cinnamon bun, or a doughnut at the mill's snack bar.

It seems that this road passes through one registered historic district after another as it approaches Cooperstown: first, the Fly Creek Historic District includes a number of buildings in town, not the least of which is Grange No. 844—better known today as the **Fly Creek Historical Society and Museum.** Built in 1899, this rectangular structure has a gabled roof and clapboard siding that date back to its construction, and it once served as a fraternal organization for local farmers who met there regularly and purchased supplies from the grange store.

As you approach Cooperstown, enter the **Glimmerglass Historic District,** which includes the village of Cooperstown and parts of Otsego, Springfield, and Middlefield. You will be within this district throughout your visit to Cooperstown.

Cooperstown

Simply saying the name "Cooperstown" to my brother is enough to bring tears to his eyes, and the same is most likely true for America's millions of passionate baseball fans. Cooperstown has many charms—more than this book can cover—but its greatest claim to fame is the **National Baseball Hall of Fame,** built near the site determined by the Mills Commission in 1907 to be where Abner Doubleday developed the method for playing the game in 1839. While considerable evidence gathered since the commission's report suggests that Doubleday was not actually the inventor of the game, the Hall of Fame, established here in 1937, continues in Cooperstown and has made this town the destination of baseball lovers for nearly a century. Here you can visit **Doubleday Field,** the baseball stadium erected at the site of dairyman Elihu Phinney's cow pasture, where Doubleday supposedly determined the rules for the national pastime, and where the Hall of Fame Classic is played—an exhibition game between Hall of Fame honorees and other retired Major League Baseball players. Believe the Doubleday story or don't as you choose, but if you love the game, you too will feel a lump in your throat and a wetness around the eyes as you enter the hallowed halls that honor every great player since the beginning.

Doubleday Field was constructed on the site where Abner Doubleday allegedly invented the game of baseball.

Cooperstown embraces its baseball heritage with great commercial gusto, providing a number of ways beyond the Hall of Fame for you to experience the excitement of being where it all began. The **Heroes of Baseball Wax Museum,** for example, provides life-size wax figures of players including Ted Williams, Jackie Robinson, Satchel Paige, Pete Rose, Joe Dimaggio (with Marilyn Monroe), "Shoeless" Joe Jackson, and many others, as well as a cafe with outdoor seating. The **Cooperstown Bat Company** will make you a custom baseball bat by hand with a laser engraving of your choice, and a number of souvenir and gift shops offer baseball-themed items, logo T-shirts, and all sorts of memorabilia. You can take a selfie at the famous **Sand Lot Kid statue**—a barefoot boy with a bat, cast in bronze—in the courtyard on your way to Doubleday Field. For those who pre-fer jewelry to bats and balls, **Cooperstown Bat** offers the exclusive Cooperstown

The Sand Lot Kid in Cooperstown may be one of the most famous statues in baseball.

Baseball Bracelet, a simple sterling silver loop that features a tiny silver or 14-karat gold baseball.

A baseball town deserves a top-notch brewery, especially in an area that once produced 80 percent of all of the hops grown in America. Cooperstown brings us **Brewery Ommegang,** a 135-acre farm that grows its own hops and turns them into Belgian-style beers. The fermentation and bottle conditioning of these beers matches the kind of processes used to produce champagne, with the addition of spices and specialty malts that make these beers distinctive. You'll find this brewery between Cooperstown and Milford on County Route 33.

If you're not a sports fan, Cooperstown provides a number of other activities and points of interest that showcase the area's history and its role in inspiring art and literature. The **Fenimore Art Museum** houses the Thaw Collection, one of the nation's finest assemblages of American Indian art. The permanent collection also features paintings from the Hudson River School, the first American-born style of landscape painting (see Route 10 for more on this), as well as genre painting—a practice of painting scenes from everyday life. The folk art collection draws visitors from across the country to one of the largest and finest assortments of paintings, quilts, weathervanes, signs, carvings, figures, and other items. Don't miss the Haida totem pole that stands in front of the museum's main entrance.

Across the road from the Fenimore Museum, the **Farmers' Museum** presents a rural 1840s village and farmstead where you can meet young farm animals and see demonstrations of combing and spinning wool, harvesting hops, weaving cloth, and other traditional farmyard activities. This living history museum provides a home to an oddity of the 19th century that never lived at all, despite the claims of its originators: the **Cardiff Giant,** a supposedly petrified 10-foot-tall man created to the specifications of a tobacconist named George Hull in 1869. Hull had the giant carved from gypsum and buried on his cousin's property, where it was "found" about a year later when the cousin hired some men to dig a well on the exact spot of its burial. Hull charged people money to see this purportedly rigidified giant, making a significant living for himself by doing so—enough, in fact, to attract a syndicate of five men to purchase the giant from him for a small fortune. Later, showman P.T. Barnum attempted to buy the giant for twice what the syndicate paid for it, but when they turned down Barnum's generous offer, he had a giant of his own made and exhibited it, claiming that the other was a fake. Syndicate leader David Hannum—not Barnum—said of this to a local newspaper, "There's a sucker born every minute." While Hull confessed to the hoax in a court of law in 1870, the carved figure still attracts a certain historical interest here at the Farmers' Museum. The museum bought the giant in 1947 after it had been used for several decades as a coffee table in an Iowa publisher's basement.

The Farmers' Museum demonstrates the skills old-time farmers used.

Beyond Cooperstown on NY 80

While the scenic route I've described here officially ends at the village of Cooperstown, a short extension to the north along the east side of Otsego Lake on County Route 31 not only provides more wonderful views of the lake and the surrounding hills, but it also brings you to a number of interesting places.

Glimmerglass State Park, with its romantic name, its beachfront along Otsego Lake, and its lush forest, would be a fine outdoor destination on its own even if it did not contain the oldest existing covered bridge in the US. **Hyde Hall Covered Bridge** crosses Shadow Brook just a few feet from the nearest parking area, providing a 53-foot crossing for the foot trail that continues from here. The bridge was built in 1823, and it features Burr Arch truss construction, which allows the arch to bear the entire load of the bridge while the kingpost truss keeps the bridge rigid. While covered bridges were built long before this one, all of the older ones have succumbed to the elements, according to information from the US Department of Transportation.

So what or where is Hyde Hall? Just up the road in Glimmerglass State Park, **Hyde Hall State Historic Site** preserves a 50-room, neoclassical mansion that has become a National Historic Landmark. Built by landowner George Clarke, the house overlooks what was once Clarke's enormous estate and contains many pieces that have been with the building and the Clarke family since the early 1800s. Clarke's records include receipts and documentation for each purchase, allowing for considerable accuracy in interpretation of the mansion's history. Architectural historians hail this site as the finest example of neoclassical style in the country, especially north of the Mason-Dixon Line. You can tour this home daily from May through early November.

Finally, if you love music, the **Alice Busch Opera Theater,** home of the **Glimmerglass Opera,** can be found at the north end of Otsego Lake. Every year in July and August, Glimmerglass brings a number of classic operas to life, running in rotating repertory to allow audiences to see several different works over the course of a weekend. All operas are presented with supertitles in English, so if you don't understand Italian or French, you can still follow the plot and enjoy the extraordinary music of Verdi, Puccini, Bizet, and dozens of other composers.

At this point, you are nearly back at US 20. Head north to reach the main road, or south on NY 80 to return to Cooperstown.

Glimmerglass State Park contains the nation's oldest existing covered bridge.

15

New York 7

Vermont Border to Troy

General description: This 26.5-mile country road leads from the Taconic Mountain range along the New York–Vermont border to the city that kicked the Industrial Revolution into high gear.

Special attractions: The Potter Hill Barn, Big Moose Country Store, Berkshire Bird Paradise, Tomhannock Reservoir, Gristmill Antique Center

Location: East of the Tri-City Capital District, from the Vermont border to Troy

Route number: NY 7

Travel season: Year-round

Camping: Greenwood Lodge and Campsites in Bennington, VT, Mickara Campgrounds in Troy, Lake Lauderdale Campgrounds in Cambridge, Deer Run Campgrounds in Schaghticoke, Broken Wheel Campground in Petersburg

Services: In Troy, Pittstown, and Hoosick

Nearby attractions: Bennington Battlefield, Grafton Lakes State Park

The Route

A leisurely ramble through gentle, foliage-covered mountains and cheerful little towns, this route provides the perfect weekend drive at just about any time of year. A dollop of Revolutionary War history and other bits of Americana emerge not far from the Vermont border, but for the most part, this drive leads to farm stands, artisans' studios, country-themed shops, antiquing, and enchanting landscapes.

Vermont to Hoosick

The **Taconic Mountains** you see around you as you begin your drive at (or perhaps just over) the Vermont border are actually part of the Appalachian Mountains, which run along New York's eastern border. Deemed one of the "Last Great Places" by the Nature Conservancy, the Taconics are sculpted in part by the Hoosic River, which you will cross shortly after leaving Vermont. Behind you, Mount Anthony rises to a height of 2,320 feet in Bennington, while **Mount Equinox,** the highest peak in the Taconic range, towers over Anthony at 3,850 feet.

The town of **Hoosick** struggled to get started back in the 1750s, as raiders from the local Indian tribes—aided by the French—broke up the first settlement during the French and Indian War. The battle of Bennington was fought here during the Revolutionary War, and after the war Hoosick settled into a long period of peace and modest growth. This Hoosick lifestyle comes across in detail at the

New York 7: Vermont Border to Troy

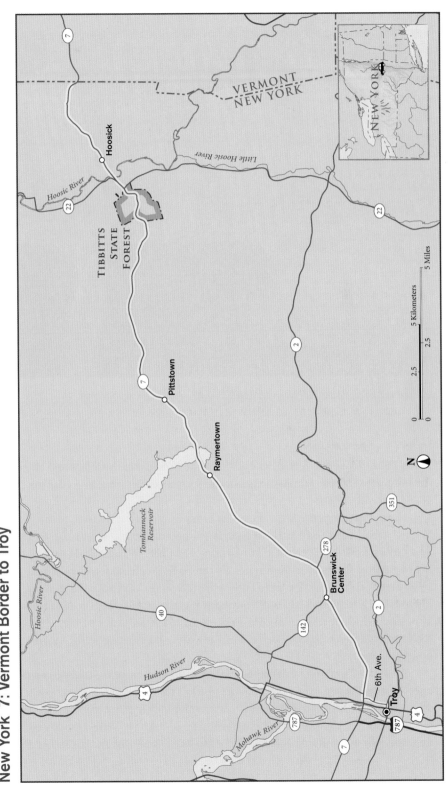

Shopping at The Potter Hill Barn will yield country crafts and unique gifts.

Louis Miller Museum in Hoosick Falls. The museum uses furnishings and other items donated by local families to provide a glimpse of Victorian life in the late 1800s and early 1900s.

Most interesting here is the dress that artist Grandma Moses wore to the White House in 1960 on her 100th birthday. Grandma Moses—whose name was Anna Mary Robertson—lived on her farm north of here in Eagle Bridge, turning to painting for the first time in her 70s. She rose to international fame when an amateur art collector discovered one of her paintings in a drugstore window in Hoosick Falls. The art collector convinced the Museum of Modern Art in New York City to include a Grandma Moses painting in a show, and soon the media took such an interest in this elderly, down-to-earth artist that her name became a household word.

For a quick trip from the sublime to the ridiculous, stop at the **Big Moose Deli and Country Store** on your way out of Hoosick. This wacky souvenir and snack stop displays more merchandise than it can comfortably fit into a store this size, in a maze of shelves snaking throughout the building. Whatever Vermont-branded item you may want, from magnets and bumper stickers to jams and cheeses or an improbable assortment of maple-flavored food varieties, you will find it here—and some of it is actually made in Vermont. Oddly enough, you won't find much in here that features New York, but you will find bacon-flavored dental floss, if that's something you desperately need. A word of warning: Many signs point you to the "outhouse," but the only bathrooms are port-o-johns behind the building.

Fields of wildflowers cover the hillsides on your way out of Hoosick, with expansive views of heavily forested mountains that turn gold, orange, and crimson in fall. Soon you'll see **The Potter Hill Barn,** a country store that warrants a stop long enough to browse with vigor. Here you'll find a wide and varied selection of country craft items for the home, including ceramics, holiday decorations for just about any season, tableware, textiles, furniture, embroidered pieces, candles, lamps, dolls, wooden signs, baskets, and a great deal more. Potter Hill is open daily year-round, so you won't miss the fun as long as you pass through during the business day.

Pittstown to Brunswick

As you approach Pittstown, **Carpenter's Touch Chainsaw Carvings and Rustic Furniture** appears on your right. It's worth a stop here to see the work of craftsman Charles Jennet, who creates more than chainsaw bears and totem poles (although these are very impressive); his work in handcrafted furniture makes use of the shape and grain of each individual section of wood, turning them into rustic pieces that bring the natural world into the home.

Tomhannock Reservoir, the water source for the city of Troy and much of Rensselaer County, passes under NY 7 as you come out of the town of Pittstown. This man-made lake holds 12.3 billion gallons of water at its peak level, and its 5.2-mile length hosts nearly 20 different species of fish, including smallmouth and largemouth bass, panfish, and walleye in abundance. To stop and enjoy the view of this shimmering reservoir, park on the west side of the causeway in the small parking area and walk out onto the bridge.

Subtle hills, fields of corn, and green pastures enhance the view as you approach Brunswick, spreading out between minimally populated areas. Watch for **Gristmill Antique Center,** a 3,400-square-foot treasure hunter's paradise on the outskirts of Troy, where more than 50 antiques vendors show their late-19th- to mid-20th-century wares. China, jewelry, glassware, furniture, military collectibles, and much more come together in one of the largest multi-dealer antiques centers in this region—and Gristmill is open seven days a week until 5 p.m., giving you plenty of opportunities to stop. Just down the road, the **Bennington Potters Factory Outlet** store features bakeware, mugs, bowls, pitchers, and serving pieces, all made in Potters Yard in Bennington, Vermont.

The views from the bridge at Tomhannock Reservoir are worth the stop.

By now you may be hankering for some homegrown fruits and baked goods, so a stop at **Tarbox Farms Earth's Bounty** will do the trick. A family now in its fourth generation of dairy, beef, and vegetable farming, Tarbox prides itself on its sustainable practices and its antibiotic and hormone-free cattle. Depending on the season, you will find apples, berries, corn on the cob, pumpkins, and vegetables here, as well as eggs, cheese, meat, maple syrup, and jellies.

As you enter the town of Brunswick and the road begins to crowd with businesses, you'll spot a small wetland on the north side of NY 7 with a parking area on its west end. This is a Department of Transportation-owned property, and the parking area and trail are not especially well maintained. If you're interested in scanning with binoculars for birds and wildlife, this may be a productive stop; otherwise, continue to Troy.

Tucked just outside of Troy, Brunswick Wildlife Viewing Area offers a natural landscape.

Mohawk Towpath Scenic Byway

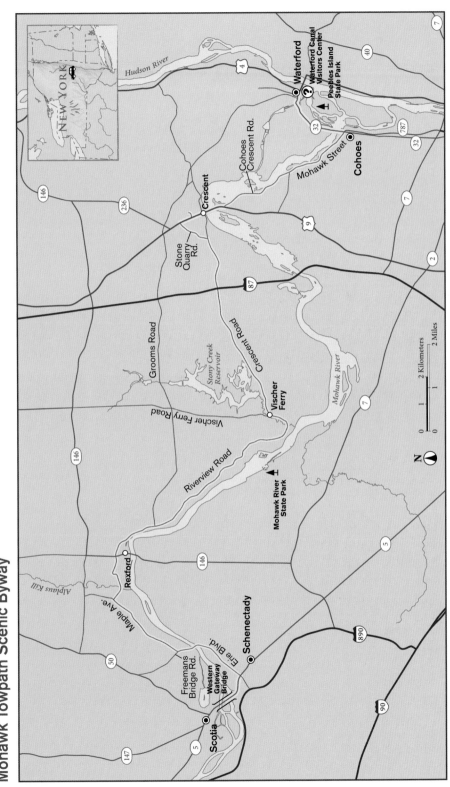

ERIE CANAL
CANAL DUG IN 1822 AND
ENLARGED IN 1842.
REMAINS OF BOTH CANALS ARE
EVIDENT. OPENED FROM
ALBANY TO BUFFALO, 1825.

When the canal opened in 1825, 82 locks along its 363-mile length allowed barges to descend the 689 feet in elevation change from Albany to Buffalo. Commerce virtually exploded along its length and beyond as goods and raw materials could reach to the ends of the Great Lakes as far away as Michigan, Wisconsin, and Illinois. The canal turned New York State into a trade hub for the entire country, generating new communities all along the waterway's length and spurring the growth of businesses that could ship their goods westward.

While the Erie Canal lost its dominance with the advent of the transcontinental railroad, its renovated iteration continues to operate as a recreational option for pleasure boaters, tour boats, and bicycles and pedestrians who walk the towpath—the trail alongside the canal, once used by horses or mules that served to pull the barges through the water. Parts of this original canal still remain along the route that you will drive today. The New York State Canal Corporation created the Mohawk Towpath Scenic Byway to make it easy to find remnants of the canal and learn about its history, and to bring you to an unusually appealing part of central New York that most visitors do not discover.

Waterford to Cohoes

Before you begin the established scenic byway, we recommend a stop at the **Waterford Harbor Visitors Center** at One Tug Boat Alley in Waterford. Here where the Hudson and Mohawk Rivers meet, the visitor center offers lots of brochures, maps, and expert commentary about the Mohawk Towpath and the things you will see along the route.

With all of this information in hand, continue across the channel to **Peebles Island State Park,** a large island from which you can see the confluence of the Hudson River flowing south, and the Mohawk River coming in from the west. Hiking trails all over this island bring you to wide vistas of the rivers and the communities above the shoreline. There's textile history here, too: Peebles Island played host to the **Cluett, Peabody & Company shirt factory,** home of Arrow shirts and collars. Arrow detachable shirt collars became a wardrobe staple for the common man of the 1910s and 1920s. Cluett, Peabody became the nation's most successful company in the 1920s, turning out four million collars a week. Extensive interpretive displays inside the building will tell you all you need to know about men's shirt manufacturing.

The original Erie Canal and the Whipple Truss Bridge.

Lock #2 on the modern Erie Canal.

Leave Peebles Island and follow the signs to **Erie Canal Lock 2,** especially if you've never seen a modern canal lock before. This is the second lock in the currently functioning Erie Canal, giving you an opportunity to see how this simple but ingenious technology has evolved since the canal's first locks were completed in 1825. The process has become more automatic and the lock's parts move under power, but the result is the same: water runs out of one side of the lock and into the other, raising or lowering the vessel as the water levels equalize. Lock 2 lifts boats 33.55 feet, from their starting level of 15.2 feet to their exit at 48.75 feet. When the lock is at rest, you can walk along its concrete walls within a fenced walkway to get a close look at the entire operation.

The paved towpath on the north side of the lock is the Erie Canalway Towpath Trail, a pedestrian and bicycle path that runs the entire 363-mile length of the canal. You can pick up the path anywhere along the route and walk as far or as little as you like, enjoying the communities you will see along the way. The path has become one of the modern canal's most popular features. Here the Erie Canal also meets the Champlain Canal, a waterway once used for shipping goods south from Lake Champlain and its environs in northern New York State. If you'd like to know more about this canal, I've detailed it in Route 1 on the Lakes to Locks Passage scenic drive.

From the Lock 2 parking area, turn left onto Broad Street, drive 2 blocks on NY 32, and turn right at the "Begin Mohawk Towpath Scenic Byway" sign. Turn left at Division Street and continue to Flight Lock Road. Turn left to see one of the two famous **Flights of Five Locks.** (There's another Flight of Five Locks in Lockport, New York, at the other end of the canal.) This remarkable configuration of locks provides the necessary navigation around Cohoes Falls, raising barges and boats 165 feet in a little more than a mile. This flight achieved the greatest lift in the shortest distance on any canal in the world—a record that stands today.

From Flight Lock Road, turn left onto Fonda Road and continue around the bed to the left. Turn left onto Halfmoon Road, going straight as it becomes Church Hill Road. There's a nice view of the bend in the Mohawk River as you turn left onto US 9, cross the Mohawk River, and enter the town of Colonie. Turn left quickly onto Cohoes Crescent Road. Follow the river on your left through a natural area and pass an old industrial dam with a man-made falls. In a moment, you'll arrive in the town of Cohoes.

Cohoes to Canal Road

Falls View Park appears on your left as you drive down US 9, the first place at which you can view the magnificent **Cohoes Falls.** Named by the Iroquois long before Europeans arrived in the New World, written about in Dutch colonists' memoirs and poets' letters since the 1600s, and sketched and painted by explorers and artists for centuries, Cohoes Falls makes an unforgettable impression from its very first viewing. This gargantuan cataract stands nearly as tall as Niagara Falls and wider than Niagara's American Falls, topping out at roughly 1,000 feet across the mighty Mohawk River. The most interesting comparative statistic, however, involves the quantity of water flowing over Cohoes' ledges: While Niagara flows at 5,000 to 21,000 cubic feet per second, Cohoes Falls routinely moves nearly five times more water, at 90,000 cubic feet per second—reaching 100,000 cubic feet per second during major storms like 2011's Hurricane Irene.

There's another viewing area for the falls just down the road at Falls View Park on School Street, where Brookfield, the area's hydropower company, harnesses the falls to churn electricity that powers 26,000 homes annually. The powerhouse uses the same hydroelectric system built here in 1915—in fact, the dam, upper gatehouse, and power canal actually date back to the 1800s. Climb the stairs to the second-floor deck for an even more expansive view.

While you're in Cohoes, walk down the road to **Harmony Mills,** now a building of trendy loft apartments and a National Historic Landmark, but formerly the

largest cotton mill complex in the world. Built in 1866, Harmony Mills produced cotton muslin and printed calico fabric in a facility considered state-of-the-art in its day. Mill No. 3 sports a mansard roof and a finely crafted façade, unusual adornments for a manufacturing facility. It also received the nickname "Mastodon Mill" because of the discovery of a prehistoric mastodon skeleton under the construction site while workers dug the mill's foundation. The skeleton now resides in the State Museum in Albany.

To rejoin the scenic byway, backtrack a bit by driving up Cortland Street (this will become North Mohawk Street, and then Cohoes Crescent Road), and making a quick right turn onto NY 9. Take the next left onto Canal Road and start driving west along the byway.

Crescent to Vischer Ferry

Crescent Park comes into view shortly as you drive along the Mohawk River. This park features a crushed stone walking path and water access for canoes and other small boats, as well as excellent views of the Mohawk River.

As you continue west on the byway, what appears to be a trench of still water covered with green duckweed comes into view on your left, alongside the river. This is a remnant of the original Erie Canal, completed in 1825 and enlarged over the course of nearly 30 years, beginning in 1834. This canal fell into disuse when the Barge Canal opened in the early 1900s, making the original canal an historic artifact. Much of it now resides within the **Vischer Ferry Nature and Historic Preserve,** the next major site on your drive, shortly after Clamstream Road becomes Riverview Road (after you pass I-87).

The 600-acre preserve contains three important elements: the remains of the original canal, a wetland ecosystem that attracts long-legged wading birds and small furry animals, and the site of the first settlement of Clifton Park.

Originally known as Canastigione, or "corn flats," this area served as farmland for the local Mohawk Indians until white settlers arrived in 1672. The newcomers established a settlement here and eventually renamed it Fort's Ferry, in recognition of the ferry run by settler Nicholas Fort. Local residents began working for the Erie Canal project in 1822, and the area became known as Clifton Park. Another settlement, Clute's Dry Dock, sprang up as a stopping place on the canal; its location is also part of this preserve.

Harmony Mills once housed the largest cotton mill complex in the world.

Also in view is the **Whipple Truss Bridge,** an 1855 bridge built from a design patented by Squire Whipple in 1841. Whipple developed the first formula to calculate the stresses in an articulated truss, according to a notation by the American Society of Civil Engineers. This bridge originally crossed the Cayadutta Creek in Johnstown, but the City of Johnstown made a gift of it to Union College, Whipple's alma mater, in 1979.

From here, continue your drive through **Vischer Ferry,** where the entire town is a National Historic District. The Greek Revival, Queen Anne, and Victorian homes and commercial buildings here date back to between 1833 and 1862, and the 1735 home of town founder Nicholas Vischer and his son, Eldret, also remains—though a Federal-style section added to the front of the building in 1806 obscures some of the colonial period detail. Eldret opened a rope ferry here in 1790, and this transportation hub quickly attracted a tavern and a store to this spot. This town thrived during the Erie Canal's heyday, but once railroads replaced the canal, Vischer Ferry found itself fairly isolated and out of the spotlight. This wasn't all bad: The town's historic buildings escaped modern development, making this hamlet an excellent place to see intact examples of 19th-century architecture.

Mohawk Landing to Rexford

After Vischer Ferry, continue along Riverview Road as views of the river become dodgy and healthy woods and meadows dominate the roadsides. Pass the Vischer Ferry Power Plant and watch for the entrance to a small park. An 800-foot crushed stone and boardwalk path at **Mohawk Landing** leads to the water's edge, where you can enjoy a sweeping view of the Mohawk River with wilderness acreage along its north banks.

Stay on Riverview Road as you come to Riverview Orchards, where you can buy local honey, fruit, and other bounty of an upstate New York harvest. Shortly after this, you will pass a mansion worthy of *The Great Gatsby*, a castlelike estate with iron gates and acres of private orchards. This is Llenroc, built for insurance magnate Albert Lawrence and his family in the 1980s. (Llenroc is Cornell spelled backward; the mansion was designed to resemble the campus center at Cornell University, Lawrence's alma mater.) Lawrence lost the home in a foreclosure in 2000, and it has changed hands several times since then. In the last reported transaction, Saratoga County foreclosed on the property because of unpaid back taxes.

Take a stroll through the Vischer Ferry Nature Preserve.

The Rexford Aqueduct.

After you pass several country clubs and a number of high-end homes, turn left onto NY 146 and watch for the small parking area on the east side of the road. Pull in here to see the upper aqueduct that carried the canal over the Mohawk River, of which remains only the two stone arches you see here. You are welcome to make an additional stop at the **Schenectady Yacht Club** to see the remains of Locks 21 and 22, which are only visible if you park and leave your car. The walls from Lock 21 are down in the water, while Lock 22 stood right in front of what is now the yacht club's clubhouse—you can only see the top of this lock, because workers filled in the lock when the canal closed. The most visible feature of the canal here is the **Rexford Aqueduct,** for which the stone arches and trough are still intact. Walk down to the water to see these, or view them from the east side of the NY 146 bridge. When you cross the river on NY 146, more arches can be seen from the parking area on the east side of the road.

Niskayuna to Schenectady

You've seen the last evidence of the original Erie Canal on this route as you leave the aqueducts and continue through Niskayuna, turning right onto Aqueduct Road. For these last few miles of the route, pass through an urban area with a good deal of evidence of industry. Aqueduct Road becomes Erie Boulevard, so named because this road replaced the original Erie Canal.

Erie Boulevard skirts a neighborhood known as the **GE Realty Plot,** a National Historic District of homes developed by executives of General Electric (GE) for the company's employees. Designed and built as part of the "City Beautiful" movement of the early 1900s, the neighborhood features gently curving streets, large lots by the era's standards, and no house built closer than 25 feet to the road. In addition, no house could be worth less than a set minimum level, ensuring that all of the homes were sizeable and well appointed. If you'd like to take a closer look at this neighborhood, turn left onto Nott Street and look for a parklike area of elegant homes, in styles from Tudor to Dutch Colonial.

The scenic byway ends in the vicinity of the **General Electric Research Laboratory,** the first industrial research facility established by an American corporation. Created in 1900 by Thomas Edison, Willis R. Whitney, and Charles Steinmetz, the lab became a model for industrial research, creating standards that many other successful corporations have scrambled to match. Here innovations including the electric fan, the tungsten light bulb filament, the first electric hotpoint range, the waterwheel generator at Niagara Falls, the portable X-ray machine, and the trans-oceanic radio system were developed. The facility still operates as GE Global Research, and recent innovations have included a fuel-efficient locomotive engine and the first 24-cylinder internal combustion engine.

FINGER LAKES
SCENIC DRIVES

Bloomfield to Bristol

Begin your drive in the village of **Bloomfield,** a small Southern Tier community that serves as a pivot point for routes to all four points in the compass. You'll find it on NY 5/US 20 southeast of Rochester. Stop here to walk or drive through the village to see more than 50 buildings dating back from 1794 to the mid-1800s, many of them designed in the Greek Revival style, but with a few Federal and Gothic homes in the mix. Four distinctive churches—Methodist, Catholic, Congregational, and Episcopal—provide examples of Gothic Revival, Romanesque, and Greek Revival architecture.

From Bloomfield, travel east on NY 5/US 20 to reach NY 64 (Bristol Valley Road), and turn right. Soon you'll drive out of Bloomfield's residential areas and into expansive farmland, where cornfields and cattle farms live side by side and horses graze in white-fenced corrals. The rolling Bristol Hills come into view to the south. As you pass **Stid Hill Wildlife Management Area,** look right to see **Bristol Mountain Ski Resort,** the ski area with the highest vertical rise—1,200 feet—between the Adirondack Mountains to the east and the Rocky Mountains to the west. In the fall, Bristol Mountain offers chair lift rides on its Comet Express to the summit of the mountain, giving you the opportunity to see the entire Bristol Valley from the summit after you enjoy a 15- to 20-minute glide upward. You can take the lift down as well, but you also may want to walk down for a peaceful experience of this impressive rise.

Your next stop could be **Arbor Hill Winery,** nestled into the countryside in a group of antique buildings in South Bristol. Here you can grab lunch at Brew & Brats, where you can enjoy a pale ale, IPA, or porter brewed at Bristol Springs in Naples, and a local sausage, dressed up with Arbor Hill's own gourmet sauces. Of course, Arbor Hill sells its wines here as well, and you'll find a wide selection of varieties, from a sparkling Chardonnay to Very Cranberry and Very Blueberry.

At the intersection with NY 21 about 2 miles after Bristol Mountain, turn right and continue south on NY 21/64.

Naples

Canandaigua Lake comes into view to your left as you head south on NY 21. Here this glacially carved lake—the fourth largest of the Finger Lakes at 15.5 miles long and 1.5 miles wide—reaches its southern end just north of the town of Naples, and this view gives you an idea of why the Seneca Indians named it Ga-nun-day-gwa, or "the chosen spot." Forested hills and farm plains surround

this lake, as does a great deal of development, but you can enjoy an unobstructed view of it at your leisure at the **Naples Boat Launch** area you see along the lakeshore.

When you leave the boat launch, watch on your left for a little house with a big sign: **Monica's Pies,** a must-do stop for anyone who visits Naples. Thirty-plus years of baking expertise make Monica Schenk the premier grape pie artisan in the area, and thanks to her careful techniques for making and preserving her Concord grape pie filling during the fall harvest, you can enjoy one of her brilliant grape pies at any time of year. Equally delicious, her cherry pies—made with fresh, whole sweet cherries—are worth breaking your diet to try. Monica has been featured on the Food Network for her extraordinary way with crust and fruit, and she even consults on bakeware with The Pfaltzgraff Co., one of the world's leading cookware manufacturers. You'll find more than 20 pie varieties at Monica's year-round, plus savory specialties including chicken potpie and quiche.

You've never heard of grape pie? The story goes that the **Redwood Restaurant** got the idea to offer the unusual flavor in 1965, borrowing the recipe from an elderly German lady in town (according to an article in the local magazine *Life In the Finger Lakes*) and featuring the pie on the menu. Soon the demand became so vigorous that local bakers started offering them as well, selling thousands of pies every fall. The dependence on fresh Concord grapes right off the vine keeps the grape pie phenomenon concentrated here, and you can still go to the Redwood or to **Bob and Ruth's Vineyard Restaurant,** the unmistakable diner at the junction of NY 21 and NY 245, for a slice with a big scoop of vanilla ice cream.

Naples serves as the western Fingers Lakes' favorite fall destination, both for its wealth of grape goodies—even the fire hydrants are purple here—and for the spectacular fall foliage that frames this appealing village. The annual **Naples Grape Festival** at the end of September attracts artists and craftspeople from hundreds of miles around to exhibit here, while bakeries, grape growers, wineries, and other food vendors share the best of the season with tens of thousands of visitors.

If you pass through Naples at any other time of year, there's still plenty here to delight visitors. **Grimes Glen County Park,** at the end of Vine Street off NY 21, offers much more than a pleasant picnic spot: On a hot summer day, dip your sneakered or sandaled feet in the water and wade up this shady creek (the water rarely gets deeper than mid-calf) to reach two spectacular, 60-foot-high waterfalls.

Finger Lakes wine country is all about grapes.

This is one of the most popular waterfall hikes in the Finger Lakes, so you will see parents with children, groups of teens, and retired couples all making their way up the creek.

Wander Naples's Main Street and find antiques stores like **Robin's Nest Antiques,** craft shops including **Artizanns: Gifts from the Finger Lakes,** country items for the home at **Carriage House Quilts,** and other interesting shopping opportunities. **Cindy's Pies,** just around the corner from Main Street on Academy Street, gets rave reviews for its sumptuous fruit and its delicate, flaky crusts.

Before you leave Naples, make a stop at **Hazlitt 1852 Vineyards and Winery,** home of Red Cat wines and many other varieties. The 1852 in the name stands for the year that David Hazlitt purchased 153 acres of land in the Finger Lakes and began a generational heritage of fruit growing, eventually leading to the late Jerry Hazlitt and his wife, Elaine, opening this winery in 1985. The winery received the Conservation Farm of the Year award in 2009 for its long history of sustainable farming practices, using cover crops instead of pesticides and turning table scraps into compost to fertilize the land. If you're not a fan of sweet wines like Hazlitt's famous red Catawbas (the Red Cats), choose the vineyard's award-winning Riesling or the acclaimed Cabernet Franc.

Naples to Canandaigua

When you're ready to head north, take NY 21/64 back the way you came and follow it up to Bristol Springs. Here NY 21 splits off from NY 64 and goes right. Take this right fork and follow the shore of Canandaigua Lake on NY 21. As you crest the next hill, the classic view of this glistening lake comes into view with the Bristol Hills in the background. **Heron Hill Winery**'s South Bristol tasting room appears just down the road, in the former South Bristol Cultural Center, where the winery opened its third location in 2010. There's plenty of room for sampling a flight of wines with friends in the spacious, high-ceilinged room, with views of the Cabernet Franc and Riesling vineyards out the huge windows.

Just north of Heron Hill, County Route 16 goes right. This is the more scenic route, so bear right to follow along West Lake Road, where you can find the occasional unobstructed view of Canandaigua Lake as you travel toward the city of Canandaigua. When you reach NY 5/US 20, turn right and continue to NY 21/332. Turn left onto NY 332 and drive into the city.

The cooling creek walk in Grimes Glen brings you to this 60-foot-high waterfall.

Canandaigua

The city of Canandaigua may seem like a tourist town gathered on the edge of a very attractive lake, but its legacy contains several historic events that had far-reaching implications. If you're an upstate New York resident, you may have heard of the Treaty of Canandaigua, an agreement between the US and the Six Nations of the Iroquois in 1794 to ensure peace and guarantee land rights between the two governing entities. Fifty sachems and war chiefs of the Six Nations met in Canandaigua with Timothy Pickering, official agent of President George Washington, and they agreed to appropriate annual payment for the land rights granted to the US: $4,500 for the annual distribution of calico cloth per year to the Six Nations, and $1,800 per year to the Oneida Nation of Wisconsin. The treaty holds today, and the tribes continue to receive these payments, including the cloth.

You can see a monument to the agreement—also known as the Pickering Treaty—on the lawn of the **Ontario County Courthouse,** where another monumental event took place in 1873. *United States v. Susan B. Anthony* examined the case in which Anthony, an activist, newspaper editor, and the nation's best-known advocate for the rights of women, registered to vote before the upcoming election, walked into a polling place in Rochester on November 5, 1872, and voted. She did not act alone, although she was the most famous among the 15 members of the National Woman Suffrage Association who voted that day. Anthony and her compatriots were arrested nine days later on the charge of voting without "the legal right to vote in said election . . . being then and there a person of the female sex." Her trial took place in this courthouse, where she was found guilty and fined $100 plus court costs, but she never paid a dime of it. Anthony gave the most famous speech of her life in this courtroom, in which she asserted that she had failed "even to get a trial by a jury *not* of my peers," because the entire proceeding had been conducted by men. She condemned the course of the trial that she felt had "trampled under foot every vital principle of our government." Anthony did not live to see passage and ratification of the 19th Amendment to the Constitution in 1920, granting women the right to vote, but she worked tirelessly to the last days of her life to make it happen.

Just down Main Street from the courthouse, the **Granger Homestead** offers an unusual opportunity to tour an 1816 Federal-style mansion that was home to Gideon Granger, postmaster general of the US under Thomas Jefferson and James Madison. Many of the furnishings and decorations in the house represent four generations of the Granger family's residency here. The homestead also features a Carriage Museum, which houses nearly 100 horse-drawn vehicles, from sleighs

At the Ontario County Courthouse, Susan B. Anthony was tried and convicted of voting while female.

to hearses—and from June to mid-October, the museum offers tours by carriage through Canandaigua's historic neighborhoods (reservations and a fee are required).

No trip to Canandaigua is complete without a visit to **Sonnenberg Mansion and Gardens State Historic Site,** where nine artfully designed formal gardens bloom throughout the spring, summer, and early fall. The gardens ornament a 40-room Queen Anne–style mansion, originally owned by New York City banker Frederick Ferris Thompson and his wife, Mary Clark Thompson. The Thompsons bought the property with a brick farmhouse on it, and expanded their living situation over the course of several decades as Thompson's business success warranted. At Sonnenberg Gardens you also can find the **Finger Lakes Wine Center,** where you can sample as many as 15 different wines from this region in the tasting room, or peruse the gift shop.

Make your last stop on this scenic drive at **New York Kitchen** at 800 S. Main St., where you can sample wines from a wide range of wineries throughout the state, take a cooking class, learn to pair wines with cheese or desserts, or have a bountiful meal from a menu featuring locally sourced ingredients. Created as a partnership between area farmers, winemakers, artisans, and others in the area's food and wine trade, this culinary center brings together New York's specialties in one place for your convenience and appreciation. Check the center's website at nykitchen.com for classes and other offerings on the day you plan to visit.

18

Seneca Lake Wine Trail & Scenic Byway

General description: More than 20 wineries, dozens of bed-and-breakfast inns, and some of New York's most beautiful state parks and forests give this 54-mile trip around the largest of the Finger Lakes the feeling of a bucolic holiday.

Special attractions: Belhurst Castle, Geneva On The Lake, many wineries (details in the text), Watkins Glen State Park, Captain Bill's Seneca Lake Cruises, Weaver-View Farms Amish Country Store, Skyland Art Barn, Wagner Valley Brewing Company, Schtayburne Farm Creamery, Seneca Harbor Wine Center, Watkins Glen International Racetrack, Seneca Harbor Park, Famous Brands Outlet Store, Hector Falls, Finger Lakes Distilling, Finger Lakes National Forest, Amazeing Acres, Seneca County Historic Courthouse Complex

Location: South of the New York State Thruway between Rochester and Syracuse

Route numbers: NY 14, NY 414

Travel season: Spring through fall

Camping: Watkins Glen/Corning KOA Campground, Cheerful Valley Campground in Phelps, Sunset on Seneca Campsites in Lodi

Services: In Geneva, Penn Yan, and Watkins Glen

Nearby attractions: Prime Outlets at Waterloo, Women's Rights National Historical Park, National Women's Hall of Fame, Erie Canal, Seneca Falls Historical Society Museum, Seneca Museum of Waterways and Industry, Canal Harbor at Seneca Falls, Seneca Meadows Wetland Preserve, Montezuma National Wildlife Refuge

The Route

If you measure your fun by the number of wineries you visit per linear mile of travel, the Seneca Lake Wine Trail and Seneca Lake Scenic Byway are about to become your favorite places on Earth. Here on the shores of the largest of the Finger Lakes, the climate lends itself to the growth of more than 30 varieties of grapes, aided in their cultivation by lakes deep enough to resist freezing and to reduce the chance of winter injury to cold-hardy vines. Growing seasons with little chance of frost provide plenty of time for grapes to grow and ripen, making for bountiful harvests that produce some of the state's most popular and desirable wines.

This route also presents us with sparkling lakeside views, country markets filled with local fruits and vegetables in late summer and fall, flame-colored foliage through October and early November, and bits of history tucked in between the wineries and trees. Of all the scenic routes through the Finger Lakes, we found this one the most satisfying.

Seneca Lake Wine Trail & Scenic Byway

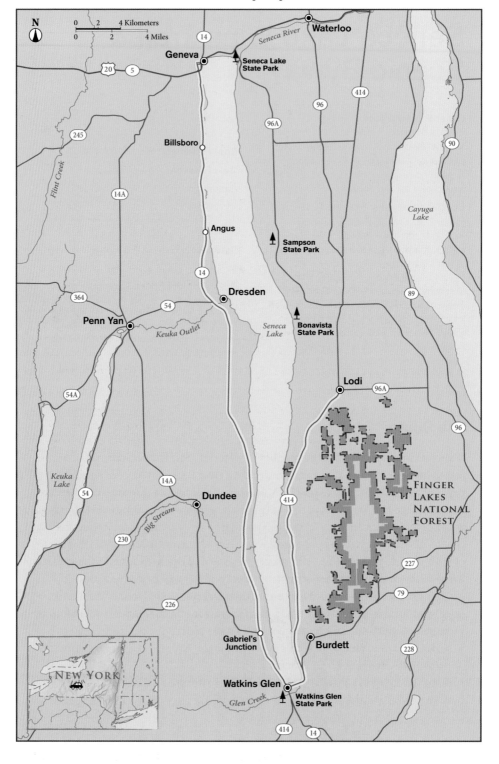

Geneva to Dresden

Pick up NY 14 south from US 20 in Geneva, where you can enjoy your first views of Seneca Lake between the downtown row houses. Pass **Houghton House,** home of the art department at Hobart and William Smith Colleges, and continue past the expansive **Geneva On The Lake** resort; if it's a weekend in spring or summer, you will almost surely see a wedding party taking place there. Soon **Belhurst Castle** comes into view, built from 1885 to 1889 as a private home and turned into an entertainment and hospitality establishment in 1933. Today this impressive mansion—which was expanded in 2003 by 30,000 square feet—features an elegant hotel, ballroom, restaurant, lounge, spa, and a wine tasting room and retail shop. If staying overnight here doesn't fit into your schedule, consider making a reservation for the Saturday or Sunday brunch, a remarkably reasonably priced feast with carving stations and a selection of 15 custom omelets.

Hardly have you begun your journey south on NY 14 before the first winery comes into view. **White Springs Winery** offers a selection of wines crafted from its 40-acre vineyard, featuring a range of whites from Riesling to Gewürztraminer, and reds including a Pinot Noir, a Blaufrankisch, and a port-style wine called Portrait of a Clipper. You'll also find **Glass Factory Brew House** here, offering tastings of its locally crafted IPA, pilsner, and Doppelbock beers.

Moving on, the red barn set back in the trees belongs to **Billsboro Winery,** which hosts the annual Plein Air Festival in mid-August. At the festival, artists spend two days creating paintings in the Finger Lakes, and their paintings are entered in a juried competition. At the end of the weekend, the paintings are sold in a silent auction at the closing gala. Needless to say, Billsboro's award-winning wines are served at the weekend's events—as well as in the vineyard's tasting room year-round.

With vineyards and other curiosities on the right, don't forget to look left for views of Seneca Lake. **Kashong Point** appears briefly, the spot at which the aging steamer *Onondaga* sank by design in 1898, when the town of Geneva loaded the boat with 800 pounds of explosives and a barrel of gasoline and detonated the lot, essentially for the entertainment of the 5,000 spectators who turned out to watch. The shipwreck—nothing but a smoldering hull at that point—went down and remains at the bottom of the lake today, as confirmed in 2012 by a pair of shipwreck hunters who use sonar to find deceased and decaying hulls under hundreds of feet of water. They, too, do this just for the fun of it.

Weaver-View Farms and Country Market comes into view as you enter Yates County. Newly moved to this location from Penn Yan, the country store features Amish quilts, fresh baked goods, homemade jams and jellies, sauces and pickled products, and local honey. Quilters will find fat quarters here, many of

them reproductions of 19th-century patterns, and the Weaver family also offers Amish-made baskets and primitive furniture.

The wineries begin to appear quickly as you continue south. **Fox Run Vineyards** offers an extensive list of varieties, and its wines have won such a long list of awards that we can barely tell you about the highlights. *Wines & Spirits* Magazine calls Fox Run one of the world's Top 100 Wineries, and the medals hanging on its walls make this a believable honor. Be sure to try the Hanging Delta Riesling, winner of Best in Class at the 2020 American Fine Wine Competition—that is, try it if it hasn't already sold out.

After Fox Run, the winery's vineyards extend nearly to the lakeshore on gently sloping green hills. Pass the junction with NY 54 at Dresden, the connecting road that once served as the Crooked Lake Canal, a 13-mile canal with 28 locks that transported cargo from one Finger Lake to the other. The canal closed in 1877, was filled in and became a railroad line, but the railroad washed out in 1972 in the destruction caused by Hurricane Agnes. Today this road is the fastest route between Seneca and Keuka Lakes.

Dresden to Dundee

Seneca Shores Wine Cellars comes into view on your left, a producer of "medieval wines" from fruits including strawberries, cranberries, and blueberries as well as grapes. **Anthony Road Wine Company** can be seen just a little off NY 14, where it grows vinifera (European varietal) grapes and produces a number of Rieslings, Chardonnay aged in stainless steel, Pinot Grigio, Gewürztraminer, Cabernet Franc, and Pinot Noir. Ask about its Devonian series, affordable blends with a light, dry style.

Note the **cobblestone house** across from Prejean Winery, a uniquely upstate New York construction method using the millions of cobbles left behind in the glacial moraine dumped here during the last Ice Age—about 10,000 years ago. The method involves setting up a frame about 20 inches wide and stacking cobbles (rounded rocks) inside, and then pouring in cement and letting it set to solidify the stone wall. It's a time-consuming process, but it creates a virtually impenetrable wall that keeps the elements out and lasts for many generations. You will see quite an assortment of cobblestone and rock-walled buildings from the Finger Lakes to the Great Lakes.

One of the oldest wineries in the area, **Prejean Winery** began as the dream of a World War II veteran and his wife who "retired" here and planted grapes beginning

Geneva's row houses are unique in upstate New York.

in 1979. Today Jim Prejean's son and daughter-in-law continue the family tradition, growing Old World grape varieties as well as some hybrid European-American crossbreeds, and producing a number of award-winning wines.

The ultra-modern **Torrey Ridge Winery** not only has some of the newest and most advanced winemaking equipment along this route, but it also enjoys one of the finest views of Seneca Lake that you will see anywhere on this drive. Its Redneck series of wines are as drinkable as grape juice and just about as sweet, but the winery also offers a number of award-winning vintages, including its Summer Delight, a strawberry-rhubarb-honey wine that wins many awards.

If you loved the Redneck wines, stop at **Earle Estates Meadery** next, where you can enjoy mead—yes, like in the days of old. Earle Estates produces honey as well, and you can watch the bees working in their hives while you enjoy a range of honey products.

Look across the road and down the hill to the left, and you'll see **Miles Wine Cellars,** with its outdoor cafe and its extraordinary setting on the edge of the lake. Miles not only features its wines in its tasting room for visitors who stop on the wine trail, but it also offers romantic overnight packages themed to match the season, complete with flowers, chocolates, wine, continental breakfast, and that awesome view of the lake.

Shaw Vineyard in Himrod may look small, but what you're seeing is the efficiency that veteran winemaker Steve Shaw brings to the process, heating his facility in part with the residual heat from underground barrels and packing the equipment and tanks into a single room. The process may be frugal, but the results confirm the method's effectiveness: Shaw's wines have made top ten lists and received recommendations from Gayot.com, *Wine Enthusiast*, and MicroLiquor .com, to name a few. The tasting room closes for the winter, but it's open seven days a week in summer.

Wineries begin to pass by quickly on your right, so if you're watching out for the one whose description intrigued you, it's time to pay close attention to the road. **Hermann J. Weimer Vineyard** is a must-stop, if for no other reason than it was one of the first wineries in the Finger Lakes—and thanks to Herr Weimer's faith in vinifera grapes' ability to grow and thrive in this climate, we now have more than 70 wineries in this region alone. The Riesling and Chardonnay here are the draw today. Nearby, **Villa Bellangelo** features one of the Finger Lakes' most celebrated Rieslings, the 2015 Berry Select, as well as an award-winning Reserve Chardonnay and a series of sweet wines called Scooter, which are sold in cans as well as bottles.

Fruit Yard Winery uses Concord and Niagara grapes as well as Chardonnay and Riesling to produce a number of sweet wines, and then branches out into a wide range of fruit flavors, from cranberry to plum, to create a menu of boldly flavorful varieties. Nearby, **Hickory Hollow Wine Cellars** offer a substantial variety of red and white wines, including its old world-style Nathan K wines, named for their highly respected winemaker, Nathan Kendall.

Dundee to Watkins Glen

With its prime real estate, including possession of a superlative view of Seneca Lake, **Glenora Wine Cellars** determined early in its existence that it should be a destination as well as a fine winery. Now offering an inn, a restaurant that specializes in local sourcing and regional cuisine, and a visitor center, this winery has made wine tasting into an all-encompassing experience. The release of the annual nouveau, the first wine of that season's harvest, takes place each year in November; Glenora is one of only a handful of New York State wineries that produces a nouveau, making this a truly special occasion.

YOUR ICE CREAM STOP: MISTER TWISTEE'S

With ice cream made from dairy products supplied by local Upstate Farms and a range of sugar-free, lactose-free, and gluten-free items, Mister Twistee's makes a stop worthwhile at the intersection of routes 54 and 14 in Dundee. The stand lives up to its name with creamy soft-serve as well as big scoops of hard flavors. Order your favorite toppings from a long list, and add candies of your choice, from M&Ms to gummy bears. Dole Whip, Italian ices, sherbet, and frozen yogurt round out the extensive menu. You'll find your new must-have flavor here.

Fulkerson Winery offers the iconic Red Zeppelin wine, as well as an ice wine and fresh grape juice each fall, while **Rock Stream Vineyards** across the road is the only winery on Seneca Lake that produces a grappa—a grape brandy with high alcohol content. The European-style chalet on your right after Fulkerson is the tasting building for **Magnus Ridge Winery,** producing a range of red and white wines from their own grapes, grown on 73 acres here in the Finger Lakes.

By the time you reach Schuyler County, you may be ready for some great cheese to go with whatever wine you bought in your many tastings. You're in luck: **Shtayburne Farm** is just down the road to the right. This family-owned dairy farm produces 15 kinds of artisan cheeses, including easy travel munchies like tomato basil cheese curds and six other curd varieties. Flavored Monterey Jack and cheddar cheeses, gift baskets, and an assortment of products from other local

Glenora Wine Cellars has some of the lakeside's best views.

farms make for convenient one-stop shopping here—and you can even meet the cows that produced the milk and cream for all these dairy products.

Barnstormer Winery offers wine tastings in its 170-plus-year-old barn, where you can sample its small-batch red and white wines made from 100 percent Finger Lakes grapes. The long, gray, one-story chalet on the left side of the road belongs to **Lakewood Vineyards,** where you can try a variety of wines including Bubbly Candeo, for "when champagne is too much and beer not enough." The winery's red and white options extend to dessert wines, featuring the sweet, rosy Borealis and the intriguingly named Glacovinum ice wine.

Watkins Glen

As you approach Watkins Glen, the crush of vineyards and residences seems to pull away and the view of Seneca Lake opens up in front of you, with the hills on the opposite shore suddenly dominating the scene. With all that we hear about

Formula One and NASCAR racing at **Watkins Glen International Racetrack,** it's easy to forget that this little town at the bottom of Seneca Lake also offers some of the most spectacular scenery in New York.

The main attraction—after the racetrack—is **Watkins Glen State Park,** a stunning gorge with a brilliantly engineered trail created by the Civilian Conservation Corps in the 1930s. The trail, its many walkways behind falling water and through solid rock tunnels, and its hundreds of chiseled stone stairs lead you past no fewer than 19 waterfalls, through a stone- and moss-covered corridor that rivals anything director Peter Jackson created for his *Lord of the Rings* movie trilogy. It's easy to believe you've found Tolkien's Rivendell when you walk through this gorge, whether you start at the bottom and work your way up, or take the shuttle bus to the top and walk down.

If you prefer a more relaxed way to take in the sights, a boat tour on **Captain Bill's Seneca Lake Cruises** may be just the thing. The narrated tours take you past expensive homes, along historic routes, and past Hector Falls, a 165-foot waterfall that can only be seen in its entirety from the middle of the lake. You can buy tickets and see the day's schedule at **Seneca Harbor Park,** which is also the best place in town to see a great deal of the lake's total length from the south end. **Seneca Harbor Station** offers waterfront dining here, and the **Watkins Glen Harbor Hotel** provides this marvelous view from many of its rooms.

If you're looking to stretch your legs with some shopping, **Famous Brands Outlet** is the largest store in downtown Watkins Glen, offering all the big outdoor brands like Patagonia, North Face, Columbia, and so on. There's a **Watkins Glen Racing store** in the town center as well, and if you wish you'd bought a bottle of wine at one of the wineries you visited earlier, you can probably pick up that vintage at the **Seneca Harbor Wine Center** in the former Iron and Agricultural Works Building.

When you're ready to move on from Watkins Glen, follow NY 414 around the lake. Pass **Hector Falls**—worth stopping to see, even though you'll only see the top half of it from the road—and be prepared to see quite a number of wineries up the east side of the lake as well. For the next 19 miles, you're driving on the official Seneca Lake Scenic Byway, a route granted New York Scenic Byway status in 2012.

Burdett to Lodi

As you approach Burdett, **Catharine Valley Winery** comes up quickly, a fairly new winery with a commitment to both domestic and Alsatian varieties. Each of the wines takes its name from a local legend or a slice of Finger Lakes area history—and the stories are as varied as the vintages. Just down the road, **Silver Springs**

The south end of Seneca Lake is in Watkins Glen.

Winery produces the Don Giovanni wines as well as a family of wines under the vineyard's name, literally bringing centuries of winemaking tradition to the Finger Lakes from winemaker John Zuccarino's Italian vineyard heritage.

Makers of distilled spirits have begun to arrive in the Finger Lakes, so a stop at **Finger Lakes Distilling** may introduce you to the region's newest craft—McKenzie sipping whiskies, Seneca Drums gin, and Vintner's flavored vodkas, all made from locally sourced materials. The modern tasting room and shop are open daily, providing samples of up to three varieties of spirits per person for a modest fee.

The views of grapevines sloping down to the lakeshore just get better and better as you continue north toward Hector. **J. R. Dill Winery**, a fairly new establishment, comes into view about six miles north of Watkins Glen. Its small-batch, handcrafted wines include Cabernet Francs and Cabernet Sauvignon, dry Rieslings, and a sparkling Cayuga white, a others.

Atwater Estate Vineyards was one of the first to establish a vineyard here, staking a claim to one of the best viewpoints on the east side of the lake and producing a range of vinifera wines as well as some yummy dessert varieties. Just beyond Atwater, **Chateau Lafayette Reneau** owns one of the largest vineyards in the area, but its list of medals from prestigious international competitions should be the real impetus for a stop here: Its dry Riesling has racked up awards since the 1990s, while judges laud the Chateau's semi-dry and sweet Rieslings as well.

You'll spot **Ryan William Vineyard** and its vines sloping all the way down to the shoreline—this small winery keeps its production limited to focus on carefully selected varieties. A stop here may provide an interesting contrast to the larger **Red Newt Cellars,** one of the best-known wineries among many upstate residents, both for its variety of excellent wines and for its espresso bar and bistro, the place to stop for coffee and a pastry or a Finger Lakes cheese and charcuterie plate. Red Newt works to promote the region's bounty through its wine club, a delicacy-of-the-season club that will send two shipments of six bottles of wine each to your door each year.

If you can tear your attention away from the lake and the wines for a bit, look to your right to see one of the area's natural treasures. The **Finger Lakes National Forest** protects 16,000-plus acres of woods with more than 30 miles of interconnected trails, including the Finger Lakes Trail, which doubles as part of the North Country National Scenic Trail (continuing to North Dakota). Few places in the entire state can match this forest for fall color, and parts of the forest are managed for blueberry, apple, and raspberry production.

The nearly new **Hector Wine Company** embraces the area's many grape varieties with its Soul blends, including medium-bodied reds and a semi-sweet white. **Leidenfrost Vineyards** comes up soon after, where you can sample a wide variety of single-grape wines and blends, all produced from estate grown grapes. Continue to **Hazlitt 1852 Vineyards,** where you can sip Red Cat Fizz or the more sophisticated Gruner Veltliner, a grape of Austrian origin that is fairly new to the Finger Lakes region.

In between the wineries, **Amazeing Acres** provides just the challenge you need after sampling wines from several vineyards: a complex hedge maze to wander through until you're good and lost, or at least well confused. The property also features a pond for paddle boating or kayaking, and a hostel for low-budget travelers.

You can't miss **Rasta Ranch Vineyards,** where the 1960s have not yet ended and the wines include Greatful Red and Arlo's Apple. The most popular variety here, however, is Uncle Homer's Red, a Concord-grape beverage that rivals the kosher-for-Passover wines we sip at the seder. On the flip side, **Sheldrake Point Winery** offers a decade's worth of award-winning estate wines, the quality of which places them among **Wine & Spirits** magazine's Top 100 Wineries year after year.

Some of us buy wines because of the labels, and **Penguin Bay Winery** may offer some of the downright cutest labels in the region with its frolicking birds of the Antarctic ice floes. Penguin Bay is part of a family of wineries that includes

Seneca Lake provides the wineries with the climate they need to produce flavorful grapes.

Swedish Hill and Goose Watch, with locations you will see as far from here as Lake Placid and Saratoga Springs.

As you reach Lodi and the end of the Seneca Lake Scenic Byway, a last spate of wineries comes into view. **Standing Stone Vineyards** has produced wine here since 1993, racking up a long list of awards and high scores from *Wine Spectator*. **Bagley's Poplar Ridge Winery** specializes in wines that are fun to drink, giving their varieties names like Busty Blanc and Pecker Head Red.

It's worth a stop at **Shalestone Vineyard** just to see the retail facility and warehouse built into the side of a hill, using wood harvested from the property and landscaped to blend into the natural scene as unobtrusively as possible. The owners built this remarkable facility themselves, and they also do the bulk of the work in the vineyards and as winemakers, specializing only in red wines.

The **Wagner Vineyards** logo will be familiar to most upstate New Yorkers, as this winery has grown grapes here for four generations and began producing wine in 1978. Wagner's 30-plus wines appear on the menus of hundreds of restaurants throughout the state, but you can try some of the lesser-known varieties by visiting the vineyard's tasting room.

The terra-cotta-colored Greek Revival building you see on the lakeshore in Lodi will make you want to come in, so stop at **Lamoreaux Landing** for the piece de resistance at the end of your scenic drive. The winery controls more than 100 acres of planted vineyards around the lake, each identified with a specific wine and managed to optimize the quality of the grape harvest. The result speaks for itself: Lamoreaux Landing nets gold medals in competitions around the world, with hundreds of medals since its first competitions in 1992. Chances are good that you'll find something here that pleases your palate.

We're ending this scenic drive here in Lodi, but the views continue as you drive up NY 414 on your way to Seneca Falls and the Thruway entrance. If you prefer, continue north to the junction with NY 96A, and turn left to head back to Geneva and complete the loop.

19

Cayuga Lake Wine Trail

General description: Follow the western shore of this Finger Lake for 42 miles from the cultured college town of Ithaca to the nucleus of the women's rights movement, stopping at state parks to see glorious waterfalls and other wonders.

Special attractions: Many wineries, Ithaca Science Museum, Cornell University, Fall Creek Gorge, Cascadilla Gorge, Sapsucker Woods, Moosewood Restaurant, Buttermilk Falls State Park, Robert Treman State Park, Cayuga Nature Center, Taughannock Falls State Park, La Romana Pottery, Bellwether Hard Cider, Myer Farm Distillers, Lively Run Goat Dairy, Deans Cove State Marine Park, Cayuga Lake State Park, Women's Rights National Historical Park, National Women's Hall of Fame, Erie Canal, Seneca Falls Historical Society Museum, Seneca Museum of Waterways and Industry, Canal Harbor at Seneca Falls, Seneca Meadows Wetland Preserve, Montezuma National Wildlife Refuge

Location: South of the New York State Thruway and east of Seneca Lake, between Rochester and Syracuse

Route numbers: NY 89, US 20

Travel season: Spring through fall

Camping: Twin Oaks Campground in Cayuga, Hejamada Campground & RV Park in Montezuma, Empire Haven Nudist Park in Moravia, Fillmore Glen State Park in Moravia, River Forest Park Campground and Marina in Weedsport

Services: In Ithaca and Seneca Falls

Nearby attractions: Prime Outlets at Waterloo, Long Point State Park, William Seward House in Auburn, Harriet Tubman House in Auburn

The Route

From the artsy college town of Ithaca to the site where the women's rights movement was born, this ramble along New York's longest Finger Lake presents some of the state's most visited state parks, a wealth of wineries, a dollop of history, and the pleasures of country living.

Ithaca

The saying goes that "Ithaca is Gorges," and even a brief visit to this town and its environs proves the truth in the motto. **Fall Creek Gorge** cuts through the middle of the Cornell University campus, loaded with hiking trails and falling water, and **Cascadilla Gorge** provides one of the most pleasant hikes in the entire Finger Lakes region with its chiseled stairs and cleverly engineered walkways, passing no less than eight waterfalls in a mile's walk. You'll find much more here than amazing waterfall views and rock formations, however, because the city of Ithaca serves as home to countless artists and musicians who come to this area for the inspiration

Cayuga Lake Wine Trail

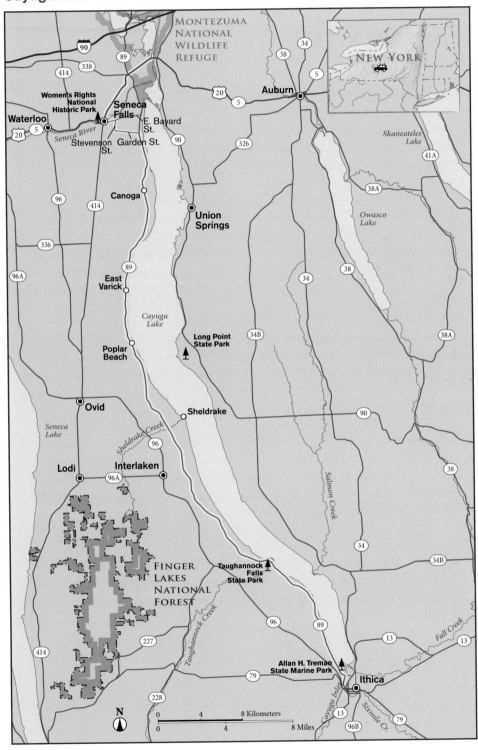

the surrounding hills and beautiful gorges provide. Ithaca caters to this population with its vegetarian restaurants, farm markets and natural foods, galleries and weekend art events, music and theater, boutiques, and outdoor activities.

The Discovery Trail unites a series of sites that explore science, nature, and local history, beginning with the **Sciencenter** and its outdoor science park. This unusual science museum attracted national attention when it created the **Sagan Planet Walk,** a 1.5 billionth scale model of the solar system—from the Sun to Pluto—that stretches for 0.73 mile through downtown Ithaca. In 2012 the Sciencenter expanded the model to include Alpha Centauri, the closest star to the Sun, placing it at the Iniloa Astronomy Center at the University of Hawaii. This made the Sagan Planet Walk the largest single museum exhibition in the world.

Also part of the Discovery Trail, the **History Center in Tompkins County** provides background on the city's development from Native American settlements to the modern cultural center we see today. **Cornell Botanic Gardens,** a 500-acre area on the Cornell University campus with landscaped gardens, an arboretum, and natural areas including Fall Creek Gorge, is open daily from sunrise to sunset for your strolling pleasure.

If you'd like to find a one-of-a-kind gift for someone special, make tracks to **Ithaca Commons Marketplace,** where you will find boutiques and galleries that feature the work of local artists, as well as new and vintage clothing, shoes and boots, fair trade imported items, and art and craft supplies. Restaurants, coffee and teashops, and other goodies have found their way into the mix, providing whatever you need to stay as long as you like.

No trip to Ithaca can be complete unless you enjoy a meal at **Moosewood Restaurant,** the world-famous vegetarian establishment that produced a line of bestselling cookbooks. A collective of 19 members has owned the restaurant since 1973, and they manage a daily-changing menu based on the availability of fresh local ingredients. You'll find the cookbooks and logo merchandise for sale at the restaurant as well, including books signed by the authors.

When you're ready to leave Ithaca, take NY 89 north along the west side of Cayuga Lake. Pass Cayuga Inlet at the southern end of the lake, and soon homes and cottages appear to your right and the woods fill in to your left. Like all of the Finger Lakes, Cayuga has its share of dense population right along the shoreline, but you will find places to pull off the road and enjoy sweeping views of the lake as well.

Cayuga Lake sparkles in fall.

Ithaca to Trumansburg

When you see a sign for the town of Ulysses, watch for **Glenwood Pines** restaurant and bar on the lake side of the road. The parking area here provides one of the nicest views of the southern portion of Cayuga Lake, so stop here for a photo if the restaurant is not busy (or stop for dinner if you like).

Cayuga Nature Center, part of the Paleontological Research Institute and one of the stops on Ithaca's Discovery Trail, offers organized outdoor education programs and day camps for students, teaching them about the natural world and our role in it. You are welcome to visit the center and enjoy the wilderness setting, perhaps sharpening your skills in identifying native plants and trees along its miles of trails. The nearby **Museum of the Earth** houses one of the largest fossil collections in the country, including the Hyde Park Mastodon, a nearly complete mastodon skeleton found downstate from here.

Trees, flowers, lakeside, and hills unfold as you drive north, leading you to **Taughannock Falls State Park** and the waterfall that stops hikers in their tracks and causes mouths to fall open in awe. This sheer 215-foot curtain of water drops straight down from a notch in a high ledge, creating a silky skein of misty whitewater that plunges deep into the pool below. You can view this natural wonder two ways: First from the Falls Overlook at the top of the gorge, to which you can drive. From the parking area, take a short stroll to the viewing platform and rock wall to enjoy a magnificent view of the entire rounded cliff edge and the falls' hypnotic descent.

Alternately, take the 1-mile Gorge Trail, an almost entirely level trail through the Taughannock Creek gorge and past a number of riffles, rapids, and one 20-foot waterfall on the way to the base of Taughannock Falls. The delightful trail provides plenty of opportunity to appreciate this most popular of all of Ithaca's gorges, and the opportunity to view Taughannock Falls from a walkway directly opposite its base makes the little bit of effort to get here more than worth the walk.

Back on NY 89 north, reach the village of **Trumansburg,** the former home of Robert Moog, who invented his Moog synthesizers in a storefront here in town. Now a favorite place for musicians to live, the town holds the **Finger Lakes Grassroots Festival of Music and Dance** every year in July at the village fairgrounds, hosted by the nationally well-known band Donna the Buffalo.

Taughannock Falls draws visitors from throughout the region.

Trumansburg to East Varick

Not only is this route part of the Cayuga Lake Scenic Byway, but it's also the Cayuga Wine Trail, and the wineries begin to appear just north of Trumansburg. **Frontenac Point Winery** has stuck to its vision of remaining a small, boutique winery, producing just 2,000 to 3,000 cases of wine annually—half of which are dry reds. Try the winery's favorites while observing and listening to Stay Sail, a 10-foot-high kinetic sculpture with chimes driven by the wind off the bow of the winery's deck. Just up the road, **Americana Vineyards** features its Crystal Lake Cafe, serving dishes made with locally sourced meat, cheeses, and produce for lunch and dinner and Sunday brunch.

Tucked in between the wineries, you'll find **La Romana Pottery,** the studio of artist Vera D. Vico. Working to capture the essence of natural beauty in her work, Vico creates functional pieces from amphorae to soup ladles, using a wide range of brilliant colors and textures.

For a different kind of experience entirely, stop at **Lively Run Goat Farm** to learn about local cheese and sample a number of varieties—and to meet the goats that provide the milk for this flavorful delicacy. With your favorite variety of chèvre, feta, or blue cheese in hand, proceed to **Lucas Vineyards,** the oldest winery on Cayuga Lake, perhaps best known for its Nautie line of sweet wines—each with a 1940s-style nautical lady on the label—and its medal-winning Tug Boat Red and Tug Boat White.

Sheldrake Point Vineyard maintains two wineries in the Finger Lakes, one on Seneca Lake in Hector and one here in the town of Ovid. Its estate wines are served at both, so you will have the opportunity to taste award-winning Riesling, Gewürztraminer, Pinot Gris, and blended wines as well as a variety of reds and ice wines.

It may surprise you to come upon a distillery in the midst of wine country, but **Myer Farm Distillers** provides a reminder that these prime soils produce a richness of healthy crops beyond grapes. Here the descendants of the first Ovid settlers (back in 1789) grow certified organic grain to create award-winning vodka, gin, corn whiskey, wheat spirit, and rye whiskey. If you hadn't considered that tasting distilled spirits could be as nuanced as sampling a range of wines, stop here and learn a little about the world of sipping whiskey.

Sheep and goat farming are popular in the Cayuga Lake area.

YOUR ICE CREAM STOP: CAYUGA LAKE CREAMERY

Lavender ice cream? How about Maple Bacon flavor? These and many other unusual concoctions, made in small batches on the premises with fresh local ingredients, make Cayuga Lake Creamery a must-stop destination while you're driving this scenic byway. You can always get the most popular flavors—vanilla, chocolate, mocha, peanut butter, coffee, and a fruit flavor—but the creative and often surprising specials bring people back to this ice cream stop on a regular basis. Whether you develop a love of Banoreo, a yummy blend of banana ice cream and Oreo cookies; Blue Hawaiian, mixing coconut ice cream with Blue Curacao liqueur; or Chilifest Chocolate, a rich chocolate ice cream blended with chili powder, it's virtually guaranteed that you will make this creamery a regular stop whenever you're in the Finger Lakes. Watch for it as you travel up NY 89.

The farther north you drive along these hills and fields loaded with blooming vines in spring and fragrant with ripening grapes in late summer, the more opportunities you have to discover a new winery and a delicious vintage. **Hosmer Winery** cultivates nearly 70 acres of grapevines, producing wines including both vinifera and French-American hybrids and offering tastings in a renovated barn across from its vineyards. **Cayuga Ridge Estate Winery,** just up the road, serves its visitors wine in a bright red barn, with Finger Lakes specialties including Riselings and Gewurztraminer and fruit wines sweet enough to be dessert.

With its first full harvest in 2012 and its 5,000-square-foot production facility completed at the same time, **Toro Run Winery** came out of the gate at a run with no less than 11 varieties of white and red wines. Now under new ownership, the winery is managed by the same people who own **Buttonwood Grove Winery** just down the road. By this time, if you've been diligent in sampling wines from a number of different wineries along this route, you may be glad to know that Buttonwood Grove Winery near the town of Romulus provides overnight accommodations in cabins that come complete with all the comforts of a hotel, but with the decor of an Adirondack great camp. Nestled in for the night in your rustic cabin, you can enjoy one of Buttonwood's dessert wines like Blackberry Briar or Riesling ice wine.

A little park called **Dean's Cove** comes up on your right as you head north. Revolutionary War buffs may recognize this site as one of the places hit by the Sullivan Expedition, a force led by American Major General John Sullivan in 1779. The expedition conducted a military campaign to drive the British and their close allies in the Six Tribes of the Iroquois Nation out of the area, using the most destructive tactics possible. While the Iroquois fled the area in advance of the approaching troops, the Sullivan Expedition arrived here at this cove and devastated everything the Iroquois left behind in their settlement. The American troops went on to burn crops, technology, and homes as part of what became known as a "scorched earth" campaign. With no homes to return to, many Iroquois attempted to find shelter with the British troops at Fort Niagara, but when winter set in, thousands of them froze or starved to death as the British struggled just to keep its own troops fed and warm in the north-country winter.

Varick to Seneca Falls

Two more wineries appear as you make your way up the last third of Cayuga Lake's length. **Goose Watch Winery,** tucked into the middle of a chestnut grove, focuses on grapes not found at many other wineries in the area. Here wines from viognier, aromella, melody, diamond, and lemberger grapes have the distinction of a number of awards and medals, making this offshoot of the much larger Swedish Hill Winery a favorite with tourists. Just down the road, **Knapp Winery** not only

The Finger Lakes provide some of the nation's best grape-growing country.

features a generous assortment of red and white wines including a Siegerrebe—a fairly rare find in the Finger Lakes—but its line of cordials includes a peach spirit, and both a limoncello (lemon) and a limencello (lime), each with the fresh citrus flavor blended with Knapp's own grappa. **The Vineyard Restaurant,** open daily for lunch and once a month for a special wine dinner, offers a menu to match the season with locally sourced ingredients, including a very popular cheese and charcuterie board with at least four local cheeses and two locally raised meats.

Three more wineries in the town of Varick top off the Cayuga Wine Trail at its northern end. The small, family-owned **Lakeshore Winery** recently released a dry Cayuga white wine, no small feat when working with one of the region's sweetest grapes. As if to offset this, Lakeshore also offers a sweet Chardonnay, another startling variety. **Varick Winery and Vineyard**—also known as Cobblestone Farm—features a country store in addition to its tasting room in its large, stone farmhouse, where you can sample sauces, jams, and jellies while enjoying a selection of wines from a Cabernet Franc to a dry Vignoles. You may have the chance to try the new Petit Verdot, a wine from a floral-scented French grape not often found in New York State wines.

The last winery on this route, **Swedish Hill** received the Top Winery honor at the New York State Fair Commercial Wine Competition in 2013. The winery has produced its own wine since 1985, but its history of growing grapes in the Finger Lakes began back in 1969, when the farm raised grapes to sell to the area's earliest wineries. Swedish Hill grew under the leadership of its original owners, Dick and Cindy Peterson, and its popularity increased significantly when their son Dave received his PhD in viticulture and joined the winery. Today Swedish Hill has two spinoff wineries, Goose Watch and Penguin Bay (on Seneca Lake), and tasting rooms in Saratoga Springs and Lake Placid as well as this one on the shores of Cayuga Lake. This location has a special treat in addition to its many wines: the opportunity to meet Doobie, the miniature donkey that bucks his way through Swedish Hill's logo. Doobie is the reason Swedish Hill features Jack Ass Red, Doobie Blues, and Smart Ass Red, three of its most popular wines.

As you come to the end of the wine trail, **Cayuga Lake State Park** provides one more expansive look at the lake—quite a different view from the one you enjoyed 40 miles south of here. Here the wooded hills slope downward to the lakeshore, ending in grassy areas, a sandy beach, and shallow waters where anglers find largemouth bass, bullheads, and carp.

Seneca Falls

When you reach the north end of Cayuga Lake, turn left onto US 20 to make a side trip to Seneca Falls.

On July 19 and 20, 1848, the first Women's Rights Convention took place in Seneca Falls at what is now **Women's Rights National Historical Park.** Here a crowd of 300 women and men, led by Lucretia Mott, Mary M'Clintock, and Elizabeth Cady Stanton, presented the nation with their Declaration of Sentiments, the document that listed the ways women in America were disenfranchised by laws that prevented them from voting, going to college, owning property after they were married, or being represented in the legislative system by their peers. The road from this date would be long and often treacherous, but this event put women of the US on a path to voting rights (not achieved until 1920), elected office, and the right to own property and hold the same jobs as those held by men. The minutes from this convention declare: "Resolved, That woman is man's equal—was

Wildlife biologists manage Montezuma National Wildlife Refuge to maximize waterfowl habitat.

intended to be so by the Creator, and the highest good of the race demands that she should be recognized as such."

A visit to this national historical park includes a visitor center and museum; the Wesleyan Chapel, where the actual convention took place; Elizabeth Cady Stanton's home; and Declaration Park, where a waterfall wall inscribed with the entire Declaration of Sentiments stretches the length of the park.

Near the national park on Fall Street, the **National Women's Hall of Fame** celebrates the lives of women who have been leaders and role models throughout history. Founded in 1969, the hall inducts a class of women every year based on their contribution to the development of the US, the national or global impact of their achievements, and the value of these achievements for the long term. As of this writing, 285 women have been inducted.

There's one more stop to make before your exploration of Cayuga Lake comes to an end: **Montezuma National Wildlife Refuge,** east of Seneca Falls on US 20. The refuge, managed for the benefit of year-round and migrating waterfowl, draws hundreds of thousands of birds annually to its main pool, marshlands, woods, and wetland areas. Shorebirds (sandpipers and plovers) gather here in spring and fall, as do many species of ducks, Canada and snow geese, long-legged waders, warblers, vireos, woodpeckers, and a number of other bird families. Muskrats build their reedy houses here and make themselves remarkably easy to see, and white-tailed deer, foxes, and other small furry animals raise their young in this refuge. You can enjoy it best by driving the 1.5-mile Wildlife Drive around the main pool, through Benning Marsh, and past newly created pools and wetlands within the refuge. A stop at Tschache Pool (pronounced "shocky") and a climb to the top of the observation tower will yield good looks at a bald eagle nest that has functioned in a tree on the opposite side of the pool for decades. Platforms on top of the high-tension electrical wires just outside the refuge's main entrance host nesting ospreys every year. Check the log at the main visitor center for that day's interesting bird and wildlife sightings.

Here our Cayuga Lake adventure ends, but if you want to continue, the east side of the lake offers some splendid farmland views and several additional wineries. If you're circling back to Ithaca, consider taking NY 90 along the lake and through the communities of Union Springs, Aurora, King Ferry, and South Lansing.

Keuka Lake Wine Trail

General description: This Y-shaped lake provides a gorgeous 22-mile driving route from Penn Yan to Hammondsport, through wine and grape country to the cradle of the US aircraft industry.

Special attractions: Indian Pines Park, Keuka Lake, Yates Cellars, Keuka Lake State Park, Hunt Country Vineyards, Chief Red Jacket home site, Stever Hill Vineyards, Sommerville Pottery, Heron Hill Winery, Dr. Konstantin Frank Winery, Bully Hill Winery, Pulteney Square Historic District, Keuka Lake Vineyards, Keuka Brewing, Greyton H. Taylor Wine Museum, Glenn H. Curtiss Museum

Location: South of the New York State Thruway between Canandaigua and Geneva

Route number: NY 54A

Travel season: Spring through fall

Camping: Keuka Lake State Park, Hammondsport-Bath KOA Resort, Camp Elmbois in Hammondsport

Services: In Penn Yan, Branchport, and Hammondsport

Nearby attractions: Watkins Glen State Park

The Route

From the top of the eastern fork of Keuka Lake to the southern end in Hammondsport, this drive passes through wooded hills, miles of grape vineyards, and some of the oldest wine country in the eastern US. Here Reverend William Bostwick planted the first vineyard in the Finger Lakes back in 1829, in Hammondsport, presumably to grow grapes for sacramental wine. His grapes thrived, and other winemakers began to arrive and to discover cultivation practices that strengthened their yield and produced flavorful wines. By 1860, the area became one of the first in the nation to establish a successful commercial wine enterprise when champagne makers from the Ohio Valley moved here and pooled their talents at Pleasant Valley Winery.

Twenty years later, a master barrel-maker named Walter Taylor arrived to make oak barrels for aging wines in the style that winemakers still use today. Within two years, Taylor established his own winery, and Taylor Wine Company flourished until it bought Pleasant Valley Wine Company and turned it into Great Western Wines. Great Western became a bastion of mass production and a major employer in the Keuka Lake area—but not everyone would agree with its winemaking practices, which included shipping in grapes from California to improve the taste of its wines. Much later, in the 1970s, a younger Walter Taylor would lose the right to use his own last name on artisan wines he produced by putting his

Keuka Lake Wine Trail

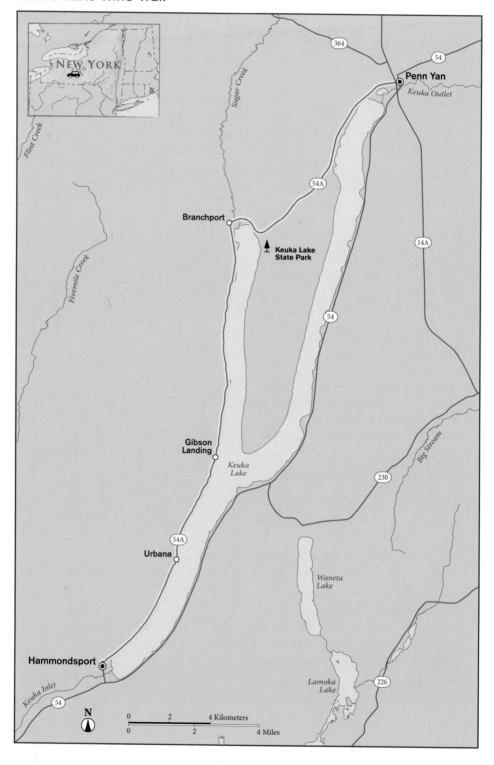

Sweeping lake views and fall colors make Keuka Lake an upstate jewel.

faith in New York's ability to produce great-tasting grapes . . . and he became one of the most infamous winemakers in the Finger Lakes when he established Bully Hill. Here he championed traditional practices to make fine wines with a decisively ironic sense of humor.

Penn Yan to Branchport

In Penn Yan, take NY 54A past **Indian Pines Park,** a great place to get a good look at Keuka Lake before following the road through residential areas along the lakeshore. This road heads south from town along the eastern tine of the fork, with views of the lake on your left and forested hills to the right. Watch for **Black Cat Bistro and Java-Gourmet Company Store** as you leave Penn Yan, a good place to pick up locally sourced gourmet foods and specialty coffees—and seven varieties of culinary flake salt, which comes from veins of sea salt below Seneca Lake. This may be the most unusual local product you can purchase as you travel the Finger Lakes, so make a point of stopping to see it for yourself.

In a few minutes, the lake fades back to the left as you cross the wetlands and woods that fill the gap between the two tines of the fork. Watch for **Hampstead Mansion,** the former home of local resident Henry Rose (of Rose Hill), built in 1838 and listed on the National Register of Historic Places. This historic home now serves as the tasting room of **Yates Cellars** winery, a small, limited-production winery with two vineyards here in Yates County.

As you reach the top of the lake's west end, **Keuka Lake State Park** comes up quickly on your left. This park features lots of lakefront and excellent lake views any time of year, but especially when fall colors paint the landscape. Take the Recreation Drive through the park to get much closer to the lake, and to enjoy some peace and quiet away from the bustle of the main road.

Alternately, a parking area on NY 54A just after the entrance to Keuka Lake State Park provides a panoramic view of the lake. When you're ready, continue on NY 54A to the traffic light in Branchport, and turn left.

YOUR ICE CREAM STOP: SENECA FARMS

Start your Keuka Lake drive by fortifying yourself at this Penn Yan creamery, where homemade ice cream flavors include Cinnamon Raisin Oatmeal—loaded with chunks of real, fresh-baked oatmeal cookies—and White Mountain Raspberry, among many others. The seasonal scooped favorite is Grape Sherbet, though Caramel Custard swirled with Soft Apple Spice crowns the fall lineup. Great ice cream requires generous portions, so you'll get plenty here.

You'll see **Hunt Country Vineyards** in Branchport, a winery long known for its Vignoles and dry and semi-dry Riesling, and also for its sweeter wines like its Remedy rosé. Hunt Country recently added a Seyval Blanc and Traminette to its already robust lineup of affordable and popular wines.

A blue and yellow New York State Department of Education sign notes that **Seneca Indian chief Red Jacket lived here,** and his mother was buried at this spot. Red Jacket served as principal negotiator with the US for land rights and other entitlements, a process that culminated in 1794 in the Treaty of Canandaigua between the Six Nations of the Iroquois and the federal government. Red Jacket was one of 50 signers of this treaty, which ceded a great deal of Iroquois land to

Finger Lakes wine country began on the shores of Keuka Lake.

the US because the tribes had fought alongside the British during the Revolutionary War.

Stever Hill Vineyards comes up on your right, easily recognizable because of the 1850s barn that serves as its tasting room. Its roster of wines includes a Marquette, one of the grapes bred specifically for colder climates, and a wide range of sweet and semi-sweet blends that are perfect for sipping on a patio in warm weather. In a moment, you will pass into Steuben County.

Pulteney to Hammondsport

Watch for the sign for **Sommerville Pottery,** a quick detour to your right as you enter Pulteney. If you love the traditional lines and substantial materials of ceramics that you can put to practical use, this studio will appeal to your sense of functionality. Choose from a range of pieces in earthy tones for your kitchen, dining table, bathroom, or craft area—the yarn bowls for knitters are quite clever—as well as lamps and home decor.

Restaurants in this area range from steaks and chops to wood-fired pizza, and they all feature a view of the lake from the waterfront or a nearby hillside. Cottages dominate the lakeshore, however, so your lake views tend to arrive in glimpses rather than long looks unless you stop for a bite to eat.

You will know you're approaching Hammondsport when you see signs for three of the area's best-known wineries: Bully Hill, Heron Hill, and Dr. Konstantin Frank. Watch for the High Road, a hairpin turn up County Route 76; swing around this sharp turn and drive up the steep hill to reach the elevated wineries and their spectacular views of Keuka Lake.

Bully Hill Winery appears first—the winery I described at the outset of this route. Here the flamboyant Walter S. Taylor built his winery on his faith in New York State hybrid grapes, eschewing his family's insistence on mixing California grapes with New York's harvest to make wines. Walter was determined to prove that hardy grapes created by crossing New York varieties with French grapevines could produce better-tasting wines than those of the Taylor Wine Company. Openly critical of his family's practices, he eventually found himself legally banished from the family business and forbidden by a court order to use the name "Taylor" on any of his products. Walter, undaunted, named his business Bully Hill, and by the late 1970s it had become the best-known winery in New York State. His self-illustrated labels for wines with names like Love My Goat Red and Space Shuttle Rosé, coupled with his unflaggingly huge personality, made Walter an icon in New York winemaking until his death in 2001. Today Bully Hill continues the tradition of making "Wine Without Fear," emblazoning this motto on the corks that seal its bottles.

You'll find Heron Hill Winery at the top of the High Road.

In contrast, **Heron Hill Winery** provides a more sedate wine tasting experience than you might enjoy at Bully Hill, but its chalet-like setting, stellar view, and long history of winemaking make this a satisfying stop. Heron Hill produced its first wine back in 1977, and it still tends to and harvests the grapes by hand to bring nearly 20 varieties of wine to the table. Enjoy a wine tasting or lunch at the Blue Heron Cafe, where the menu features dishes made with local ingredients and the wine list includes many Heron Hill specialties.

Finally, one of the oldest wineries in New York State resides here on the hill: **Dr. Konstantin Frank's Vinifera Wine Cellars,** repeated winner of awards including Winery of the Year at the New York Wine and Food Classic, and famous for its Rieslings, Gewürztraminer, and a number of other varieties. Dr. Frank was instrumental in bringing European wine grapes to the Finger Lakes region, and his descendants continue to run the winery to the standards he established early in the area's wine producing history. A stop here should be a requirement on any wine lover's tour.

When you've had your fill of these three distinctly different wineries, head down the hill and back to NY 54A and continue south to Hammondsport.

Hammondsport

A place that I enjoy so much that I wrote a romance novel with this town as the setting, Hammondsport presents just the right mix of history, charm, and accommodations for its guests. Here the turn-of-the-20th-century town square—also known as the **Pulteney Square National Historic District**—features a cluster of shops, restaurants, boutiques, antiques stores, and all the necessities of small-town living, surrounding a true town square park complete with a gazebo. Here you'll find restaurants that serve grape pie, the most localized of all the area's delicacies, and places to purchase country crafts, jewelry and handbags, Scandinavia products, candles, collectibles, and many other gift items.

The elegantly European-styled **Pleasant Valley Wine Company,** precursor to many of the wineries you've visited today, provides a window into the wine industry's past, while the **Glenn H. Curtiss Museum** fills in a piece of aviation history: the leap from the Wright Brothers' discovery of the secret of flight to the use of this brand-new technology for military planes and other aircraft. Curtiss, an inventor who earned the title of "Fastest Man on Earth" in 1907 when he built and tested a motorcycle that clocked at 136.3 miles per hour, became one of the fathers of human aviation when he performed the first publically observed, officially recognized manned flight in America in 1908. In 1909 he went on to pilot an aircraft for 24.7 miles in competition, establishing a new world distance record and becoming the nation's foremost aviation pioneer.

You've reached the end of the scenic drive described here, but if you want to continue your exploration of Keuka Lake and eventually return to Penn Yan, head north up the east side of the lake on NY 54.

You can see sailboats on Keuka Lake throughout the spring, summer, and fall.

GREAT LAKES
SCENIC DRIVES

21

Great Lakes Seaway Trail, Part 1

Pennsylvania Border to Youngstown

General description: The 114-mile first leg of the Seaway Trail follows the eastern coast of Lake Erie, as well as the entire US shoreline of the Niagara River. Beaches, lighthouses, well-appointed estates, Concord grape vineyards, and the nation's largest and mightiest waterfalls are all prominent features of this uncommon driving experience.

Special attractions: Niagara Falls State Park, Barcelona Harbor and Lighthouse, Vinewood Acres Sugar Shack, Lake Erie Wine Trail wineries, Point Gratiot Park and Dunkirk Historic Lighthouse, Dunkirk Historical Museum, The Stagecoach West western wear and equine gear store; Evangola State Park, Graycliff Estate, Friends of Lake Erie Seaway Trail Center, Tifft Nature Preserve, Buffalo Outer Harbor, Buffalo Grain Elevator, Buffalo Harbor Lighthouse, Buffalo-Erie County Naval & Military Park, Herschell Carrousel Factory Museum, Devil's Hole State Park, Niagara Power Project Power Vista, Aquarium of Niagara, Seneca Niagara Casino, Joseph Davis State Park, Fort Niagara State Park

Location: The western portion of the Seaway Trail actually begins at the Ohio-Pennsylvania border, but our route picks up the trail in North East, Pennsylvania, at the New York border. It follows the western edge of New York State along Lake Erie through Buffalo and Niagara Falls to the northwestern-most corner of the state at Fort Niagara State Park. Two more sections of the trail are covered in this book.

Route numbers: NY 5, NY 266, NY 265, Robert Moses Parkway, NY 104 East, NY 18F North

Travel season: Year-round, though winter and early spring provide the least-obstructed water views and the most potentially hazardous driving. Summer and fall are great for views of the vineyards and other crops, while fall presents the most spectacular foliage displays.

Camping: Lakeside Campground in Ripley; Westfield/Lake Erie KOA Campground in Barcelona; Blue Water Beach Campground in Westfield; Lake Erie State Park; Evangola State Park; Point Breeze RV Resort

Services: In North East, Ripley, Westfield, Barcelona, Dunkirk, Silver Creek, Point Breeze, Hamburg, Buffalo, Tonawanda, Niagara Falls, Lewiston, and Youngstown

Nearby attractions: Chautauqua Institution, Jamestown Audubon Nature Center and Roger Tory Petersen Institute, National Comedy Center, Lily Dale Assembly, Buffalo & Erie County Botanical Garden, Theodore Roosevelt Inaugural National Historic Site, Buffalo Transportation and Pierce Arrow Museum, Darwin Martin House

The reconstructed Oak Orchard Lighthouse, a replica of a 19th-century light, opened in 2010.

Great Lakes Seaway Trail, Part 1: Pennsylvania Border to Youngstown

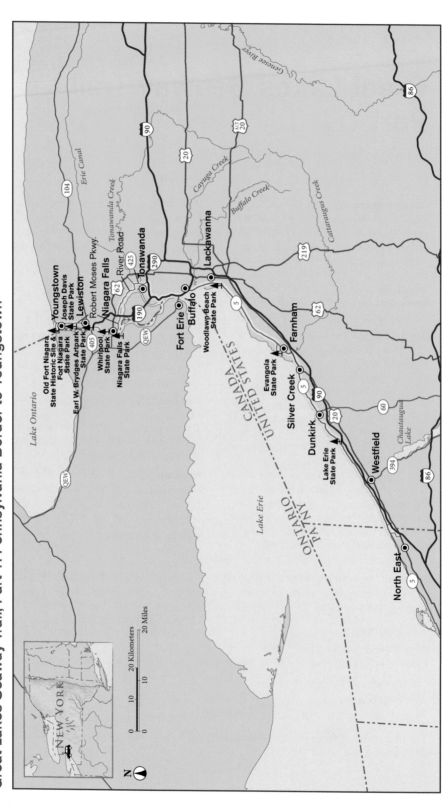

N

0   10   20 Kilometers
0   10   20 Miles

NEW YORK

Lake Ontario

Erie Canal

Old Fort Niagara
State Historic Site &
Fort Niagara
State Park
Joseph Davis
State Park
Earl W. Brydges Artpark
State Park
Youngstown
Lewiston
Whirlpool
State Park
Niagara Falls
State Park
Robert Moses Pkwy.
Niagara Falls
River Road
Tonawanda
Tonawanda Creek
Cayuga Creek
Buffalo Creek
Cattaraugus Creek
Genesee River
Lackawanna
Buffalo
Fort Erie
Woodlawn Beach
State Park
Farnham
Evangola
State Park
Silver Creek
Dunkirk
Lake Erie
State Park
Westfield
North East
Chautauqua
Lake
Lake Erie
CANADA
UNITED STATES
ONTARIO
PA / NY

86
90
ALT 20
20
104
62
425
290
190
QEW
405
5
219
62
5
60
394
86
90
20
5
QEW

The Route

Of all the scenic routes in New York State, the Great Lakes Seaway Trail provides the greatest diversity of subjects, the widest range of panoramic views, and the longest actual ride. Winding along the western border of the state for 518 miles (454 miles in New York state alone), it begins in Pennsylvania and continues along the shores of Lake Erie, the Niagara River, Lake Ontario, and the St. Lawrence River until it terminates at the Canadian border in Rooseveltown. More than 100 outdoor "storyteller signs" provide the details you may miss from your car window: natural and maritime history, the locations of lighthouses, and information about unusual agricultural crops or striking architectural styles that you will see along the route. The Seaway Trail sets a standard for all of the scenic byways in the state with its well-crafted interpretive content, its clearly marked twists and turns, and its wealth of sights and places to explore.

We've broken this long route into three manageable pieces, each of which provides a solid day's drive or a fun weekend with plenty of interesting stops. If you're thinking of taking on the entire trail—i.e., all three of the sections that we describe in this book—plan on at least a week's journey, and maybe longer to be sure that you don't miss any of the area's fascinating maritime history. New York became a pivotal point of growth and commerce for an entire nation because of its two Great Lakes, the river and waterfalls that generate enough power for the state's entire western segment, and the seaway and canal that helped open commerce in the nation's Midwest.

This first section leads from the Pennsylvania border at North East, Pennsylvania, to Youngstown, New York, on the Lake Ontario shoreline at Fort Niagara. New York State's role in the War of 1812 comes into focus as you skirt the eastern shore of Lake Erie, a waterway that became a pivot point in the US Navy's ability to take on the British fleet. While Commodore Oliver Hazard Perry's famous victory over the British took place many miles from here off the north coast of Ohio, battles on and around Lake Erie caused reverberations all the way to Buffalo, as the British tore through the city to burn down neighborhoods in retaliation for American aggression.

The area's military history began long before 1812, of course, and Old Fort Niagara saw a great deal of that action. Built in 1726, the fort guarded the mouth of the Niagara River to secure access to the Great Lakes, first for the French and then for the British until the end of the Revolutionary War. The British took the fort back from the Americans in 1813 but had to give it back in 1815 when the War of 1812 ended with the signing of the Treaty of Ghent in Washington, DC. Today the restored fort serves as the keeper and interpreter of the military history that shaped this entire region.

Amidst the tales of war and other conflicts, the Seaway Trail has many more contemporary charms. Today's peaceful Great Lakes feature a number of easily accessible lighthouses for your photographic pleasure, and state parks with lengthy beaches and wide views of quiet lakeshores. Seabirds congregate in harbor areas that never freeze over in winter, giving you plenty of opportunity to pick through gulls with your scope until you find the uncommon Iceland or glaucous gull. Open areas provide chances to see all kinds of small, furry animals, from groundhogs galumphing along the roadside to white-tailed deer munching on last year's corn in a farmer's field.

Perhaps best of all, the Seaway Trail supplies access to nearly a dozen wineries along the Lake Erie Wine Trail, where the frigid winter climate suits the growth of Concord grapes—the kind used in grape jelly and jam—as well as catawba, Delaware, ives, and Niagara grapes. You'll find the better-known Riesling, Chardonnay, Merlot, and Cabernet grapes wine here, and some French varietals thrive in western New York's fields as well. Fields of grapevines make this area look like France or Germany as you drive along the country roads, especially against the distant backdrop of the Allegheny Mountains.

North East to Barcelona

Begin your drive in North East by taking US 20 east to Shortman Road. Turn north onto Shortman and continue until the road ends at NY 5. Turn east (right). Now you're on the Seaway Trail, and you've crossed into New York State.

Lake Erie comes into view in the distance, just past the farms to your left. In the foreground, fields of grapevines dominate the landscape, and you soon see signs for the **Lake Erie Wine Country Trail** (some signs may say CHAUTAUQUA WINE TRAIL). Signs for various wineries pop up along this route, so keep an eye out if you want to sample some of the local varieties. In particular, **Sparkling Ponds Winery** is famous for its Woman Pleaser Blush, a Niagara wine with a little cranberry in the finish. **Noble Winery,** a little south of the Seaway Trail in Westfield, presents a panoramic view of Lake Erie wine country from its lengthy patio along with a nice selection of sweet and dry wines.

Drive through farmland and wooded areas as you approach Westfield, where the Daniel Reed Memorial Pier (what the locals call **Barcelona Pier**) offers your first close views of the lake. Stop here to see the **Barcelona Lighthouse,** the first lighthouse in the US to be powered by natural gas. The US Lighthouse Board

Don't miss Buffalo Light.

decommissioned the light in 1859 when it discovered that there was no actual harbor at Barcelona, making it unnecessary to provide a guiding beacon for incoming ships. The building became a private residence in 1872, and it remains one to this day. You are welcome to photograph this house, but not to trespass on the surrounding land.

While you're in Westfield, pay a visit to the **Vinewood Acres Sugar Shack,** which is open daily in the afternoon. The farm's signature fruit syrups—which are delicious on ice cream—include flavors like wild currant raspberry and cherry rhubarb, as well as maple syrup made from the farm's own trees. Vinewood doesn't provide its recipes for private labeling by big manufacturers, so you can really get something special here.

Westfield to Dunkirk

Cross Corell and Slippery Creeks, and you'll soon find yourself at **Lake Erie State Park,** an excellent place to stop and enjoy the best views yet of this Great Lake. Two hundred forty-one miles in length from this point to (roughly) Toledo, Ohio, Erie is the world's 12th largest lake, created by two different Ice Ages—the first more than one million years ago, and the second just 12,600 years back. Geologists tell us that these glaciers gouged the lake out of rock layers that are at least 400 million years old, originally formed as a tropical ocean reef when much of the North American continent was under water. The layers of prehistoric rock surrounding the lake today produce abundant quantities of sand, gypsum, and limestone, all of which are used in building construction.

Here at Lake Erie State Park, you can enjoy lake views from the tops of high bluffs, or comb the beach for interesting stones among the sandy gravel (swimming is not allowed here). Picnic tables and pavilions provide great places to relax and take in the expansive view before you continue up the coastline.

As you enter the City of Dunkirk, Seaway Trail signs will direct you to turn left at Light Street. This takes you to **Point Gratiot Park,** where the views of Lake Erie are only one of the attractions. Drive through this city park on the one-way road to **Dunkirk Historic Lighthouse,** where you also will find the city's **Veterans Museum & Light Keeper's House,** a building packed with an assortment of artifacts from the lighthouse's long history. As a major thoroughfare for more than 250 years for settlers and commercial traffic that opened the

The first lighthouse on your Seaway Trail tour is Barcelona Light in Westfield.

American Midwest, Lake Erie also became one of "the graveyards of the Great Lakes," as hundreds of ships ran into violent weather, unexpected obstacles, and even one another in their determination to reach the distant shore at any cost. The museum at Point Gratiot displays bits of cargo washed ashore and discovered by locals, as well as military artifacts and items collected from the lighthouse keeper's home.

The warmest and shallowest of the five Great Lakes, Erie provides an extraordinarily productive breeding ground for native and nonnative fish. Anglers enjoy smallmouth bass and walleye fishing out of **Dunkirk Harbor,** wading out into the lake or taking a kayak or a small motorboat just a few hundred yards from shore. Visit the **City Pier**—a quick left onto Central Avenue—and you're almost sure to see fishing boats leaving or coming into the harbor, especially in late summer when the warmer waters attract fish that spend cooler months in tributary streams. If you come through in fall or winter, you may spot unusual birds feeding on the harbor's mudflats—this area regularly attracts American avocet, white-winged gulls like the Iceland and glaucous species, and even the occasional phalarope, a little shorebird that spins in place while it feeds. The City Pier features a short boardwalk with a pub, gift shops, a cafe and ice cream parlor, public restrooms, and an ATM.

Dunkirk to Point Breeze

Wooded areas, corn and cabbage fields, vineyards, and some scattered homes line the road as you head northeast along the lakeshore from Dunkirk. Watch for an unmarked inlet and an RV park on the left; this is **Sheridan Bay,** an indentation in the shoreline that affords some nice but brief views of the lake. In a moment you'll pass County Road 79, where you may want to detour to sample the wares at a number of Lake Erie's wineries. In addition to an award-winning semi-dry red wine and a number of other varieties, **Liberty Vineyards and Winery** features a collection of sweet wines in its "Rock and Roll" series, with irresistible names like Lucy's In The Sky, White Side of the Moon, and Purple Haze. **Willow Creek Winery** serves up an outdoor experience along with its popular chocolate wines and 16 other varieties, with its popular gazebo and pond and the waterfalls along Willow Creek. **Merritt Estate Winery** was one of the first wineries in New York State, opening in 1976 on land that the Merritts have owned since the 1860s. Don't miss

Stop in Point Gratiot Park to see Dunkirk Historic Lighthouse.

their Bella Ice and Bella Rosa wines, award winners in national and international competitions for multiple years.

Pass a parking area with picnic tables (or stop if you like), and enter Silver Creek, a village first settled in 1803 and now home to about 2,700 people. If you stop to explore this little village, you may come across a **monument to a black walnut tree** at the corner of Ward Avenue and US 20. The celebrated tree, said to be the largest one east of the Rocky Mountains in its day, became even more famous after it blew down in 1822. A local merchant took a 13-foot-tall, 30-feet-around section of this tree and hollowed it out, making it an addition to his store. Legend has it that this section could seat 20 people, and a man actually rode a horse through it. Eventually the merchant sold this tree section to some businesspeople who took it on tour, and the tree changed hands several times before it finally ended up in a museum in London, England—but when the museum burned down, the tree met its much delayed end.

As you leave Silver Creek, keep an eye out for **The Stagecoach West,** the largest western apparel and equine gear store east of the Rockies. Even if you're not a horse lover, there's plenty of interesting shopping here in the apparel, shoes, gifts, and jewelry departments. If you're hauling a camper or trailer, you can find lots of useful accessories here as well.

Cross Cattaraugus Creek on a steel bridge and enter the Cattaraugus Indian Reservation; stay on NY 5 as US 20 splits off and goes south. Watch for the sign to turn left onto the Seaway Trail, leaving NY 5. The trail doubles back for a bit until you reach Lake Shore Road, where it turns northeast once again. Here the road leads through woods to **Evangola State Park,** where you can find camping, swimming in Lake Erie, places to enjoy a picnic, and a chance to stretch your legs on a hiking trail.

The route continues through Point Breeze in the town of Angola, where **Castaways Restaurant** and a popular dogs-and-burgers stand are the immediately recognizable landmarks. Here you will spot Pioneer Camp & Retreat Center, the first of a series of such centers that offer church groups, youth organizations, families, and others the opportunity for relaxation, team building, and reflection as a group. The lakeshore is a popular place for such activity, as you will see by the number of centers like this one along this route.

Niagara County produces some of the state's sweetest and most popular white wine grapes.

Grandview Bay to Lackawanna

Once you've passed Point Breeze, the neighborhoods along the lakeshore begin to increase in density. Watch for the Seaway Trail to make a left turn onto Lake Shore Road as it passes St. Vincent de Paul Camp; cross Big Sister Creek and turn left at Dennis Road (still following the Seaway Trail signs toward Buffalo). **Wendt Beach Park** soon appears on your left, followed by the Erie County Water Authority building at Sturgeon Point. Private owners dominate this area, affording only short glimpses of the lake beyond their estate-size residential properties.

After the St. Columbia Center and Diocesan Retreat, there's an exciting surprise for those interested in Arts and Crafts period architecture and furnishings. **Graycliff Estate** offers you the chance to tour a home designed by renowned architect Frank Lloyd Wright for Isabelle R. Martin, wife of industrialist Darwin Martin, between 1926 and 1931. Here you can appreciate Wright's concept of a "natural house," one that so complements the landscape that it does not disrupt the natural character of the surrounding area. The house itself—recently restored to its original glory after an order of Roman Catholic priests used it as a motherhouse for nearly 30 years—was built of materials indigenous to western New York, and features sunken gardens, a fountain and pond, an expansive terrace and esplanade, and the stylistic choices that make Frank Lloyd Wright's designs so distinctive and appealing. Tours are by reservation only, so call ahead when you plan your Seaway Trail drive. (Darwin Martin's year-round home, also designed by Wright, can be found at 125 Jewett Pkwy. near Delaware Park in Buffalo.)

Cross Eighteenmile Creek and enter a neighborhood of fairly affluent residents and lakeside estates. When you can see the water between homes and their surrounding woods, the city of Lackawanna comes into view across this northeastern tip of Lake Erie. Turn left at the junction with NY 5, and make a stop at the **Friends of Lake Erie Seaway Trail Center** in the former Wanakah Water Works building as you enter the town of Hamburg. Open Thurs through Sun in summer and weekends only during the off-season, this information center can supply you with literature, maps, public restrooms, and up-to-date road conditions for the trail's western end and its nearby attractions.

After the visitor center, **Hamburg Town Park** provides the wide-open water views you haven't seen for some time, as well as a good, close look at a modern wind power installation across the water in Lackawanna. These 14 giant windmills are known as **Steel Winds,** in part because they rise over the site of the former Bethlehem Steel plant. The plant stopped producing in 1983 and shut down the last of its operations in 2000, leaving a contaminated site that required an extensive, costly cleanup. The urban wind farm, the first of its type when installed in

2007, used incentive funds and expertise provided by the New York State Brownfields Cleanup Program to repurpose the site. Today this power generation tract produces 50 million kilowatt hours of electricity each year, enough to power 9,000 homes in western New York.

Buffalo and Tonawanda

Stay on NY 5 as you enter a major industrial area and the road becomes a highway. As you pass through Lackawanna, the "scenery" is more instructive than attractive for a while, but you can see the influx of trades that have helped this city recover from the loss of the steel industry back in the 1980s. Eventually the highway passes the lovely **Tifft Nature Preserve** (a great place for short hikes and birding) and **Buffalo Harbor State Park,** the first state park in the metropolis and the newest in New York State at the time of this writing.

Stay on NY 5 until the Seaway Trail signs direct you to get off at Delaware Avenue, putting you at the **Buffalo and Erie County Naval & Military Park** at Buffalo's Erie Basin Marina, where Lake Erie meets the Niagara River at the end of Pearl Street. If you're concerned that you might not find the museum, just keep an eye open for the **USS *Little Rock,*** a Galveston-class guided missile cruiser used in peacekeeping missions in southern Europe, the Middle East, and Santo Domingo in the 1950s and 1960s. As you get closer to the battleship, you'll see the **USS *Croaker,*** a Gato-class submarine that saw action in the Pacific theater during World War II. The *Croaker* sank a cruiser and five freighters and damaged a sixth freighter in six war patrols on the Yellow Seas, and went on to lifeguard duties in the Luzon Straits and South China Seas. Tours of the *Little Rock* and the *Croaker,* as well as other ships in the harbor, are available through the museum.

While you're at the waterfront, take note of the towering grain elevator behind the military museum. In the 1920s, a time long forgotten by more recent generations, Buffalo processed 300 million bushels here in the **Grain Elevator District,** making the city a pivotal point in the storage and transport of grain by land and sea. Two of the elevators continue to function today; you can tour the operation when you visit the harbor.

From here, the Seaway Trail passes through one of Buffalo's oldest neighborhoods, now infused with ethnic restaurants, unusual shops, and residents of every background. As you pass Columbus Park, you can't help but take note of the **Connecticut Street Armory,** the castlelike building constructed in 1899. Designed by architect Isaac G. Perry, the imposing structure virtually glows with the warm red of impenetrable Medina sandstone, and its four- to six-story towers would scare off just about any would-be intruder. The armory houses the 74th Regiment of the

New York National Guard, and the castle is listed on the National Register of Historic Places.

The Seaway Trail turns left at the junction with NY 266, entering Tonawanda. Watch for a blue history marker at the corner of Amherst and Niagara Streets. If you're not familiar with the War of 1812's **Battle of Black Rock,** you may be surprised by what you learn here: On December 30, 1813, the British attacked the small community of Black Rock and burned it to the ground in retaliation for an attack led by Brigadier George McClure of the New York State Militia 20 days earlier. McClure had decided to abandon Fort George, just inside what is now the Canadian border, so he determined that the nearby village of Newark (now Niagara-on-the-Lake, Ontario) must be destroyed before the Americans left the area. He gave the townspeople only a few hours to clear out before he and his men burned down all but one of the 150 buildings in Newark, forcing them from their homes in the midst of an upstate winter.

This aggressive and seemingly merciless act angered the British. A few days after the burning of Newark, British forces led by Major General Phineas Riall destroyed the American towns of Lewiston, Youngstown, Manchester, and Tuscarora. When the American forces burned a bridge to keep the British from entering Buffalo, the British carried their boats around Niagara Falls and made their way in anyway, burning all the buildings in the town of Black Rock—now commemorated by a pocket park. The British went on to torch Buffalo as well, destroying all of the homes and buildings except for two: the jail, and the hotel and adjacent cottage owned by Margaret St. John. What magic Ms. St. John used when she pleaded with Major General Riall to spare her home and livelihood, we will never know, but the general relented—at least temporarily. The British returned on January 1 and burned the hotel anyway, though they did leave Margaret her cottage—one of only four structures in the entire city that survived the attack.

At George Washington Park, the **Niagara River** comes into view. You've left Lake Erie behind at this point, though the lake's water supplies the river and tumbles over Niagara Falls a few miles north. Here the **Shoreline Trail,** a paved biking and hiking trail, parallels the river through scrub woodland and pocket parks, and even past a landfill that has replaced some of the heavy industry that crowded this area in decades past. If you need a treat at this point, **Mississippi Mudds** at 313 Niagara St. in Tonawanda provides a menu full of guilty pleasures, a rooftop dining area, and Perry's ice cream as well as frozen custard.

Buffalo and Erie County Naval & Military Park features several warships.

At Seymour Street, turn left onto NY 265, cross the Erie Canal, and enter North Tonawanda, an area that once led the nation in the production of carousels. Beginning with the Armitage-Herschell Company in 1873, the merry-go-rounds produced here included special portable models for use by traveling carnival operators. A visit to the **Herschell Carrousel Factory Museum** can include a ride on the 1916 carousel sitting astride one of 36 hand-carved horses, as well as a stroll through the collection of 20 animals from four different eras of carousel production.

Pass Veterans Park in Tonawanda and continue to follow the Niagara River through Wheatfield and into the City of Niagara Falls (turn left at the end of River Road onto Buffalo Street, as Seaway Trail signs will indicate).

Niagara Falls

The largest and mightiest waterfalls in North America thunder here on the US–Canada border, a set of three falls that provide an unparalleled spectacle and a massive amount of hydropower. Here on the New York side of the Niagara River, you can enjoy gorgeous views of the **American Falls,** a 1,060-foot-wide cataract that varies from 70 to 100 feet in height, depending on the position of large boulders at the bottom of the cascade. You have many viewing options, including several platforms in **Niagara Falls State Park** and the nearby Rainbow Bridge, which provides both vehicular and foot traffic with a direct route to Ontario, Canada, and the best views of both **Horseshoe** (2,600 feet wide) and **Bridal Veil Falls** (56 feet wide).

Despite their girth and the astonishing average of four million cubic feet of water that flows over the crest line every minute, these falls are youngsters in the perspective of geological time. They formed at the end of the last Ice Age—about 10,000 years ago—when water from Lake Erie sculpted the Niagara River to connect with Lake Ontario. The water flowed along the Niagara Escarpment, a bedrock formation that borders part of three Great Lakes: Ontario, Huron, and Michigan. When it reached the edge of the escarpment, the water tumbled over the cliff and created these extraordinary falls, then continued to wear away at the bedrock and create the **Niagara Gorge,** flowing with renewed force as it continued north. Don't miss the hiking opportunities the gorge offers north of the falls—you can find trail maps and information in our book, *Best Easy Day Hikes: Buffalo* (Falcon Guides), or at the visitor center in Niagara Falls State Park.

The Seaway Trail takes you directly to the entrance of the state park parking area, where you will pay a fee to leave your car while you walk to view the falls or explore the rest of the park. It's a fairly short stroll from the parking lot to the free viewing area; if you'd like an even more spectacular view, the park charges a nominal fee to go up onto the enclosed observation deck over the Niagara River.

Niagara Falls provides extraordinary views in any weather, at any time of day.

The most thrilling way to see the falls, however, is from the deck of the **Maid of the Mist,** arguably one of the most legendary and popular tourist attractions in any park in the world. The locally owned operation brings passengers from a dock on the Niagara River to within a few feet of the bottom of the falls, where you can experience an impressive fraction of this natural wonder's full power and be drenched to the skin in the process. The Maid's operators provide a free souvenir rain poncho to every passenger, but expect to get pretty damp around the edges.

If you plan to cross into Canada to see Horseshoe and Bridal Veil Falls, be sure to bring your US passport. Since the terrorist attacks on September 11, 2001, the US Congress passed a law requiring everyone crossing this border to provide proof of citizenship, even if you are only going to see the rest of Niagara Falls in the Canadian provincial park. Thanks to this additional regulation, you may experience lengthy wait times in line at the border. I highly recommend leaving your car in the parking area and walking across the **Rainbow Bridge** to Niagara Falls Park in Ontario—a total walk of just under 3.5 miles if you walk all the way to the top of Horseshoe Falls and back.

Before you get to the falls park, you will drive through much of the city of Niagara Falls. Back in the 1800s and early 1900s, this city provided much of western New York with the electricity its homes and businesses required, and the hydropower used by all manner of manufacturing operations. You can still see the remains of the **Schoellkopf Power Plant,** the first major power project founded here in 1853 and one of the earliest producers of direct current electricity. (The plant collapsed into the river in 1956 in a landslide.) The power plant constructed by Westinghouse Electric in 1895 still stands: the **Adams Power Plant Transformer House** is a National Historic Landmark, the last remnant of the alternating current facility based on the work of scientist and inventor Nikola Tesla. By 1896, plants in Niagara Falls supplied power all the way to Buffalo, 20 miles away. New hydroelectric stations built in the 1960s include the Niagara Power Authority plant, where you can visit the **Niagara Power Project Power Vista,** enjoy more than 50 interactive exhibits, and stand on the observation deck for stunning views of the Niagara River Gorge from 350 feet above the river.

It's no secret that the city of Niagara Falls has seen better days since many industries pulled out of the city in the 1960s after the Schoellkopf plant collapsed. Others followed in the 1980s and 1990s when labor became cheaper overseas; you will note the result in the number of empty storefronts and vacant buildings along NY 104 East as you continue on the Seaway Trail. In a few minutes, follow the trail signs onto NY 18F North and into the Village of Lewiston.

Lewiston to Youngstown

Drive through the distinguished neighborhoods on the outskirts of the village to Center Street, the main thoroughfare of this small community. If it's getting close to dinnertime and you're looking for a casual meal, the **Brickyard Pub & BBQ** and the adjacent **Brickyard Brewing Company** serve up hearty plates of ribs, brisket, or chicken with all of your favorite sides; or try **Casa Antica** for homestyle Italian dishes—and leave room for dessert at **Hibbard's Custard** (see "Your Ice Cream Stop" page 239). Antiques shops, galleries, a bookstore, and clothing boutiques make this town a fun place to stop for a bit.

YOUR ICE CREAM STOP: HIBBARD'S CUSTARD

The Hibbard family has a secret: a custard machine that pumps less air into the mix than the ice cream made by other soft-serve producers. The result is richer, more flavorful, and creamier custard that Hibbard's whips up fresh every day, with chocolate, vanilla, and black raspberry on tap any time you visit. The flavors don't stop there, however—on any given day you might find peach, cinnamon, cotton candy, crème de menthe, creamsicle custard, or one of more than two dozen other flavors. You'll find this ice cream stand at 105 Portage Rd. in Lewiston—and it's open daily until 11 p.m., so you can make it an after-dinner treat.

As you leave Lewiston and begin to drive along the Niagara River again, a blue history sign marks the spot where the British Regulars came ashore on the night of December 18, 1813, and began their march north to capture Fort Niagara. Stinging from an American assault on the British-held town of Newark on December 10, the Regulars began a retaliatory strike that took the American forces entirely by surprise on the night of the 19th, while Fort Niagara's commander, Nathanial Leonard, was absent from the fort visiting family in Lewiston. In a cascade failure of the fort's defenses, the picket soldiers left to guard the fort had succumbed to the cold and gone inside. The British disarmed the Youngstown pickets easily and without bloodshed, gained entrance to the fort itself when the gates opened to admit an American, and found just about the fort's entire complement fast asleep. By sunrise, Fort Niagara was a British outpost. The Regulars used the fort as a base of operations as they advanced to destroy Youngstown, Lewiston, Manchester, Fort Schlosser, Black Rock, and Buffalo.

Do you have a sudden urge to play Frisbee golf? **Joseph Davis State Park,** just outside of Lewiston, provides a 27-hole course as well as fields, woodlands, a nature trail, and picnic areas. If you fish, you can catch largemouth bass in the pond near the park entrance, or a variety of freshwater species from the dock on the lower Niagara River.

Youngstown, in the top northwesternmost corner of the state, sits at the mouth of the Niagara River and provides your first wide views of **Lake Ontario.** From here, you can see the town of Niagara-On-The-Lake, Ontario, just across the Niagara River—and while you can't see it, Toronto, Ontario, stands directly across Lake Ontario from Youngstown. Even today, when the US has an entirely peaceful relationship with Canada, Youngstown resides in a strategically advantageous position, hosting a US Coast Guard station that has been in service since 1893.

Here stands **Old Fort Niagara,** the longest continually occupied military site in the US and the oldest building on the Great Lakes. Built in 1726, the fort site began operating as a military post much earlier, protecting French interests in the area from the late 1600s until the British captured it in 1759 during the French and Indian Wars. They held it until they lost the Revolutionary War, when the newly established US Army took over the fort and kept it until December 19, 1813, the day the British staged a surprise attack and took it back. The Regulars were forced to give up the fort in 1815 under the Treaty of Ghent, which ended the War of 1812. Once secured by the Americans again, the fort remained an active military post until it became part of **Fort Niagara State Park** in the 1960s. The opportunity to tour a fort built in 1726 will likely be irresistible, and you may do so for a reasonable fee on any day except for New Year's Day, Thanksgiving, and Christmas.

If you can't wait to continue your drive along the Seaway Trail from here, the next major segment takes you all the way to Oswego.

You can drive right up to Fort Niagara Lighthouse.

22

Great Lakes Seaway Trail, Part 2

Youngstown to Oswego

General description: Continue your journey for another 159 miles along Lake Ontario to discover War of 1812 and French and Indian War history, hidden lighthouses, wineries and cheese, fresh local produce, and panoramic views of the easternmost Great Lake.

Special attractions: Wilson Tuscarora State Park, Wilson Pier, Tuscarora Bay, Chateau Niagara Winery, Black Willow Winery, Schulze Vineyards, Zehr's On the Lake Farm Market, Winery at Marjim Manor, Singer Farms Market, Golden Hill State Park, Thirty Mile Point Lighthouse, Oak Orchard Lighthouse, US Militia State Historic Site, Hamlin Beach State Park, Braddock Bay Park, Braddock Bay Hawk Watch, Braddock Point Lighthouse, Ontario Beach Park, Durand Eastman Park, Irondequoit Bay, Simply NY Marketplace and Gifts, Whispering Pines Mini-Golf Course, Gosnell Big Woods, Whiting Road Nature Center, Webster Park, Kent Park Arboretum, Salmon Creek, B. Foreman Park, Beechwood State Park, Sodus Point, Sodus Bay Lighthouse Museum, Alasa Farms and Cracker Box Palace, Lancaster's Farm Stand, Thorpe Vineyard, Chimney Bluffs State Park, Kutchen's Farm Market, Wolcott Falls Park, Wager's Country Apple Farm Market, Fair Haven State Park, Sterling Renaissance Faire (in season), Sterling Heritage Park, Ontario Orchards Farm Market and Cider Mill, Fort Ontario

State Historic Site, Battle Island State Park, H. Lee White Marine Museum, West Pier Lighthouse, Fort Oswego, Oswego Railroad Museum

Location: Along the Lake Ontario shore from the northwestern corner of the state in Youngstown to the northward bend at the eastern end of the lake

Route numbers: NY 18, Lake Ontario State Parkway, NY 104, CR 4, CR 101, CR 143, NY 104A

Travel season: Spring through fall

Camping: Daisy Barn Campground in Wilson, Willow Beach RV Park in Porter, Hughes Marina and Campground in Williamson, Cherry Grove Campground in Wolcott, Fair Haven State Park, Shady Shores Campground in Fair Haven

Services: In Youngstown, Irondequoit, Webster, Pultneyville, Sodus, Fair Haven, Oswego

Nearby attractions: Iroquois National Wildlife Refuge, Niagara County Historical Museum, Lockport Caves and Underground Boat Ride, Lockport Locks and Erie Canal Cruises, Genesee Country Village and Museum, Jell-O Gallery Museum, Strong National Museum of Play, University of Rochester Memorial Art Gallery, Seabreeze amusement park, Susan B. Anthony House State Historic Site, Ontario Heritage Square Museum

Great Lakes Seaway Trail, Part 2: Youngstown to Oswego

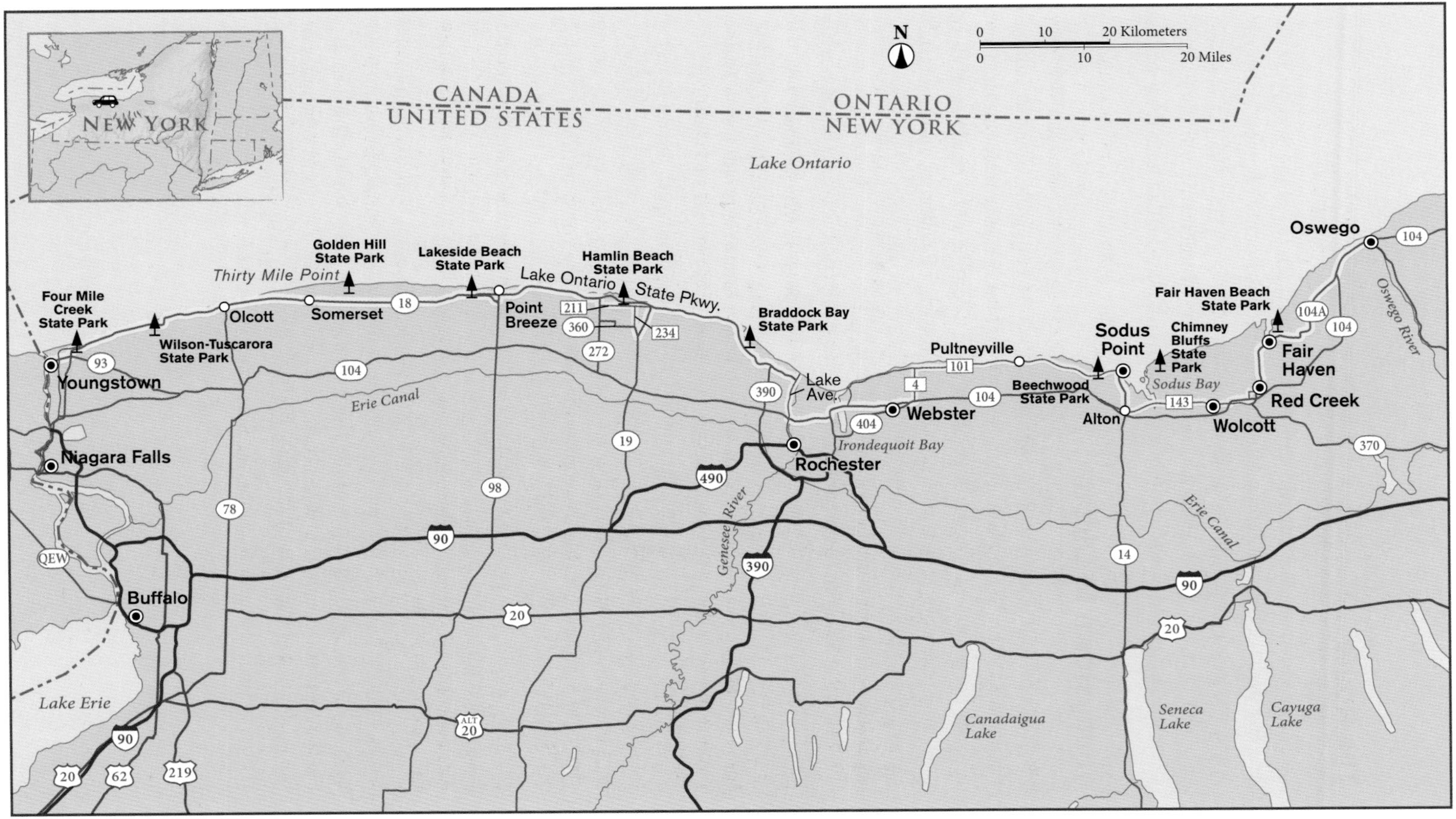

The Route

Sweeping views of Lake Ontario highlight this next stretch of the Seaway Trail, keeping the lake on your left and upstate New York's bounty of grape vineyards, apple and peach orchards, cornfields, and dairy farms on your right. The route also transects some of western New York's sweetest rural towns with their cobblestone buildings, old-world churches, and farm markets loaded with local produce.

Youngstown to Olcott

Head out of Youngstown on NY 18F east, and cross Four Mile Creek as you pass **Four Mile Creek State Park.** Here NY 18F ends at NY 18; continue east. The town of Porter appears on the edge of the park. From here the road passes through one small (even tiny) town after another, each with a few homes and large tracts of plowed fields; in spring and summer, this area can be very pleasing to the eye with its uniform rows of corn, beans, and cabbage.

Arrive at **Wilson-Tuscarora Park** on the shores of Tuscarora Bay, a heavily wooded park with hiking trails and a marina for pleasure and fishing boats. The eastern and western branches of Twelvemile Creek form the boundaries of this park, carrying local watershed directly into Lake Ontario through the cleansing natural filters of the park's wetlands and foliage. As NY 18 arcs to the north, it brings you closer to Lake Ontario and to the **Wilson Boatyard,** once a major ship-building center from 1845 to 1876. Wilson's location on the sheltering Tuscarora Bay, its abundant supply of lumber from nearby forests, and its equally generous supply of manpower made this a prime location for the construction of nearly 20 major ships that carried cargo up and down Lake Ontario and into ports to the west. Today you can stop here and enjoy the lake view and a meal at the Boat House Restaurant on the pier.

Past Wilson, farmland dominates the landscape, and you may find yourself beginning to crave a piece of the fruit you can see hanging from trees and vines along this route. Watch for one of many farm stands that pop up in summer and early fall, many of them right in the front yards of people's homes. You'll find berries, apples, squash, tomatoes, corn, and many other fruits and vegetables of the local harvest—often just picked a few hours before. Some of these folks must return to their fields to continue the harvest, so if you see a farm stand operating

You'll find all kinds of fresh produce along the Seaway Trail between Youngstown and Hamlin.

on the honor system, pay for your purchase by slipping your cash into the appropriate receptacle.

What would western New York be without a few vineyards among the farms? **Schulze Vineyards** is the first you will see as you enter the town of Burt, where sweet wines are among the most celebrated: Thirty Mile Point Niagara took the double gold medal at the Taster's Guild International competition, and Ruby wine took the gold medal in its class at the same event. Don't miss Schulze's dessert wines, each with its own string of honors. Just down the road, the 43-acre **Black Willow Winery** not only produces a number of red and white wines from their local grapes, but it also provides three varieties of mead—a golden wine made from honey—with Norse mythology-inspired names like Odin's Nectar. One of the area's newest wineries comes into view in Newfane. **Chateau Niagara** planted its first grapes in 2006 and turned them into three wines: a Riesling, Gewürztraminer, and Chardonnay; its red grapes went into the ground in 2007 and began racking up honors and awards a few years later (be sure to try the Saperavi, a grape rarely found in New York state wines).

As you enter the Eighteen Mile Creek watershed, Lake Ontario and the picturesque Olcott Beach area come out from behind all the foliage and farmland. **Olcott Beach Carousel Park** features a 1928 Herschel-Spillman carousel and five vintage children's rides—the kind that old fogies like me remember riding in Roseland Park in Canandaigua. If you're looking for a little more mature entertainment, the **Lakeview Village Shoppes** in Olcott are open daily from Memorial Day through October, and include vintage clothing, gift shops, boutiques, and an ice cream parlor.

Burt to Point Breeze

The temperate climate along the lakeshore provides as many as 220 growing days per year, just the environment required for many northern fruits—earning this area the moniker of "Fruit Belt" and drawing many farmers to work to capitalize on these excellent conditions. **Singer Farms** is a prime example of the success that fruit growers can achieve here: It's a family farm established in 1915, growing nearly 80 different varieties including a number of named apples, peaches, cherries, and plums. In early summer, you can come here to pick your own cherries and to sample tart cherry juice made right on the farm. Singer sells most of its fruit wholesale to farm markets, but you can stop in and fill up your market basket throughout the summer.

Singer Farms provides its fruit locally as well, particularly to **The Winery at Marjim Manor** down the road in Appleton. The stately Marjim Manor, built in 1854 and once used as a summer retreat for the Sisters of Saint Joseph, now provides a sprawling 9,500-square-foot footprint to house the tasting room, a

Babcock House is a fine example of the stone construction unique to upstate New York.

wrap-around enclosed porch, a number of cats, and a few ghosts—enough that the building has been featured on two television shows: *Ghost Hunters* and *Most Terrifying Places in America.* Marjim's wines come from grapes and a number of alternative fruits, including apples, cranberries, apricots, berries, cherries, plums, peaches, and even currants.

Somerset follows Newfane on NY 18. Watch for a large farmhouse with walls made entirely of sand-colored cobblestone; this is **Babcock House,** built in 1848 by farmer Jeptha Babcock who later became a New York State assemblyman. Babcock used the most modern farming methods of the time, most of which involved horses and all that required working by hand. On one weekend every year, Babcock House hosts a farm festival with live demonstrations of these time-consuming and laborious work methods; on most other days in summer and early fall, the completely refurbished house serves as a museum and welcome center for the town of Somerset.

Just before you reach County Line, **Golden Hill State Park** gives you the option of making a left turn and heading to the lakefront to see one of the Seaway Trail's few lighthouses that are open to the public. **Thirty Mile Point Lighthouse**

Thirty Mile Point Lighthouse opens its keeper's quarters to overnight guests.

served to warn ship captains of the shoals along the coast of the lake, and its natural limestone construction and Victorian Gothic style make it a particularly striking figure on the lakeshore—thanks in part to a partial renovation in the mid-1990s. If you've dreamed of being a lighthouse keeper, you can rent the second floor of the keeper's house for a week and see if the actual job might be to your liking.

As you approach **Oak Orchard State Marine Park** after Point Breeze, you will see a sign for the War of 1812—one of the markers New York State has placed along the Seaway Trail and in other places to let you know that something important happened there more than 200 years ago. Finding the actual descriptive signs for these events can be tricky, however, taking on the feeling of a scavenger hunt as you leave the main road to hunt for them. This one can be found in the parking area and turnaround point at the beginning of the Lake Ontario State Parkway, which starts just after Oak Orchard Park.

This War of 1812 spot tells the story of the *Hamilton* and the *Scourge*, two merchant ships acquired by the US Navy as the War of 1812 looked to be close at hand. Reoutfitted at Sackett's Harbor with heavy military artillery, the two ships became so top-heavy that sailing them was a challenge at best, and dangerous at worst. The danger came to be realized when both ships sank off the coast of Hamilton, Ontario, on August 8, 1813, when a bad Great Lakes squall toppled them. One hundred and sixty years would pass before technology made it possible to locate these ships on the bottom of the lake, and Canada has designated their resting place a National Historic Site in honor of the 80 men who died in the wrecks.

Lake Ontario State Parkway to Rochester

Here come the long views of Lake Ontario, the ones that tell you just how vast and far-reaching a Great Lake can be. **Lake Ontario State Parkway** provides a scenic alternative to the highways that connect western New York State to Rochester, arcing along the southern edge of the lake and traversing wetlands, the edges of small towns, and the bays and inlets that provide calm water for wildlife viewing. When you can't see the lake for the trees, ponds and wetlands come into view, often laden with mute swans and Canada geese as well as migrating waterfowl in spring and fall. Hawks circle overhead and ride thermals on their way north or south, and turkey vultures create "kettles" of anywhere from three to dozens of birds as they survey the area for carrion they can secure for dinner.

Driving east on the parkway, keep an eye out to your left for a sign for the US Militia State Historic Site at the Albion/Point Breeze exit, where the newly reconstructed **Oak Orchard Lighthouse** (see photo, page 220) stands. The actual lighthouse vanished in a storm in 1916 seven years after it had been decommissioned, but nearly 100 years later, residents of Oak Orchard formed a committee and raised funds to build a perfect likeness. The new Oak Orchard Lighthouse opened in 2010 and welcomes visitors on weekends from May through mid-October.

Returning to the parkway, continue east past remarkable views of the lake to **Hamlin Beach State Park,** where another War of 1812 marker directs you to the parking area just off the road. Most New York State residents probably are not aware of the role the state's militia played in the War of 1812, but the signpost here at the park helps to tell this story. Militia men had little training, often did not have regulation uniforms, and did predictably poorly in armed combat until the spring of 1814, when General Jacob Jennings Brown insisted that his troops refrain from combat for three months while they received intensive military training. His caution proved its worth on July 3, 1814, when Brown and his troops captured Fort Erie and held it through a British siege until the opposing forces finally withdrew on September 21.

After Hamlin Beach, lake views alternate with wooded areas until you reach an exit for Lighthouse Road. Turn left from the parkway onto Lighthouse Road and continue to Clearview Avenue, and turn right. When you see **Braddock Point Lighthouse Bed & Breakfast,** you may be surprised (we were!) to see the now privately owned Braddock Point Lighthouse, restored to its 1896 condition and open to guests of the house for tours and a climb to the top.

As long as you've made the turnoff, **Braddock Bay Park** should be your next stop. Here the **Braddock Bay Bird Observatory** runs its annual Hawk Watch from the platform in the middle of the park, from which professional observers and plenty of local birders bring their binoculars and spotting scopes and watch tens of thousands of hawks migrating overhead in spring and fall. Positioned on the Atlantic Flyway, the main corridor through which hawks and many other migrants pass every year, Braddock Bay provides prime viewing of dozens of raptor, waterfowl, and smaller bird species, especially in March and April. There's no fee for joining the observers and they love meeting other bird enthusiasts, so bring your optics and climb on up.

You can return to the Lake Ontario parkway at this point, or take a slower but more attractive and interesting route from here. If you'd like to see more of the lake, drive toward the lake to County Road 130 (Edgemere Drive), and turn right. With the lake to your left, watch for a series of ponds that appear on your right: Cranberry Pond, Long Pond, Buck Pond, and Round Pond as you pass the City of Rochester Water Authority building. Here Edgemere Road becomes Beach Avenue and one remarkable lake house appears after another. Pass the Lake Shore Country Club and continue to Ontario Beach Park—but first, stop at the corner of Lake and Beach Avenues for ice cream at **Abbott's Frozen Custard** (see "Your Ice Cream Stop" below), a family-owned Rochester institution since 1926.

YOUR ICE CREAM STOP: ABBOTT'S FROZEN CUSTARD

It's a no-brainer: Abbott's super-creamy, ultra-thick frozen custard is the best in the state, and maybe beyond. The chocolate, vanilla, and chocolate almond custard are enough to have people standing in line outside of the stand in Charlotte for as long as it takes to get a dish of these extraordinary confections, but Abbott's also offers a number of specialty flavors at each of its many locations. What's the secret to the creaminess and luscious flavors? The owners won't tell, but it's the same recipe Arthur Abbott perfected back in 1902 and peddled from one place to another while he pursued his love of horse racing. Just like his customers more than 100 years ago, you'll want to come back every week.

Braddock Point Light is on the grounds of a bed-and-breakfast guesthouse.

Charlotte to Webster

Your route from **Ontario Beach Park** in Charlotte (pronounced Shar-LOT, by the way) to the continuation of the Seaway Trail on the other side of Rochester gets tricky, mainly because of a bridge at Irondequoit Bay that closes from April 1 to October 31 every year to allow boats to have access to the lake. Here's how the route works:

At the corner of Beach and Lake Avenues, Ontario Beach Park (also known as Charlotte Beach) is directly in front of you. The park contains a vintage Dentzel menagerie carousel, a wooden boardwalk along the beach, gazebos and picnic pavilions, and a bathhouse. Here you can walk out into the lake on a wide concrete jetty to the light tower at the end, gaining a view of Lake Ontario that you can't access anywhere else. If you take this walk, try to imagine the fierce military activity that took place at this very spot in May 1814, when British sailors made their fourth raid in two years for provisions from the village of Charlotte. The townspeople, tired of giving up their meat and flour without attempting to resist, decided to stand their ground with the help of two cannons they obtained from the US military. They assembled a local militia and trained them for combat, built a breastwork between Charlotte and Rochesterville, and even rigged a bridge to fail when the British attempted to cross it. When British ships appeared on May 14, 1814, they faced a line of men with guns and enough cannon fire to turn a British gunboat back to sea. The opposing force, meeting the first real resistance they had ever encountered here, decided not to pursue their usual run for provisions. The Charlotte militia chalked up a victory.

To continue your drive, turn right from Beach to Lake, and proceed south on Lake Avenue past the Charlotte Genesee Lighthouse, an octagonal lighthouse built in 1822, to Pattonwood Drive. Turn left onto Pattonwood. Cross the Genesee River on the Colonel Patrick O'Rorke Bridge (named for the Civil War officer who helped defend Little Round Top at Gettysburg). You may need to wait at this drawbridge if you cross in summer, when it goes up on the half-hour to accommodate boat traffic.

Continue on Pattonwood to Culver Road, and turn right. Almost immediately, turn left onto Lake Shore Boulevard. Drive through **Durand Eastman Park,** with the lakeshore and beach on your left and the park's small lakes, arboretum, and wooded areas on your right. This parkland once belonged to a doctor named Henry Durand, and he and his friend George Eastman, the founder of Eastman

East of Rochester, you'll enter New York's apple country.

You can walk out to the light at the end of Ontario Beach pier.

Kodak Company, saw the need to create a park along the lakeshore to preserve this open land and give people access to the beach. The two men bought up land around the Durand property and offered it to the city of Rochester free of charge for this purpose. If you have time to wander the trails in this park, you'll discover some of the nearly 400 plant species that grow here, including the arboretum filled with flowering fruit trees. You are almost certain to see squirrels, chipmunks, wild turkeys, and white-tailed deer, and during the spring and fall migration and in winter, interesting waterfowl and shorebirds collect at the lakeside outlet for the VanLare Wastewater Treatment Plant.

Leave the park on Sweet Fern Road, and turn right onto Culver Road as you come to the end of the park drive. Here you will see the **Parkside Diner,** a great place for breakfast or a quick lunch, and the **Whispering Pines miniature golf course,** the oldest continually operating mini-golf course in the US.

Follow Culver Road south to Empire Boulevard (NY 404), and turn left. (You should see Seaway Trail directional signs along this route.) Continue on NY 404 along **Irondequoit Bay** and past **Lucien Morin Park** on your right and **Abraham Lincoln Park** on your left, until you reach Bay Road. Turn left onto Bay Road (County Route 16) and follow this until it ends at a T intersection on Lake Road. Turn right onto Lake Road and continue your journey along the Lake Ontario shore. That's the end of the confusing part of this route; you'll stay on this road for 30 miles until you reach Sodus.

Here in Webster, you can glimpse the lake between the upscale homes along the shore, but there's much more natural treasure here as well. On your right, three "forever wild" areas provide birding, nature walks, picnic areas, and even a hiking trail that connects all three properties to give you a grand day out on foot. **Gosnell Big Woods,** protected by the Genesee Land Trust, enjoyed the protection of the Gosnell family for generations until they decided to make it a permanent nature preserve. Here some of the oldest trees in New York State continue to thrive in the face of lake-effect snowstorms and evidence of climate change, filling this area with green leaves and shoots in spring and extraordinary colors in fall. Nearby, **Whiting Road Nature Center** adds shrub-seedling and sapling-pole forest, mature woods, fields of grasses and wildflowers, and a beech forest, making this a prime stopover point on the Atlantic Flyway for songbirds and other forest dwellers. Finally, **Webster Park** blends creeks and lake views with forest, offering lots of fruiting shrubs, cone-producing trees, and shelter to attract birds from the Adirondack and Canadian forests to overwinter in this more temperate climate.

Just a country block south of Lake Road on Schlegel Road (between Salt Road and Basket Road), the **Webster Arboretum** brings together a number of community organizations to plant and maintain showpiece gardens in this concentrated environment. Take a short walk here to admire the gardens and learn about plant species that grow well in the northeastern climate, particularly the native species that attract birds, bees, and butterflies.

Ontario to Sodus Point

As you leave Monroe County and enter Ontario, older neighborhoods quickly give way to corn and bean cropland and apple orchards, with row after row of short trees with crazily angled limbs blooming white in spring, and bearing green and red fruit in late summer. Pass the R. E. Ginna Nuclear Power Plant, now owned by Exelon Generation, and watch for the sign for the **Heritage Square Museum,** a living history museum in Ontario that brings a mid-19th-century crossroads town to life. Open from June to early October, the museum at Brick Church Corners preserves a number of buildings from the 1800s including a Baptist meeting house, a log cabin, a train station, and the Ontario Lock Up, telling the stories of professions including apple growers and processors, ore miners, farmers, and others.

As you approach **Pultneyville,** a blue and yellow New York state history sign comes into view. Here a British warship anchored offshore during the War of 1812 and kidnapped two locals—Noah Fuller and a Captain Church, whose first name does not appear in records of the day—and forced them to assist the ship in navigating the port of Pultneyville. Fuller and Church did as they were told, and they were released unharmed once the boat had made it safely into the dock.

Make a quick left on the Seaway Trail in the small town of Pultneyville and come around the bend at the Pultneyville Deli Company, and you'll spot a War of 1812 marker. The day after Charlotte residents decided to stand up to their British foes, so did the inhabitants of Pultneyville, no doubt frustrating the British fleet to the maximum. This time, however, the US militia under General John Swift was busy conducting training drills in the lakeshore fog when the mist suddenly lifted, revealing the British fleet just offshore and getting ready to send troops to the beach. Swift's 130 militiamen ran for cover—not exactly the maneuver for which Swift had trained them—but when the British sent a delegation to shore to negotiate an American surrender, Swift refused and went about regrouping his forces. In the meantime, the villagers had hidden their provisions in a nearby ravine, leaving only about 100 barrels of substandard flour for the British to take from them. The British troops, realizing they were being duped, attempted to raid other buildings in town, and the villagers leapt to their own defense. By the time the encounter ended, many buildings sported cannonball holes, but no Americans and only one British soldier died in the gunfire. The British retreated and sailed off, their second defeat in two days by ragtag bands of local farmers and merchants.

All history aside, what really makes Pultneyville a favorite stop for upstate residents is the view of Lake Ontario as we round the bend in the middle of town. Stop at **B. Foreman Park** if you want to savor this sight before you continue along Lake Road to Sodus Point.

On your way out of town, you'll see cobblestone houses and some of western New York's Italianate architecture, a style that became popular in the 1840s and 1850s when architects Alexander Jackson Davis and Richard Upjohn began using it in prominent homes as an alternative to the Greek Revival style that dominated so many neighborhoods at the time. Look for flat, projecting roofs supported by corbels, and a central tower creating an additional story at the top of the house.

Sodus Bay Lighthouse Museum is the visitor center for
Big Sodus Light.

As you approach Sodus Point, a number of bed-and-breakfast establishments and historic inns begin to line the road, providing plenty of overnight options especially if you're passing through in the off-season. Watch for signs for the **Sodus Bay Lighthouse Museum,** a left turn onto Ontario Street from Lake Road. Here you can see **Big Sodus Light,** the second lighthouse on this spot; the first one was completed in 1824. The big light served mariners from 1871 to 1901, when the navigable channel actually came very close to this bluff. Shifting sands and construction of the breakwater changed the proximity of the lighthouse to the shore, a situation made more pronounced by the construction of homes between the light and the newly formed shoreline. Today a new lighthouse stands at the end of the cement pier that extends into the bay, providing the assistance boaters need to find the channel to the harbor. The lighthouse keeper lived nearby in a house represented here only by four piles of stones that mark the corners of the former foundation.

The War of 1812 visited Sodus Point and rained destruction down on the village on June 19 and 20, 1813, when a militia of trained and untrained men tried to resist the British forces foraging for supplies. The British attacked under cover of rain and darkness, not expecting to encounter a fairly organized group of about 60 men with guns who fired a single volley, saw the flash of the British guns returning fire, and used that momentary sighting to take better aim and hit more of their targets. When the Americans retreated into the woods, the British returned to their ships and made a second attack in the morning, this time cleaning out the town's supplies and burning all but one of the buildings to the ground. Only two American men died in the battle, but Sodus Point residents had lost everything they owned.

Today's Sodus Point has become a resort town, and as such it can be a great place to spend an afternoon poking through nautical shops and having a bite to eat at **Captain Jack's Goodtime Tavern.** In summer, with the light breezes coming off the lake, the tropical drinks served on the patio at every bar, and country music coming through the speakers in most of the harbor-side eateries, you may drift off for a moment and believe yourself to be in the Everglades City, Florida, or Myrtle Beach, South Carolina. This is as close as upstate New York gets to that kind of casual waterfront atmosphere—so pause here and enjoy the ambiance. That being said, bring a sweater; even in the sweltering days of midsummer, it's usually 10 to 15 degrees cooler at the lakeshore than it is in nearby towns.

Sodus to Oswego

When you're ready to move on, leave Sodus Point on NY 14 south, following alongside the marina and Sodus Bay. The road climbs very briefly to an area called Sodus Bay Heights, with homes on a bit of a bluff that provides prime bay viewing for the residents.

In a moment, you'll pass **Alasa Farms,** a 600-acre natural area rescued from potential development by Genesee Land Trust in Rochester. Alasa Farms provides a home to abused and neglected farm animals at its **Cracker Box Palace,** a place to meet horses, cows, sheep, goats, and others that have been rescued by the good people at this welcoming place.

Turn left onto NY 14 south and continue straight on Ridge Road, leaving NY 14. On Ridge Road, you'll see a beautiful cobblestone church: Alton United Methodist Church, constructed in 1837. The town of Huron comes up quickly after this, and soon you see one farm market after another offering local produce, New York State cheeses including Helluva Good Cheese, and other locally made treats. When you see the sign for **Chimney Bluffs State Park,** be sure to stop and check this one out: The bluffs are a natural phenomenon of wind and weather on the shores of Lake Ontario, and they are disappearing in the wake of winter blizzards and summer storms at a rapid rate. If you've visited before, the bluffs will look different this time, even if only a year has passed since your last look at them. Easy trails trace their way along the top of the bluff to give you access to the best views of the Lake Ontario shoreline from this height.

Thorpe Vineyards had the good sense to locate here back in the 1980s, taking advantage of the long growing season the lake provides to produce a number of wines, some of them fairly unusual for New York. Its Evening Glow wine combines Diamond and Chancellor grapes, not the usual varieties found in New York wines, while Hunter's Moon sweetens the French Maréchal Foch grape to achieve a casual red that's a natural with a burger.

The town of Wolcott began, like so many towns in this area, with a sawmill and a gristmill built near a natural waterfall that settlers harnessed for power. In the middle of the town, **Wolcott Falls Park** provides a pleasant view of this waterfall around which the first neighborhoods in town grew. Turn left onto Mill Street (NY 104A) to follow the Seaway Trail signs past this little park. When you're ready to go on, continue on NY 104A, crossing NY 104 and maintaining a straight course through fields of corn, beans, sunflowers, and meadow grasses.

Pass through Red Creek, turning left at the Cornerstone Restaurant and Bar to stay on NY 104A. Soon you're back to open fields and forest until you see the Holiday Harbor RV Park at the waterfront. Enter Cayuga County at the town of Fair Haven.

Best known for the **Sterling Renaissance Faire** that returns for weekends in July and August every year, the Fair Haven area also provides a state park with an extended beach and lots of campsites. An encapsulated history of the neighboring town of Sterling resides on the second floor of the **Little Red Schoolhouse** in town, a building on both the New York State and National Registers of Historic Places. Cross Sterling Creek on NY 104A and look to your left to see the waterfall created there by the town dam.

Continue to follow this route into Oswego County, where NY 104A ends and the Seaway Trail turns left onto NY 104.

Oswego

If you've been waiting for a tale of a real battle in the War of 1812, you've come to the right place. Oswego served as a key location on the supply route for virtually all of the US military along Lake Ontario and down into the Hudson River Valley to New York City, making this a contested location as far back as the French and Indian War in 1756, when defenders lost both Fort Oswego and Ontario to the Marquis de Montcalm and the French troops.

In 1814 America's primary naval military base resided in Sackett's Harbor, just a quick trip by boat across a lake inlet, so supplies coming up the channel into Oswego could be transported fairly rapidly to the main base. The winner of this pivotal port would win the war, and both sides knew it, so neither wanted to attack until it had a major arms advantage over the other. Both the British and the Americans spent years fortifying their holdings, building ships and arms until one finally decided to attack. The resulting battle on May 5, 1814, swung in the British navy's favor after a rocky start, and the Americans lost Fort Ontario to their enemy . . . but the bulk of their military supplies were stashed 12 miles downriver, so the Americans still managed to transport all of these heavy, iron munitions over land to Sackett's Harbor—a heroic feat if ever there was one. By July 1814, the Americans had completed the new ships they needed to trounce the British later that year.

The War of 1812 and other period history abounds in Oswego, where you can visit a line of historic watercraft the length of Oswego's West First Street pier at the **H. Lee White Marine Museum,** and view the **West Pier Lighthouse** from shore (the lighthouse itself is not open to the public). You can see the site where the *David W. Mills*, a Great Lakes steam-powered cargo ship, ran aground on Ford Shoals on August 11, 1919, when forest fires in Canada created dense smog here.

View the West Pier Lighthouse from shore in Oswego.

The boat could not be rescued and eventually succumbed to a fall storm, cracking and sinking into the lake later the same year.

This concludes the second segment of the Great Lakes Seaway Trail. If you are continuing north along Lake Ontario, we will continue to narrate your journey in the next route of this book.

23

Great Lakes Seaway Trail, Part 3

Oswego to Massena

General description: This last, 160-mile leg of the trail bends around the eastern end of Lake Ontario and continues north along the St. Lawrence Seaway, where it explores the Thousand Islands region.

Special attractions: Mexico Bay, Selkirk Shores State Park, Sandy Island Beach State Park, Southwick Beach Park, North Sandy Pond, Henderson Bay, Westcott Beach State Park, Black River Bay, Long Point State Park, St. Lawrence River, Burnham Point State Park, Grass Point State Park, Cedar Point State Park, French Creek Bay, Thousand Islands Arts Center (home of the Handweaving Museum), Antique Boat Museum, Rock Island Lighthouse, Thousand Islands Winery, Alexandria Bay, Boldt Castle, Keewaydin Point State Park, Thousand Islands State Park, Jacques Cartier State Park, St. Lawrence Park, Robert Moses State Park, Eisenhower Lock, St. Lawrence–FDR Power Dam

Location: This route travels the northwestern edge of northern New York State, following the east end of Lake Ontario to

the northern border between the US and Canada.

Route numbers: NY 104A, NY 104B, NY 3, NY 12E, NY 12, NY 37

Travel season: Spring through fall

Camping: Dowie Dale Campground & Marina in Mexico, Yogi Bear's Jellystone Park Campground in Mexico, Chedmardo Campsites in Mexico, Selkirk Shore State Park in Pulaski, Bedford Creek Marina and Campground near Sackett's Harbor, Black River Bay Campgrounds north of Sackett's Harbor, 1000 Islands Campground on Mullet Creek Bay, Lisbon Beach and Campground in Ogdensburg, Coles Creek State Park south of Massena

Services: In Sackett's Harbor, Cape Vincent, Clayton, Alexandria Bay, Chippewa Bay, Morristown, and Massena

Nearby attractions: Battle Island State Park, Robert Wehle Park, Wellesley Island State Park, Kring Point State Park, Galop Island, St. Lawrence State Park

The Route

Forts, castles, lighthouses, and feats of engineering provide the stops along this segment of the Seaway Trail, and while the road itself does not deliver the scenic impact you've seen on the first two sections of this drive, side roads take you to startling views of Lake Ontario and the St. Lawrence Seaway.

Great Lakes Seaway Trail, Part 3: Oswego to Massena

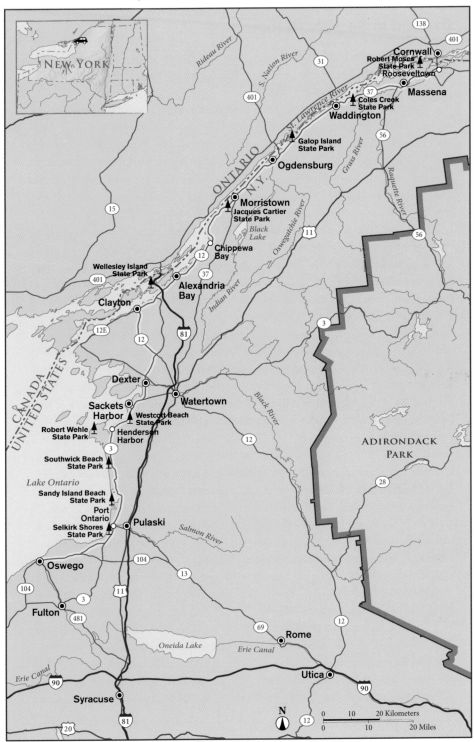

NEW YORK

Rideau River

S. Nation River

St. Lawrence River

138

401

Cornwall

Robert Moses
State Park

Rooseveltown

Massena

31

401

37

Coles Creek
State Park

Waddington

Galop Island
State Park

56

Ogdensburg

Grass River

Raquette River

ONTARIO

N.Y.

Morristown
Jacques Cartier
State Park

Black
Lake

Oswegatchie River

11

56

15

Chippewa
Bay

12

Wellesley Island
State Park

401

37

Alexandria
Bay

Indian River

3

Clayton

12E

12

81

Dexter

Watertown

Black River

Sackets
Harbor

Westcott Beach
State Park

CANADA
UNITED STATES

Robert Wehle
State Park

Henderson
Harbor

ADIRONDACK
PARK

Southwick Beach
State Park

3

12

Lake Ontario

Sandy Island Beach
State Park

28

Port
Ontario

Selkirk Shores
State Park

Pulaski

Salmon River

104

Oswego

13

104

3

11

Fulton

481

12

69

Rome

Oneida Lake

Erie Canal

12

Erie Canal

90

Utica

90

Syracuse

81

20

N

12

0   10   20 Kilometers

0   10   20 Miles

Oswego to Sackets Harbor

Leave Oswego on NY 104 and continue east to NY 104B in New Haven. Turn left onto NY 104B and follow this to Mexico Point; turn left onto NY 3. This is the road you will follow to Sackets Harbor.

Watch for the signs for **Derby Hill Bird Observatory,** one of the most dependable and renowned places in New York State to observe the raptor migration. Hawks, falcons, eagles, vultures, and harriers all pass through this point on their way north or south, and visiting birders often see rare or uncommon species here that may not turn up at Braddock Bay to the west, or even at Hawk Mountain in Pennsylvania. If you're passing through when the migration is not in full swing, you may still see interesting resident birds from this point.

Back on NY 3, head north to **Selkirk Shores State Park.** This park provides some of the finest views of Lake Ontario in the entire state, looking due west at sunset for unbroken, horizon-to-horizon water vistas. Swimming is not allowed here, but if you really need a dip, head down the road to **Sandy Island Beach State Park,** where there's a lifeguard on the beach during scheduled swimming hours.

If you called Port Ontario a fishing village, you would not be wrong; the Salmon River passes through here, and anglers line the bridges on NY 3 in season or head out onto the lake in chartered boats with experienced guides. Cabin rentals cater specifically to people who fish, offering locations right on the river or close enough to walk to it. If the day you visit doesn't provide the weather you planned on, a side trip east to Altmar to the **Salmon River Fish Hatchery** or the **Salmon River Visitor Center and International Fishing Museum** may satisfy the angler in you.

A War of 1812 marker lets you know that you've reached the site of the Battle of Big Sandy, one of the most impressive American victories of the entire war—followed by a demonstration of grit and tenacity that could only lead to the Americans finally winning domination of Lake Ontario. Here on Sandy Creek, US Captain Melancthon Woolsey set a trap for the British pursuing his convoy of 19 bateaux packed with shipbuilding materials. Lining the banks of the creek with armed militiamen and Oneida tribesmen, Woolsey overpowered seven boats filled with British soldiers, killing or wounding 70 men while only two Americans were wounded (one died a few days later). The remaining British men became prisoners, and all of their munitions and supplies fell into American hands.

This was all well and good, but the main contingent of British ships still held the lake, and the Americans had stockpiles of heavy equipment and supplies to move to Sackets Harbor for shipbuilding. With all the militiamen they could spare, the Americans loaded these materials onto carts and transported them by land—all except a cable weighing nearly five tons. It took 84 men to carry the 600-foot cable the 20 miles to Sackets Harbor, with as many as 120 more joining in en route to spell the men when they tired out. This heroic effort became known as the Great Cable Carry, and the story still widens the eyes of those who read about it here at Sandy Creek.

NY 3 continues through healthy woodland, broken by cropland and a number of creeks. By now you have likely noticed that there's a surprising lack of "seaway" along the Seaway Trail, as woods and development obscure the view of Lake Ontario along most of this route—and this will continue to be true as you follow the St. Lawrence Seaway farther north. To see the water, you will need to turn left and leave the trail, visiting the small lakeshore towns and parks that have greater access to the waterfront.

In **Henderson Harbor,** you will see a marked pull-off with interpretive signs about a French stronghold in this area during the French and Indian War. This region served as a critical link between France and its colonies in the New World in the 1750s, but British interests often created obstacles to transportation and communications. In an effort to drive the British out of nearby Oswego through harassment and interception of supply shipments, Captain Coulon de Villiers and roughly 600 men set up camp here in July 1756, receiving additional reinforcements until the number of troops here swelled to more than 4,000. On August 6, the French army marched on Oswego, overwhelming the British forces at Oswego and achieving a quick surrender.

Lake views emerge through the foliage as you approach Sackets Harbor. For some great views, pay a visit to **Robert Wehle State Park** or **Westcott Beach State Park** to see Henderson Harbor and spot the lighthouse on Galoo Island some distance offshore.

If you're a fan of War of 1812 history, the name **Sackets Harbor** will be more than familiar to you. Here the Americans built most of their warships and maintained the base of its naval operations, taking advantage of the deep water in the harbor and its strategic location near the British naval base across the seaway in Kingston, Ontario. That proximity offered both positive and negative effects: the British chose Sackets Harbor as a primary target at the very beginning of the war in July 1812, and returned to the port in May 1813 to attempt to take out the Americans' newest warships and destroy its navy yard. In both cases, however, the British failed in their cause—though the second attack did result in considerable destruction of American armament (mostly because a young lieutenant ordered half a million dollars' worth of naval supplies burned rather than ceding them to the British). Sackets Harbor remained in American control for the duration of the war.

Your visit to Sackets Harbor should begin with a stop at the **Seaway Trail Discovery Center,** which you will see as you enter the town. Located in the circa 1817 Union Hotel, the Discovery Center provides background and exhibits on the military and maritime history of this area, as well as information about New York State's coastal agriculture, historic architecture, and natural history.

Tour the **Sackets Harbor Battlefield State Historic Site** with a guide or on your own, and visit the restored Navy Yard and Commandant's House. The nearby Military Cemetery is believed to contain the remains of General Zebulon Pike, a Revolutionary War soldier under George Washington who went on to win the battle for York (now Toronto), Ontario, even though it cost him his life. Many other soldiers are buried here—some identified, and some unknown—who fell during the battles that took place here, and in other wars at home and abroad.

As you leave Sackets Harbor, take NY 180 to the junction with NY 12E. Continue on NY 12E into the Thousand Islands.

The Golden Crescent to Cape Vincent

At Lake Ontario's northeastern end, the lake and surrounding coastland create the world's largest freshwater bay by combining four separate inlets: Chaumont Bay, Three Mile Bay, Sawmill Bay, and Black River Bay. So rich in resources is this area—from the wealth of fish in its waters to the sunsets on its western horizon—that it became known centuries ago as the **Golden Crescent,** a moniker that local residents work to maintain and live up to just about every day of the year.

The villages of Dexter, Limerick, Chaumont, and Three Mile Bay provide the head, heart, and hub of the Crescent, four small, residential towns that provide services to the many anglers, hunters, boaters, and campers who come here from early spring well into late fall. Many of these services close up for the colder seasons, but some stay open year-round to serve the residents and intrepid passersby. Locals and visitors alike swear by the food at **Wise Guys** and **The Blue Heron** in Chaumont, two restaurants across the street from one another on NY 12E.

As you travel through the Golden Crescent, you'll see upstate New York's famous stone houses, as well as carefully preserved examples of Greek Revival and Victorian architecture. A quick right on NY 12F east of Dexter brings you to Brownville, where you can visit one of the oldest buildings in the area: the **home of War of 1812 hero General Jacob Brown.** General Brown served as colonel of the 108th regiment of the New York Militia, moving up the ranks to brigadier general as the war got under way. This position came with challenges, however, making Brown a model of leadership under hardship—Brown defended the frontier from Oswego all the way to St. Regis, 300 miles north, with a regiment of 600

Tibbett's Point Lighthouse marks the confluence of Lake Ontario and the St. Lawrence River.

untrained recruits. After the war, he maintained his postwar headquarters here at this home until he moved to Washington DC in 1821. This 22-room Georgian mansion now holds the village of Brownville's offices and library.

From Three Mile Bay, continue on NY 12E into Cape Vincent. Once in town, NY 12E becomes Market Street; stay on this until the junction with Broadway (County Route 6). Turn left onto Broadway and stay on it as signs warn that it's a dead end. This long residential road ends when the land comes to a point, at the exact spot where Lake Ontario ends and the St. Lawrence Seaway begins.

It only stands to reason that a lighthouse should punctuate this spot, so **Tibbett's Point Lighthouse** stands here as it has since 1827. This lighthouse contains the only original, working Fresnel lens in a light on Lake Ontario, giving it distinction among the many lighthouses on this route. There's a hotel here at the lighthouse if you'd like to stay out here overnight.

When you return to NY 12E, watch for a paved parking area along the lakeshore with a War of 1812 sign in it. From here, you can see **Carleton Island,** the former site of Fort Haldimand, a bastion built by the British to protect its holdings in Kingston, Ontario, during the Revolutionary War. After the war, the British were required as part of Jay's Treaty to cede all of its military holdings in Lake Ontario, but Carleton Island somehow was overlooked, leaving it open for British occupation once again during the War of 1812. While it seemed advantageous to have this stronghold, the British did not make the most of it, losing the island to three freelancing American sailors without putting up much resistance. The island became the only land gained by either side in the War of 1812. Today the fort is gone, and no one lives on the island.

You may be pleased to know that from Cape Vincent to Clayton, NY 12E becomes a remarkably scenic route along the St. Lawrence Seaway. At **Burnham Point State Park,** you can look out over the water to see the **Wolfe Island Wind Farm,** a project owned and operated by the Canadian Renewable Energy Corporation. The 86 wind turbines here have the ability to generate nearly 600 gigawatt-hours of wind power each year, enough to power 75,000 homes. A study also shows that this wind farm struck and killed 602 birds in six months in 2010, well above industry standards for bird strikes. The construction of wind farms continues to be contentious throughout New York State and in other areas through which birds migrate in spring and fall.

The Thousand Islands: Clayton to Chippewa Bay

Site of the 1813 Battle of French Creek—an impressive but short-lived victory for the Americans—the town of Clayton now heralds your entrance into the Thousand Islands region with a full complement of museums, shops, restaurants, and places to stay. *Coastal Living* magazine named Clayton a "Best Small Town," and *Budget Travel* proclaimed it one of the "Coolest Small Towns in North America," so you can expect to find plenty to keep you entertained here whether you stop for an hour, a weekend, or even a season. Here you can take a boat tour of Wellesley and Grindstone islands, just across the seaway, and visit **Rock Island Lighthouse,** one of the few lights at this end of the Seaway Trail that is open to the public. The town's **Antique Boat Museum** houses the largest collection of antique and classic boats in North America, as well as artifacts of many periods in nautical history. It's the **Hand-weaving Museum,** however, that really sparks curiosity: Located in the Thousand Islands Arts Center, this museum preserves the traditional art of handmade textiles, curating a collection of more than 2,200 pieces from around the world. Don't miss the retail store in this building, showcasing the work of more than 100 artists.

James Street in Clayton features some terrific shopping as well, including **Gold Cup Farms/River Rat Cheese,** where you can find all kinds of food products made in New York State including Adirondack sausage, pure maple syrup, and a wide variety of cheeses. Stop at the **Thousand Islands Museum** to see its collection of vintage decoys and its military artifacts, and shop for the local St. Lawrence tartan—a plaid you can purchase nowhere else—in the gift shop.

Head north on NY 12E as you leave Clayton, and watch for **Thousand Islands Winery,** producing nearly 30 varieties of wine to accompany the spectacular view from its tasting room and vineyard. You may want to take a detour across the seaway to **Wellesley Island,** one of the few islands in this region that you can reach by car, to visit Wellesley Island and Dewolff Point State Parks. When you continue north, **Keewaydin State Park** offers sweeping seaway views, campsites, and steep rocky points from which to watch sea vessels heading north and south on the St. Lawrence.

Alexandria Bay serves as the mainland point of departure for trips to many of the 1,864 islands in the St. Lawrence River. The resort town is most famous for its proximity to Heart Island, the home of **Boldt Castle,** the extraordinary dream house of hotel owner George Boldt, who started the project as a gift to his beloved wife, Louise. Months before the castle's completion, Louise died of a sudden illness and George, his dream shattered, ceased construction of the home. The castle remained vacant for more than 70 years, but it now serves as one of the Thousand Islands' most popular tourist attractions, open for visitors from mid-May through mid-October.

Just about any time you visit during the summer months, Alex Bay hosts a number of special events from its annual River Run Motorcycle Rally to its craft fairs and music concerts. Scuba divers flock here to dive the many shipwrecks under the St. Lawrence's surface, and anglers know that these waters make Alex Bay one of the top ten fishing locations in the US. These attractions explain why this area has more than 1,000 hotel rooms and 32 restaurants, acting as a hub of tourist activity throughout the summer months.

Another castle comes into view as you reach Chippewa Bay: **Singer Castle,** built by millionaire Frederick Gilbert Bourne, head of the Singer Sewing Machine Company. The Bourne family actually lived in the castle for many decades, entertaining such luminaries as Cornelius Vanderbilt, Vincent Astor, and neighbor Frederic Remington, the famous painter and sculptor. The massive compound can be reached by boat tour to Dark Island from Chippewa Bay; on arrival, you'll take a 45-minute guided tour of four floors of the castle and the grounds. If you have money to burn, you can spend the night in the castle's Royal Suite, furnished with all the modern comforts and overlooking the St. Lawrence—even from the bath.

As you leave Chippewa Bay, you'll find a War of 1812 sign directing you to a viewpoint where you can see Singer Castle (in winter, anyway) and learn about the **Wilkinson campaign.** James Wilkinson's name may not be immediately familiar to you, but in his day he made himself one of the most notorious leaders of American forces in the War of 1812—and not in a good way. Wilkinson, a governor of the Louisiana Territory, blackened his reputation before the war by becoming involved in a plot to create an independent nation with Vice President Aaron Burr. He regained some credibility early in the war when he seized Mobile (now in Alabama) from Spain, leading his friend John Armstrong, then US Secretary of War, to offer him a command up north on the St. Lawrence River. Wilkinson proceeded to lead a slipshod, ill-planned campaign to take Canada that finally ended horrendously at Crysler's Farm on November 11, 1813. He attempted another attack on Canada early the following year, failing miserably once again, and this time he was relieved of command.

Morristown to Waddington

As you reach Morristown, signs direct you to the **Stone Windmill,** probably the most recognized landmark in this town. To reach the windmill—which was built in 1825 and is the only remaining windmill on the American side of the St. Lawrence River—take NY 37 and turn right onto High Street, then left onto Morris Street. Along with the windmill, you'll see a War of 1812 sign detailing the battle between the American ship *Julia* and the *Earl of Moira*, a British vessel. The *Julia* engaged the *Earl of Moira* and the *Duke of Gloucester*, another British warship, here in the waters opposite Morristown, and the intrepid ship *Julia* hit the *Earl of Moira* with enough cannon fire that the British finally pulled back, retreating to the Canadian side of the seaway. The *Julia* accompanied several schooners from Ogdensburg to Sackets Harbor and safety.

Clayton has a fun and interesting town center with museums, shops, and restaurants.

From Morristown, continue on NY 37 east and cross the Oswegatchie River, then approach the former site of **Fort de la Présentation.** A mission rather than a military outpost, this fort was constructed in 1749 by French priest Abbé François Picquet as a shelter in which to convert Native Americans to Catholicism. Picquet gathered quite a parish of people from several Iroquois tribes throughout the 1750s, but when the French began to pull out of the area and other forts fell in the face of British aggression, Picquet was forced to abandon the fort and his work there. The British used the fort during the Revolutionary War, finally ceding it to the Americans in 1796.

Soon **Ogdensburg** comes into view, the site of a battle of February 22, 1813, in which 500 British-led troops handily took over Ogdensburg and defeated a small contingent of Americans at what was now called Fort Presentation. Here the 2.2-mile **Maple City Trail** provides a pleasant walk along the St. Lawrence and Oswegatchie Rivers, connecting a number of buildings that date back to the early 1800s. The large, stone **US Customs House** has stood here since 1809–10, and the **Oswegatchie River Dam and Pump Station** provide a look back at early endeavors to use the river's power for energy and manufacturing. The lighthouse you can see here is privately owned and not open to the public.

Probably the most well-known landmark in Ogdensburg, however, is the **Frederic Remington Art Museum,** housing a large collection of artist Remington's paintings, sketches, and sculptures on western and military subjects. Remington served as an illustrator for *Harper's Weekly* and other major magazines in the 1880s and 1890s, bringing scenes of the west to life to accompany stories written by staff and contributors. While he produced more than 3,000 illustrations, he is probably best remembered for his bronze sculptures, including *The Bronco Buster*, perhaps the most recognized of his three-dimensional work. Much of his art is displayed here in the home his wife, Eva, lived in after Remington's death in 1909.

From Ogdensburg, drive along NY 37 through farmland with occasional views of the river. Waddington is the next sizeable town, and as you leave NY 37 to drive along the town's Main Street, it becomes clear that this village hosted a great deal of entrepreneurial leadership in its heyday—a history that Waddington has worked hard to preserve. Take the **historic Waddington walking tour** along six blocks of the town's most interesting areas, and follow the signposts to learn more about the businesses and industry that sprang up here many years ago.

The Stone Windmill is the most recognized landmark in Morristown.

Massena to Rooseveltown

Continue on NY 37 north through cropland, crossing an inlet of the St. Lawrence River before you approach Massena. When you see the junction with NY 131 to your left, take it and continue along the seaway to **Robert Moses State Park** and the **Eisenhower Lock.**

Partly on the mainland and partly on Barnhart Island, Robert Moses State Park requires you to drive through a tunnel under the Eisenhower Lock to get to the largest part of the park's spacious lands. Here the expansive Barnhart Beach offers the best views of the St. Lawrence River that you will find anywhere along the Seaway Trail, as well as a marina, plenty of picnic space, campsites and cabins, and the opportunity to see white-tailed deer, wild turkeys, groundhogs, and many other woodland animals. Short-eared owls hunt in broad daylight in this park, and the Hawkins Point Nature Center provides information about trails and the best places to see various species of birds, plants, and animals.

Here the **Franklin D. Roosevelt Power Project,** functioning since 1958, began a legacy of hydropower generation in partnership with Canada that continues to power both nations today. Its 32 turbine generators are divided equally at the international border, and each side operates independently of the other. The stateside 16 turbines can produce more than 900,000 kilowatts of electricity—more than enough to light a major city of more than half a million people.

At the northernmost point of the US shipping channel in the St. Lawrence River, the **Eisenhower Lock** is the first lock on the seaway that is solely operated by the US. Five Canadian locks and two US locks take ships through the channel from Montreal, Quebec, south to Lake Ontario, where they can continue through the Great Lakes all the way to Lake Superior. From the Atlantic Ocean to Duluth, Minnesota, this all-water route takes ships 2,038 nautical miles. As modern as it looks, the Eisenhower Lock works just like the locks on the Erie Canal: Water flows into the lock or out of it, depending on whether the ship inside is traveling upstream or downstream. When the water is equalized on both sides of the lock, the gates open and the ship continues on its way.

From here, the Great Lakes Seaway Trail continues to the beginning of NY 131 in Rooseveltown, where there's a border crossing to Canada if you have an interest in continuing north. There this 454-mile road trip ends, not with a bang but with a bit of a fizzle. If you're looking for a different route to take south, we recommend heading east on NY 131 to NY 37, and turning south on NY 37 to go through Malone. From there, head through the Adirondacks on the drive described in Route 6 of this book.

Robert Moses State Park offers easy wildlife viewing.

HUDSON VALLEY
SCENIC DRIVES

24

Palisades Parkway to Bear Mountain

General description: The New York State segment of this National Historic Landmark road emerges from State Line Lookout, just over the New Jersey border, and continues north for 26 miles, all the way to Bear Mountain.

Special attractions: Bear Mountain State Park, Anthony Wayne Recreational Area, State Line Lookout, Stony Point Battlefield State Historic Site, Appalachian Trail, Nyack Beach State Park, Rockland Lake State Park, Fort Montgomery State Historic Site, Knox Headquarters State Historic Site

Location: From the New Jersey border through Rockland and Orange Counties in southern New York State, north of New York City

Route numbers: Palisades Parkway

Travel season: Year-round

Camping: Harriman State Park (north of the Palisades)

Services: Food and beverage service at State Line Lookout; service area with gas and conveniences at 12.8 miles (1.8 miles north of New Jersey border)

Nearby attractions: Harriman State Park, Storm King State Park, Sterling Forest, Goodspeed Mountain, Washington's Headquarters State Historic Site, Minnewaska State Park, New Windsor Cantonment, Sterling Forest State Park

The Route

Named for the New Jersey Palisades, a line of ridges and cliffs skirted by this winding road, the Palisades Parkway traveled a rocky route to its opening over the course of more than 20 years. Developer William A. Welch first conceived of a scenic road that would follow the Hudson River from the New Jersey border to the state parks along the river in New York, and he inspired industrialist John D. Rockefeller to donate 700 acres of his land along the river to the project as far back as 1934. It looked like road design and construction would get under way almost immediately when the Civil Works Administration accepted the project with the influence of President Franklin Roosevelt—a supporter of a parkway in the Hudson Valley since he headed the Taconic State Park Commission in the 1920s. Everything came to a halt, however, when the New Jersey Highway Commission determined that it did not wish to see such a road built at that time.

Don't forget to stop and look at the scenery while you're in the Hudson Valley.

Palisades Parkway to Bear Mountain

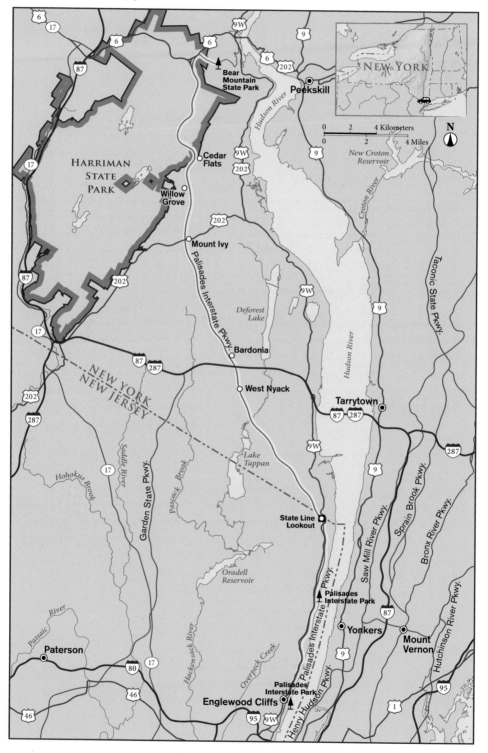

When Rockefeller picked up the ball again in the 1940s and began to seek supporters for the parkway, he chose Robert Moses, the extraordinarily powerful urban and suburban planner who developed New York City's system of highways and parkways. With Moses at the helm, the project moved forward quickly, with a groundbreaking for the New York segment on April 1, 1947. The last segment saw completion in 1958. In 1965, the National Park Service named Palisades Interstate Parkway a National Historic Landmark.

Today the parkway seems a little narrow, with its complete lack of shoulders and its canopy of native and nonnative trees hugging the road closely on both sides. As a respite from New York City's highways, however, it serves its purpose well, directing drivers to one state park, historic site, or wilderness area after another. Your journey may not be very long—a mere 26 miles in New York State, and just 12 miles more in New Jersey—but it satisfies the need for green space, clear air, and places that don't echo with the roar of bus horns and dense traffic.

State Line Lookout to Nyack

What better place to start than right on the New Jersey border, where you can look across the Hudson River and see the ridge of the Palisades? Here at **State Line Lookout,** the highest point on the New Jersey Palisades Cliffs—532 feet above the Hudson—you can take in the spectacle of the opposite bank from a platform right off the parking area, or stop at the Lookout Inn for lunch, a snack, and a browse through the bookstore and gift shop. The Works Progress Administration built this inn in the 1930s during the Great Depression, making it an open-air facility originally—but the realities of New Jersey winters soon set in, so an enclosure with many windows soon surrounded the snack stand. It's open year-round with cozy fireplaces burning in winter, so you may want to linger here over a hot chocolate.

The exit from the parkway to State Line Lookout isn't numbered, so keep an eye out for it if you've entered the parkway from a little farther into New Jersey. From here, it's easy to join the parkway going north. Cross into New York and watch for the first of the stone arch bridges that have become the hallmark of Robert Moses's construction projects. By the time Moses championed the Palisades Parkway, he had already completed the Long Island parkway system, a network of roadways designed to be more picturesque and pleasant to drive than the urban highways built in and around Manhattan, or the bullet-straight, high-speed, military-inspired roads found in Europe. As the Long Island State Park Commission explained at the New York World's Fair in 1964, its parkways were "of the same high standard as the parks and no less useful to the public." The masonry bridges with decorative stone facing certainly fit this description.

Pass exits for the many residential communities that offer suburban living for those who work in "the city"—there's no need to specify what city here—and make a stop in the village of **Nyack** (exit 8). Rockland County gathers up the best of its artistic and cultural offerings and puts them forward here, in a town center that makes you want to slow down, stroll through shops, chat with gallery owners, sample some intriguing restaurants, and take in a concert or a show.

There's something about the light here in Nyack as it comes into town off the Hudson River—something that made painter Edward Hopper spend his life here and paint exactly what he saw. The **Edward Hopper House** is now an art center, and you can tour it with a docent if you arrive on a weekend afternoon. It may be the light that attracted a bevy of famous artists from many different genres to West Nyack in the 1940s, where they founded what is now the **Rockland Center for the Arts (RoCA)**—luminaries like Aaron Copeland, Helen Hayes, Kurt Weill, Lotte Lenya, Paulette Goddard, and Maxwell Anderson all had a hand in developing this celebration of creativity. Check the RoCA website at rocklandartcenter.org for events scheduled during your visit.

Nyack to Stony Point

Return to the parkway and continue north, crossing I-87 and I-287. If you're looking for a place for a picnic, exit 13 provides access to **High Tor State Park,** a day-use park with capacious views of the Hudson Valley. This is also the exit for **Hook Mountain State Park,** an undeveloped park that features a brisk walk to the 730-foot summit. The National Audubon Society designated this prime hawk-watching destination as an Important Bird Area back in 1997; if you're here in spring or fall during the hawk migration, you may catch glimpses of Cooper's, sharp-shinned, broad-winged, red-shouldered, and red-tailed hawks from the summit.

At exit 15, **Stony Point State Historic Site** provides a slice of Revolutionary War history that's not at the forefront of the common narrative. Here in July 1779, General Anthony Wayne led the American Corps of Light Infantry in a surprise midnight attack on the British Regulars, capturing the point in about 33 minutes. Today this artfully landscaped site features walking paths to the **Stony Point Lighthouse** and around the battleground, a military museum, and pleasant trails through trees, wildflowers, and a small wetland. The lighthouse, built in 1826, is the oldest one on the Hudson River, and it offers long views of the Hudson from

You can climb the stairs in Perkins Memorial Tower for more great views.

its post above the river. This state historic site closes on weekends through the fall and winter, but it's open seven days a week from mid-April through Labor Day.

Visitor Center to Bear Mountain

When you return to the parkway and continue north, watch for the **Palisades Interstate Park Commission Visitor Center** and bookstore on the median after exit 16. You'll find displays here about the **Appalachian Trail,** the 2,180-mile footpath that begins at Springer Mountain, Georgia, and ends atop Mount Katahdin in Maine. Eighty-eight miles of the trail are in New York, passing through Sterling Forest, Bear Mountain, and Harriman State Parks, all of which are along the parkway. You can pick up maps of the trail—and of just about any other trail in the area—in the bookstore at this visitor center.

Exit 17 provides access to the **Anthony Wayne Recreation Area,** named for the American general who scored such a great success at Stony Point. This unit of Harriman State Park provides picnic grounds, ball fields, and hiking trails in a pretty valley surrounded by the local mountains, making it a nice stop if you're looking for a place to enjoy your lunch. If you prefer a more secluded setting, however, exit 18 gives you the easiest access to the rest of **Harriman State Park,** which at roughly 44,000 acres is the second-largest park in the New York State Parks system. Thirty-one bodies of water grace this park, from pristine lakes surrounded by dense foliage to reservoirs that supply water to New York City. Rocky streams, trails through fascinating geologic formations, challenging but manageable trails, and views of the Hudson Highlands from atop many hills make this park a more than agreeable place to spend a day or a weekend.

If scrambling over boulders and traversing natural areas on foot do not appeal to you the way they do to me, you can still enjoy the best of the Palisades by driving to the top of **Bear Mountain**. Take exit 19 (Seven Lakes Drive) and follow the signs to Perkins Memorial Drive, the road to the summit. In about ten minutes—perhaps longer on a high-traffic day—the winding road ends at a large parking area at the mountaintop. You'll find plenty of vantage points from which to enjoy the expansive view of the Hudson Highlands and Harriman State Park. If you like, climb the **Perkins Memorial Tower** for even more spectacular vistas.

Once you've seen the main attraction, take time to make a satisfying exploration of the rest of Bear Mountain State Park. An easy, winding nature trail leads

Stony Point Lighthouse is part of a state historic site of the same name.

Bear Mountain provides romantic sunsets far above the Palisades.

you to four **Trailside Museums,** where you can learn about the Palisades region's natural features through exhibits on the area's geology, ancient and colonial human history, warm-blooded animals, and reptiles and amphibians. Between these museums, you'll pass a black bear den and exhibits that contain a live bobcat, porcupine, coyote, fox, beaver, otter, and white-tailed deer, as well as a number of birds of prey.

When you return to the parkway, you'll soon reach its end at a roundabout that includes exits for the Bear Mountain Bridge and for US 9W North, another scenic route along the Hudson River that we have detailed in this book. You may want to continue your exploration of the river and its significant influence on life north of New York City—especially for the wealthy and powerful—by driving along the Hudson from here.

25

Hudson River Valley

Poughkeepsie to Kingston

General description: This 29-mile drive introduces you to one of the most pleasant areas along the Hudson River, stoked with historic sites and tempered by shopping and dining experiences.

Special attractions: Walkway Over the Hudson, Culinary Institute of America, Home of Franklin D. Roosevelt National Historic Site and Presidential Library, Franklin D. Roosevelt Nature Preserve, Clinton Vineyards, Eleanor Roosevelt National Historic Site, Vanderbilt National Historic Site, Mills-Norrie State Park, Mills Mansion State Historic Site, Rhinebeck Antique Emporium, Wilderstein Historic Site, Beekman Arms & Delamater Inn, Historic Kingston, Hudson River Maritime Museum

Location: Along the Hudson River's downstate west bank

Route numbers: US 9, NY 199, NY 9W

Travel season: Year-round

Camping: Mills-Norrie State Park in Staatsburg, Clarence Fahnestock State Park in Carmel, Sylvan Lake Beach Park in Poughkeepsie

Services: You are never away from services on this route. Concentrations are found in Poughkeepsie, Hyde Park, Rhinebeck, and Kingston.

Nearby attractions: Winnakee Nature Preserve, Roosevelt Farm & Forest, Pinewoods Park, Poet's Walk Park, Dutchess Wine Trail, Old Rhinebeck Aerodrome, Montgomery Place, Opus 40, Delaware and Hudson Canal Museum, Glebe/Clinton Houses

The Route

If you measure your favorite byways by the number of historic sites and interesting stops per linear mile, this Hudson River Valley route may be the New York State winner. Here in the cradle of genteel twentieth-century civilization, the ultra-wealthy Vanderbilt family built its fabulous mansion, the Roosevelts preserved many acres of natural land and used Hyde Park as a northern White House, industrial leader Ogden Mills built the family's Greek Revival estate home, and a descendant of the Beekmans and the Livingstons, two prominent families of the 17th and 18th centuries, constructed a Queen Anne-style country house with one of the finest views on the river. This is the place to discover how the wealthiest one-thousandth-of-one-percent lived in the times of our nation's greatest growth.

Poughkeepsie to Hyde Park

Begin your ride with a walk, one that provides the views of the Hudson River you simply cannot see from the road. The **Walkway Over the Hudson** in Poughkeepsie

Hudson River Valley: Poughkeepsie to Kingston

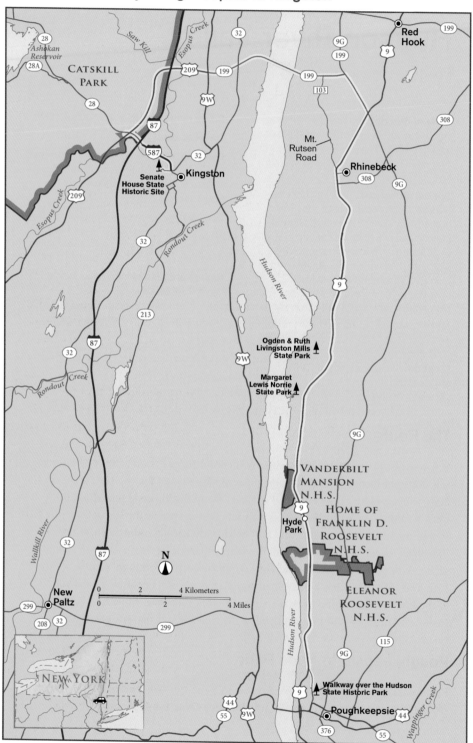

repurposes the old Poughkeepsie-Highland Railroad Bridge, a 19th-century railroad bridge that served for many decades as a major rail corridor. When fire severely damaged the bridge in 1974, the structure stood dormant until a group of citizens joined with the state and federal government to repair it and transform it into a new state park. Opened in the fall of 2009, the wide, smooth, modern walkway now stands as the longest elevated pedestrian walkway in the world, 212 feet above the river's surface. Expect to encounter crowds if you visit here on a sunny Sunday in spring or fall, and on just about any day during the summer.

When you've enjoyed the walkway to your heart's content, begin the drive up US 9 north. It won't take long to realize that US 9 in itself is not a particularly scenic road, but there's plenty of interesting human development to see along the way.

In a few minutes, enter Hyde Park, one of downstate's toniest residential areas. Here stands the New York campus of the **Culinary Institute of America,** recognized by many as the premier college for chefs in the entire world. The next generation of top chefs learn their craft here, and you have the opportunity to sample their creativity and admire their skill by dining in one of several restaurants on campus. Reservations are strongly recommended for the American Bounty Restaurant ("inspired foods of the Americas"), the Bocuse Restaurant (French), and Ristorante Caterina de'Medici (Italian), but you have the option of dropping into the Post Road Brew House for a craft beer and a pub meal, or to the Apple Pie Bakery Cafe for fresh-baked delicacies and casually elegant fare.

The **Home of Franklin Delano Roosevelt National Historic Site** sits adjacent to the **Franklin Delano Roosevelt Presidential Library and Museum,** so if you're an FDR fan or if you want to learn more about the president who held the office longer than any other person in history, you can immerse yourself in Roosevelt information for days at this site. Roosevelt gave us Social Security and the Federal Deposit Insurance Corporation, dug the country out of the Great Depression with a number of stimulus programs, put people back to work through the Works Progress Administration and the Civilian Conservation Corps, and saw the US through World War II. While he ran into many of the same kinds of controversies over his policies that we see in our own Congress today, he accomplished a great deal—including the New Deal—for working-class Americans, all of it after polio placed him in a wheelchair in 1921. He died on April 12, 1945, just a few weeks after his inauguration to his fourth term as president, and he and his wife, Eleanor Roosevelt, are buried here on the grounds of the estate.

Eleanor also maintained a home of her own, called Val-Kill, and the National Park Service now preserves this modest house as the **Eleanor Roosevelt National Historic Site.** Here the wife of the president established Val-Kill Industries, a factory that provided rural families with income during the winter, making furniture, cloth, and pewter items right here in the First Lady's household. The program

became a model for some of the initiatives Roosevelt would enact as part of the New Deal. Mrs. Roosevelt turned the factory into her home after the Great Depression, moving into it permanently after her husband's death. This is where she lived while she served as the first chair of the United Nations Commission on Human Rights, and as chair of the Presidential Commission on the Status of Women under President John F. Kennedy.

In sharp contrast to Eleanor Roosevelt's understated home, the **Vanderbilt Mansion National Historic Site** may be everything you might expect of the home of one of the nation's richest industrial magnates. This mansion is one of the region's oldest estates on the Hudson River, built in the late 1800s in the classic American Beaux-Arts style and still furnished with many of the pieces purchased by the Vanderbilts themselves. Just visiting the formal gardens gives you an idea of the kinds of lives the elite class could live at the time, but you really must go inside and take the tour to fully comprehend the divisions between the very wealthy people of the Gilded Age and the rest of us. In addition to this marvelous estate, the historic site also owns the original estate records, ledgers, diaries, and photos that inform the preservation of the buildings and grounds, lending a superlative level of authenticity to the park service's management of the estate as a historical resource.

If you feel the need to extend the sense of the luxurious life beyond your tour of the mansion, make a stop at **Clinton Vineyards** and sample the gold medal-winning cassis, a full-bodied black currant dessert wine. The vineyard's seyval blanc, a single-grape white wine, is a well-reviewed favorite, while its Jubilee and Seyval Naturel use seyval blanc grapes to create a sparkling wine in the traditional champagne-style method.

As you leave Hyde Park and approach Staatsburgh, you will pass **Mills-Norrie State Parks,** a pair of adjoining parks created from the estates of Margaret Lewis Norrie and Ogden and Ruth Livingston Mills. These thousand acres provide walking and cycling trails, woods, a marina and boat launch on the river, and some of the best panoramic views of the countryside that you'll find in the Hudson Valley.

Staatsburgh to Rhinebeck

In the town of Stattsburgh, the don't-miss stop is the **Staatsburgh State Historic Site,** the former home of Ogden Mills and his wife, Ruth Livingston Mills. The Mills family made their money in banks, railroads, and mines, investing in promising enterprises and seeing those investments pay off, and Ruth Livingston

Drive or walk across the FDR Mid-Hudson Bridge to get from Poughkeepsie to Highland.

inherited this property originally acquired by her great-grandfather Morgan Lewis, the third governor of New York State. Today you can tour this sprawling, 65-room Beaux-Arts mansion with its French-style interior design and its many pieces from the 1600s and 1700s, and get a sense of the period called the American Renaissance. The gift shop here, by the way, is one of the top-rated in the county by local residents.

From this historic site, look out across the Hudson River to see **Esopus Meadows Lighthouse,** a small lighthouse surrounded by water on a foundation of 250 40-foot-long poles driven into the riverbed. The area required a lighthouse at this spot because of mud flats to the west on the river, which presented a potential hazard for boat traffic. This lighthouse was constructed in 1871 with a 53-foot-high light tower, and it's the only remaining lighthouse on the river with a wood frame. Extensive renovations have restored this buillding to its original structural integrity and design, with some modernization to ensure its continued sturdiness.

The Catskill Mountains come into view on your left as you drive north through Staatsburgh, passing the famous **Belvedere Mansion** hotel and the **Rhinebeck Antique Emporium.** Continue north toward Rhinebeck.

Take a left onto South Mill Road and drive through a wooded neighborhood to reach **Wilderstein Historic Site,** perhaps the most unusual of the mansions-turned-museums because of its Queen Anne style. When Thomas Holy Suckley bought this land in 1852, he and his wife prized the natural setting with its varied terrain and its stunning views of the river, and they built an Italianate villa on the site. Nearly four decades later, the Suckleys' son and his wife transformed the villa into the elaborate home we see here, with its five-story circular tower and its multi-gabled attic. When you see the outside, you will want to know how the inside fits together and how New York City decorator Joseph Burr Tiffany made the most of the design with his interior choices.

When you return to US 9, turn left and continue north into Rhinebeck, the town that became the center of international attention in the summer of 2010 when Chelsea Clinton, daughter of former President Bill Clinton and Secretary of State Hillary Rodham Clinton, married Marc Mezvinsky at Astor Courts, on John Jacob Astor IV's former **Ferncliff estate.** If you'd like to see the mansion where the wedding took place, turn left onto Montgomery Street in Rhinebeck, and take the first left onto Astor Drive. The property is privately owned and is not open for tours; please respect the owners' privacy.

Even on the heavily trafficked US 9, one extraordinary home after another slides into view, most of them repurposed as bed-and-breakfast establishments, inns, and shops. More than 400 homes in this town are listed on the National Register of Historic Places, and the town itself is a designated National Landmark District—and part of the Hudson River Valley National Heritage Area, just to give

The Wilderstein estate is a fine example of Queen Anne architecture.

it some extra panache. Dutch settlers arrived here in 1686, including Henry Beek-man and Casper Landsman, two men whose names are still on many landmarks in the area. William Traphagen built the first tavern here on what would become US 9 back in 1706, and his son relocated the tavern in 1766. The Bogardus Inn, as it was known then, changed hands a number of times until it became the **Beekman Arms Inn**—albeit with extensive renovations. Today the Beekman Arms is the old-est continually operating inn in the US.

You'll find a wealth of places to eat and shop here in Rhinebeck, including the **Hammertown Barn** for art, antiques, and collectibles, and **Winter Sun & Summer Moon** and **Warren Kitchen & Cutlery** for home furnishings, housewares, and gifts.

Bridge to Kingston

When you reach the junction with NY 9G north of Rhinebeck, turn left and con-tinue to the junction with NY 199. Turn left and cross the Hudson River on the **Kingston/Rhinecliff.** Once you have crossed, take the exit for NY 9W south/

Kingston. Pass through some general American mercantile and follow the signs as NY 9W jogs left and gets on Frank Koenig Boulevard, a divided highway. In a moment, follow the signs for **Kingston's Historic Waterfront District.**

If you're looking for a place to end your day with a good meal, an attractive view, some fun shopping, and maybe a lesson or two in history, Kingston's waterfront can provide the entire package. Here the **Hudson River Maritime Museum** tells the story of the shipping industry that once dominated the river, and Kingston's role as a critical port between New York and Albany. From here, you can take a boat tour to see the **Kingston Lighthouse,** an 86-year-old structure that helped guide ships through a tricky part of the river. More than a dozen restaurants offer everything from Hudson Valley produce and cheeses to Mexican, Japanese, and Italian delicacies, and antiques stores and galleries tempt shoppers with unusual finds. Complete your afternoon or evening with a quiet stroll along Rondout Creek on a brick walkway, watching the ducks and the occasional boat pass by on the water.

If it's still early in the day and you'd like to see more of the area, we recommend that you continue another 10 miles south on NY 9W to New Paltz, and take the Shawangunk Ridge Scenic Byway (Route 11 in this book) to truly appreciate the beauty of the nearby mountains.

26

Bronx River Parkway

General description: This 23-mile drive provides a short-lived but welcome respite from the urban jungle, deep in New York City's northernmost borough.

Special attractions: Kensico Dam Plaza County Park, Bronx River Reservation, New York Botanical Garden, Bronx Zoo, Bronx Park

Location: In the Bronx, beginning at the Taconic State Parkway and ending at the Bruckner Expressway

Route numbers: The Bronx River Parkway does not have a number.

Travel season: Year-round

Camping: None in the immediate area

Services: In White Plains, Scarsdale, Hartsdale, Crestwood, and Tuckahoe

Nearby attractions: Silver Lake Preserve, Greenburgh Nature Center, Old Croton Aqueduct State Historic Park, Grassy Sprain Reservoir, St. Paul's Church National Historic Site

The Route

So you're driving through the Bronx, one of the nation's most populated and congested urban centers, and you've had just about all the bumper-to-bumper traffic, cluttered streetscapes, and crowded sidewalks you can handle. On a whim, you make a quick right turn . . . and the buildings and the people vanish. You're on the startlingly green, tree-lined Bronx River Parkway. In minutes you feel yourself relax as you match the pace of the drivers around you—all of whom treat the 50-miles-per-hour speed limit as an amusing suggestion—and watch the woods close in as flashes of light against water signal glimpses of the Bronx River along the road to the east.

The river gives the parkway its name, but it also played the pivotal role in the road's origin. Back when Native Americans of the Weckquasageek and Siwanoy tribes used this river—which they called the Aquehung, or River of High Bluffs—for drinking water, fishing, and annual ritual baths, this river ran clear and sparkling through a densely wooded landscape. In the early 17th century, Dutch trappers arrived to hunt and gather pelts from beavers, mink, otters, and other animals, and when they could not keep up with the demand from European merchants for these pelts, the Dutch settlers turned to milling and other more industrial pursuits. By the mid-18th century, more than a dozen mills got their power from the river. It did not take long for these activities to begin to mar the clarity and purity of Bronck's River—named for a Swedish businessman who bought this land from the Native Americans in 1639.

By 1906, when the first major segment of the Bronx River Parkway was constructed, the river that poet Joseph Rodman Drake had called "a ravishing spot

Bronx River Parkway

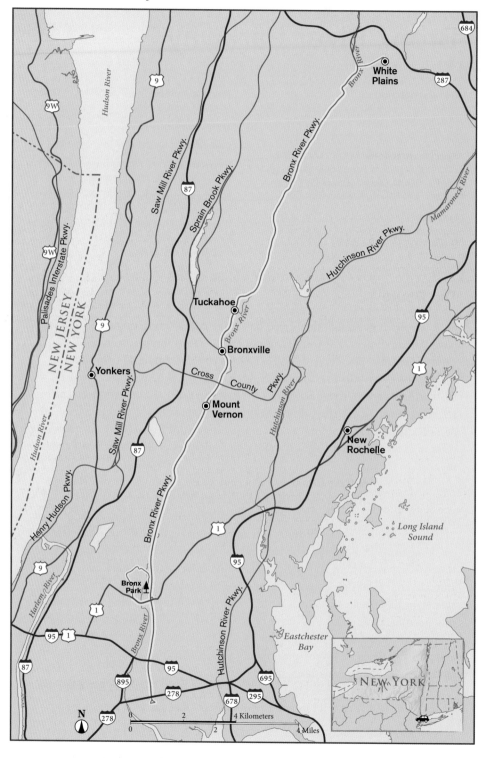

White Plains

684

287

Hudson River

9

9W

9W

Saw Mill River Pkwy.

Sprain Brook Pkwy.

Bronx River Pkwy.

87

Palisades Interstate Pkwy.

NEW JERSEY
NEW YORK

Mamaroneck River

Hutchinson River Pkwy.

95

9

Tuckahoe

Bronx River

Yonkers

Bronxville

1

Cross County Pkwy.

Mount
Vernon

Hutchinson River

Saw Mill River Pkwy.

Hudson River

New
Rochelle

87

Henry Hudson Pkwy.

Harlem River

9

Long Island
Sound

Bronx River Pkwy.

1

Bronx
Park

95

Hutchinson River Pkwy.

Eastchester
Bay

1

95

1

87

895

95

278

678

695

295

N

278

0   2   4 Kilometers

0   2   4 Miles

NEW YORK

Bridges across the Bronx River Parkway create the feeling of a country road.

formed for a poet's dwelling" in 1817 now had a more apt descriptor: the newspapers called it an "open sewer." Decades of residential and commercial waste transformed this waterway in ways that seemed irreversible, and while some efforts were made toward conservation, industrial dumping and other injurious activities repeatedly undid what little that restoration-minded individuals could accomplish.

Something permanent had to be done, and in 1974, a lasting solution finally took hold. A group of concerned citizens created an organization called the Bronx River Restoration, partnering with governmental agencies, other nonprofit organizations, and hundreds of like-minded volunteers to clean the river and keep it as pristine as its urban location will allow. Today you can drive along this meandering waterway and see trees, mowed lawns, flowers, and birds where mills once belched pollutants into the current.

Just 23 miles long, this parkway seems to go by in the blink of an eye—especially at modern roadway speeds—so I do recommend that you make a stop or two along its length, pulling off at one or more of the exits and circling back to park and stroll through some of the Bronx River Reservation.

White Plains to Hartsdale

Before you start your drive south on the parkway, pay a visit to **Kensico Dam Plaza County Park.** The 300-foot-high dam on the south end of Kensico Reservoir stands as one of the area's most impressive construction projects, mainly because of the feat of engineering and material movement required to create it. Using turn-of-the-20th-century transportation and technology, the largely Italian immigrant workforce moved stone from the quarry at nearby Cranberry Lake Park, and hauled away construction debris to landfills on a railroad built exclusively for this project.

Here in this Westchester park, you can also visit **The Rising,** the county's September 11 memorial. It's easy to find in the park—an open structure with a tall spire that becomes unmistakable as you move toward it. The memorial contains the names of all the Westchester residents who perished in the terrorist attack and the collapse of the World Trade Center towers, as well as a quote about each of the victims, supplied by their families. It can be approached from any direction, and its structure allows visitors to move in, through, and around it to view all of the names and quotes.

From here, it's easy to get onto the Bronx River Parkway. Follow the signs and start driving south. You'll notice almost immediately that this road seems narrow compared to most highways in New York City, because it was built long before sport utility vehicles were even considered by car manufacturers. Originally, when the parkway first opened in 1925, drivers would maintain a leisurely 35 miles per hour on the parkway, to give them the chance to admire the scenery and the "rusticated" stone bridges that arch across the road at each exit.

Harstdale offers visitors a number of interesting stops. **Ferncliff Cemetery** serves as the final resting place for a long list of celebrities including Ed Sullivan, Basil Rathbone, Judy Garland, Jerome Kern, Joan Crawford, Jam-Master Jay, Heavy D, Aaliyah, Oscar Hammerstein, Thelonious Monk, Paul Robeson, and Malcolm X. John Lennon and Jim Henson both were cremated here, as was former New York State governor Nelson Rockefeller. Captain of industry Tom Carvel (born Carvelas) is buried here, not far from the site of his very first Carvel Ice Cream store (see "Your Ice Cream Stop" page 297) on Ridge Road in Hartsdale. The 1936-built store closed in 2008 and was torn down when developers bought the land for other purposes.

If you have a passion for Revolutionary War history, you may want to pass by **Odell House** (425 Ridge Rd.), the headquarters of Comte de Rochambeau, commander in chief of the French expeditionary forces, in the summer of 1781. The 7,000 French troops virtually doubled the size of General George Washington's army, making it possible for the Continental Army to seize Yorktown and win the Battle of the Chesapeake—and hence, the war for American independence.

Hartsdale to Tuckahoe

From the parkway itself, the view consists almost entirely of leafy trees and occasional glimpses of the Bronx River, but the adorable village of **Tuckahoe** makes exit 3 a worthwhile stop. If you're old enough to remember the television situation comedy *Maude*, one of Norman Lear's several *All in the Family* spinoffs, the Findlay family lived here in this tony Westchester County community.

Tuckahoe became a center of commerce in the early 19th century when miners unearthed a vein of bright-white marble beneath the town. Builders and architects sought such a material for high-end municipal construction projects, so the marble quarry soon provided jobs to immigrants from Italy, Ireland, and Germany in the 1840s, and later to recently freed African Americans after the Civil War. Two train depots opened nearby, and for more than 60 years this little town thrived with carloads of its prized metamorphic rock leaving daily for New York City and Washington, DC. By the early 20th century, however, the vein had been harvested beyond its capacity, and the marble industry shrank to a shadow of its heyday.

Bronx River Park is the result of a massive river restoration project.

Today the 0.5-square-mile town center features shops, restaurants, and services for the 6,000 or so residents, as well as access to the Bronx River Reservation, the parkland that runs along the eastern edge of the parkway. Tuckahoe provides on-street parking and some lots where you can leave your car and walk along the paved path that parallels the Bronx River. Joggers, skaters, cyclists, and dog-walkers all use this trail, so you are likely to be in good company, even in the middle of a weekday afternoon.

Bronx Park

Back on the parkway, it's only a ten-minute drive to the interchange for Bronx Park, where the **New York Botanical Garden** occupies 250 acres with more than one million plants in 50 separate gardens and collections. Take exits 9W-E or 8W and follow the cloverleaf around to Dr. Theodore Kazamiroff Boulevard, which leads to the park entrance at 2300 Southern Blvd. Just about every season produces a different spectacle here, from the azalea garden that begins to bloom in April to the chrysanthemum beds in fall. In winter, the conservatories produce gorgeous flowers and exotic plants that you can tour in the cozy warmth of a well-tended greenhouse. The park also features a 50-acre forest, a tiny sample of the natural woods that covered this entire area when the Weckquasageek fished in the Aquehung.

Central Park gets all the attention, but **Bronx Park** rivals it in plant and animal diversity, bird populations, and scenic quality. Here the Bronx River creates a deep gorge, where a floodplain forest and a red maple swamp shelter the river along the gorge's floor. Walking along the river, fishing, birdwatching, and leaf-peeping all attract visitors from throughout the five boroughs of New York City, and chances are good that you will hear a number of different languages spoken here as you enjoy the natural surroundings in the heart of the Bronx.

If you've got an urge to see an aardvark, a collared lemur, or an Asian elephant before you leave the park, pay a visit to the **Bronx Zoo,** where 265 acres of habitats will provide you with enough animal entertainment to fill your entire afternoon. Choose the Total Experience Ticket to add the Butterfly Garden, Congo Gorilla Forest, Wild Asia Monorail, and other special attractions to your day, and plan to spend the time you need to enjoy as many exotic creatures as you can.

From Bronx Park, the parkway continues just 4 miles to the Bruckner Expressway, while the Bronx River empties into the East River in another 2 or 3 miles.

LONG ISLAND
SCENIC DRIVES

27

Montauk Highway

Southampton to Montauk Point

General description: Cropland, vineyards, and farm stands on this 32-mile route create a stunning paradox with tony towns and shopping for the ultra-fashionable on the southern outskirts of Long Island. Sniff the salty air of marshes along Block Island Sound, load up on just-picked apples and grapes, and wend your way to the lighthouse on the tip of the island's south shore.

Special attractions: Montauk Point State Park, Camp Hero State Park, Hither Hills State Park, Shadmoor State Park, upscale shopping in Southampton, Water Mill Museum, wineries, Georgica Pond, Cedar Point County Park, Amagansett National Wildlife Refuge, Amagansett Marine Museum, Miss Amelia's Cottage, Napeague State Park, ferry to Block Island

Location: On the southeast end of Long Island. Begin in Southampton, NY; end at

the southern tip of the island at Montauk Point.

Route number: NY 27

Travel season: Year-round, though summer and fall are the most active times

Camping: Sears Bellows County Park in Hampton Bays, Cedar Point County Park in Easthampton, Shinnecock East County Park in Southampton, Hither Hills State Park and Montauk County Park in Montauk

Services: In Southampton, Water Mill, Bridgehampton, Sagaponack, Wainscott, Montauk. It's a good idea to get gas before you start driving this route, as gas prices skyrocket the farther east you go on NY 27.

Nearby attractions: Whaling and Historical Museum in Sag Harbor, Conscience Point National Wildlife Refuge, Shinnecock Reservation

The Route

The southern tip of Long Island looks deceptively easy to reach on maps: Just one driving route goes all the way out to Montauk Point, and the dense population that clogs Nassau and western Suffolk Counties all the way from Queens seems to dissipate as you head to this eastern promontory. What we must take into consideration, however, is the extraordinary popularity of eastern Long Island and the proximity of this lovely, remote place to the most populated city in the US. Even if a tiny fraction of 1 percent of this population decides to head out to Montauk on a beautiful summer day, it results in tens of thousands of people on this one road.

Now that I've put that statement out there, let me say this: Go anyway. First, it's a treat to see how that tiny fraction of 1 percent lives in this breathtakingly

Once you pass through Amagansett, the scenery changes to coastal grassland.

Montauk Highway: Southampton to Montauk Point

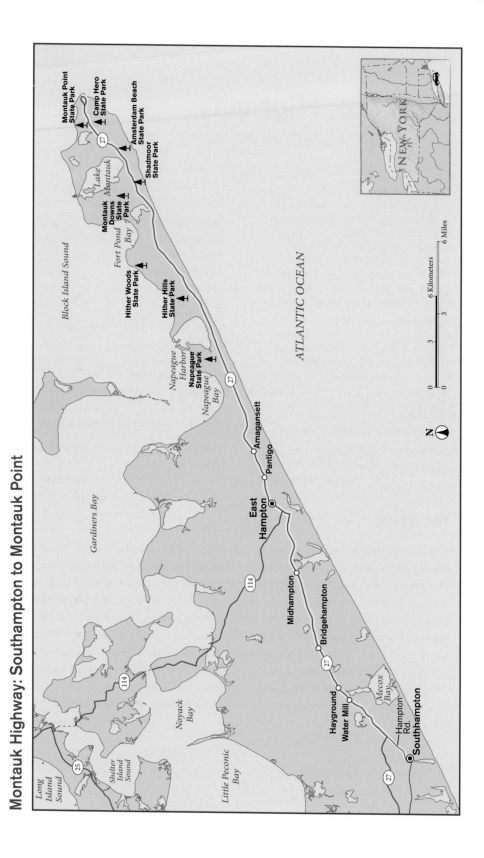

expensive and exclusive area. Second—and much more compelling—people in New York State who will never be able to afford even a hotel room in this area still deserve to experience its pleasures. Sleek beach views, acres of grapevines, marshes filled with birds, weathered gray-shingled homes, and causeways over rippling inlets are sights for city-weary eyes, regardless of the visitor's income level.

In between the natural sights and the well-appointed homes, truly great shopping awaits. Whether you enjoy poking through thrift and consignment shops, searching antiques shops for lucky finds, or browsing the racks at LoveShackFancy, you will find plenty of satisfying entertainment in the town centers of communities like Southampton, Amagansett, and Montauk.

We mentioned it in the notes above, but it bears repeating: Fill your gas tank before you reach Southampton. Gas prices climb precipitously once you're in the Hamptons, and most of us think twice before paying 20 to 70 cents above the state average rate per gallon.

Southampton to Water Mill

The first thing you may notice about **Southampton,** especially if you drove through the Hamptons along thickly wooded roads to get here, is that the homes in this town are remarkably visible. Lining the main road with carefully managed and landscaped yards, these meticulously maintained, gray-shingled homes tell a complete story about this community on their own. People here are likely to take the Long Island Railroad in from New York and walk around town, so the homes, restaurants, shopping, and other services are clustered here in a way that seems almost old-fashioned. The architecture carries this perception through as well, much of it dating back to the 1800s.

A number of houses in and around town have been listed on the National Register of Historic Places, and while most of these are still private residences, you are welcome to drive by them to appreciate the style and impeccable maintenance. The Second Empire–style commercial office building at 300 Hampton Rd. (NY 27A) was constructed in 1875 for Captain C. Goodale, a well-to-do ship captain. **Balcastle,** on the corner of Herrick and Little Plains Roads, features an ivy-covered, one-and-a-half-story octagonal tower to complete its resemblance to an Irish castle; builder and cabinet-maker Joshua Edward Ellison Jr. designed and built this home to share with his wife, Emma Rose, of a prominent local family. At 115 Hill St., the condominium building known as **Whitefield** originally served as a summer residence for engineer James Breese. The 1858 mansion featured a 72-foot music room and formal gardens.

If you'd like a close look at some of this period architecture, pay a visit to the **Rogers Mansion Museum Complex** and **Southampton Historical Museum** at

17 Meeting House Ln., a right turn on North Sea Road from NY 27. The Rogers family settled here in 1648, and the 12 buildings in the complex are all listed on the National Register of Historic Places. Most of the buildings were constructed in the late 1800s, but the mansion itself originates in 1750. The Sayre Barn, built in 1739, became part of the British holdings in this area during the Revolutionary War, making it a symbol of tyranny for the local residents.

The highway leads through Southampton's vibrant shopping district, where you'll find men's and women's clothing stores, upscale gift boutiques, galleries, ice cream and candy stores, and the Southampton Hospital Foundation Thrift Shop—incongruous but welcome amidst the tonier brand-name wares.

YOUR ICE CREAM STOP: THE FUDGE COMPANY

If you can make it past the fudge counter in this corridor-shaped confectionary without blowing all of your cash on melt-in-your-mouth chocolate, the ice cream is, if anything, even more satisfying. This is the only place in New York where we found Honey Hill Farms frozen yogurts, with indulgent flavors like Moon Pie (with graham crackers and cinnamon swirled through it along with the marshmallow), butter toffee popcorn, birthday cake, and snickerdoodle cookie dough. There's full-fat ice cream, too, from the hard-to-find Schrafft's brand that once dominated the New York City ice cream scene. This establishment calls itself "the candy and frozen dessert shop for the rich and famous," so you can breathe the same rarified air as the fabulously wealthy while enjoying something yummy.

Take NY 27 east as you leave Southampton, and watch for a smattering of wineries that chose the South Fork instead of the more popular North to pursue the wine craft. **Duck Walk Vineyards** comes into view fairly quickly, its chateau reminiscent of one you might see in France. It's appropriate that this is the first winery you see, as this vineyard is one of the oldest and most established in Long Island's vibrant wine scene. Its large tasting rooms, award-winning wines, and lovely grounds make a stop here an excellent introduction to Long Island's many vineyards.

From the moment you set foot on its sidewalks, Southampton feels like a world apart.

As you enter the hamlet of **Water Mill,** the big windmill in the town park lets you know that milling played a major role in this area's development. In fact, that heritage extends all the way back to 1644, when the town gave colonist Edward Howell 40 acres of land here on which to build a gristmill, giving local settlers a place to grind their grain. The mill, first constructed on a pond a little north of the town park, continued to work for residents well into the 1800s. When it fell into disuse in the early 1900s, the local ladies' auxiliary raised money for its renovation and preservation. Today you can visit the **Water Mill Museum**—listed on the National Register of Historic Places—at 41 Old Mill Rd., a left turn from NY 27.

Once you're past Water Mill, the continued route becomes remarkably rural. Farm stands and markets edge the road as hundreds of acres of farmland extend behind them, most probably reaching all the way to the shores of Long Island Sound. Stores along this stretch include woodworking supplies and specialty items for boats, with the occasional antiques dealer in the mix.

Bridgehampton to East Hampton

As you enter the hamlet of Bridgehampton, a sign identifies this stretch as part of the Bridgehampton Heritage Area, first settled in 1656. If you want to know more, head for the **William Corwith House**—which doubles as the Bridgehampton Museum—at 2368 Montauk Hwy. (NY 27). The Corwith House, built in 1830, served as a boardinghouse and underwent a significant expansion in the 1880s when interest in the Hamptons as a vacation destination increased. Boarders could walk the 2 miles to the beach or take a horse-drawn jitney that left from right in front of the house. Today your visit to the house includes exhibition galleries and period rooms, which are open Mon through Fri (plus Sat in summer).

Watch for another older house on the corner of Montauk Highway and Ocean Road. The **Nathaniel Rogers House** now bears the name of its architect, but it was originally the home of Abraham T. Rose, who had it built in 1824. Rogers himself remodeled it in 1840, and other families renovated, redecorated, and added on to the house throughout the 19th century. The Bridgehampton Historical Society recently took over stewardship of the house, and will supervise a major restoration and turn it into a headquarters for their organization.

A thriving town center offers plenty of fun shopping at boutiques for women's clothing, jewelry, and hats (seriously, hats), some brand-name men's clothing and housewares shops, and interesting places for lunch or dinner.

The big windmill lets you know that you're in Water Mill.

As you leave Bridgehampton, make a left at the first traffic light on Sagg Road and drive about 200 yards to reach **Wölffer Estate Winery.** Founded in 1987, this 55-acre winery has a Tuscan look and feel, and considers itself "an American winery in the classic European tradition." Making use of the unusual combination of fertile glacial moraine and cool Atlantic Ocean breezes, the winery produces award-winning vintages that are acclaimed as companions for a wide range of cuisines. The elegant tasting room makes a great place to spend some time sampling.

When you return to Montauk Highway, pass through the village of Sagaponack and watch for a parking area outside of Wainscott on the edge of **Georgica Pond.** You'll need to park and walk into the reeds a bit to actually see this very pretty coastal lagoon, where you will likely share the view with canoeists, kayakers, and boating guides. If you're a fan of Broadway shows or a fanatic for Kennedy family lore, you may recognize the name of this pond as the location of the **Grey Gardens estate** chronicled in the 1975 documentary and Tony-winning 2006 show of the same name, where relatives of Jacqueline Bouvier Kennedy lived as eccentric recluses with as many as 52 cats. (The mansion itself is at 3 West End Rd. in Easthampton, and has been completely renovated; it is a private residence, so please respect the owners' privacy.) Other luminaries who have lived or still live in the Georgica Pond neighborhood include Stephen Spielberg, Martha Stewart, Calvin Klein, and Ronald Perelman. President Bill Clinton and First Lady Hillary Clinton vacationed here at the Spielberg home in 1998 and 1999.

Across the road on the left, signs direct you up Stephen Hands Path to Northwest Road, where you'll find **Cedar Point County Park.** If you're carrying lunch, this is a great place to enjoy it in the park's picnic area, where a snack bar and general store can provide cold drinks and munchies. Best of all, this 607-acre park offers open views of **Gardiner's Bay,** often without the crowds you may find at Montauk.

When you return to Montauk Highway and turn east once again, East Hampton becomes your next destination. Not quite as chic as Southampton but still decidedly upmarket, the town boasts a windmill in its central square and a variety of older homes with a deliberately weathered, coastal tone to their otherwise impeccably maintained exteriors. This is the most likely place on the South Fork to spot very wealthy residents and their guests from New York City, Hollywood, and other centers of commerce. As I write this, East Hampton stands as the hot vacation spot of the moment for people with more money than they can spend—and it's not uncommon for them to spend $80,000 and more per month to rent a house

Georgica Pond is the home of many famous people, as well as the Grey Gardens mansion.

at the height of the season. It's no wonder that the shops in the town center carry designers like Stacey Bendet, Zimmerman, Alexandre Birman, Altea, and Elie Tahari, along with a number of one-of-a-kind boutiques with merchandise at staggering prices. The cost may be out of our league, but it's still great fun to see what everyone's wearing at the Hamptons this season.

Amagansett to Montauk Point

On your way into Amagansett, pass the **Bayberry House & Garden Center,** a nursery and landscaping establishment that started here back in 1959, long before this branch of Long Island became the playground it is today. As nurseries go, this is one of the grandest, so if you're a fan of trees and shrubs, make a stop here to stroll through the 14-acre landscaped grounds and see what's growing.

You're nearly at the end of your journey to Montauk Point, but Amagansett presents a number of interesting opportunities to stop. The Amagansett Historical Association operates three museums, including the one at **Miss Amelia Cottage,** a 1725 cottage on the land owned by the men who founded this town. The **1850 Lester Barn** stands on the same property, and the **Phoebe Edwards Mulford House,** built in 1805, is also open to the public.

Nearby on Bluff Road, you'll find the **Marine Museum** with its collection of artifacts and information on the history of whaling on Eastern Long Island. It's worth driving around the neighborhoods here to get a sense of Long Island coastal living that you won't necessarily absorb from Montauk Highway. Amagansett is essentially your last stop before the drive to Montauk Point (which is just a few miles down the road), so you may want to linger here a bit before rejoining the traffic out to the eastern end.

From here, the road takes you along a narrow sand spit with woods on both sides. This is **Napeague State Park,** a predominantly pine woodland, and you can watch the trees get shorter the farther east you go—the result of winds, weather, and shallower roots as you head toward the point. You can see water on either side as well: the **Atlantic Ocean** to your right, and Gardiner Bay to the left.

Keep an eye out for two seafood restaurants, **Clam Bar** at Napeague and a house-size restaurant with a big blue sign that says "Lunch," just after the East Hampton Nature Preserve. At Clam Bar, you can sit outside and enjoy the fresh ocean breezes while you munch on locally caught clams, shrimp, mussels, lobster, and today's fresh fish. "Lunch" has another name: **The Lobster Roll,** and in addition to its namesake dish, you'll find just about every seafood favorite you could want to try. Just down the road, **Morty's Oyster Stand** offers a little more upscale menu of seafood, burgers, salads, and a raw bar featuring East Coast oysters.

After the densely populated areas bisected by Montauk Highway since your drive began in Southampton, the upcoming respite from houses and packed town centers may seem almost lonely in comparison. **Hither Hills State Park** comes up quickly after the restaurants, with a sandy ocean beach that can be jammed with bathers on hot summer days. Hither Hills and the neighboring Napeague State Park share stewardship of a Bird Conservation Area, where pelagic species (birds that almost never come ashore on the mainland) and at-risk shorebird species, including the endangered piping plover, can rest and nest on protected land. Just offshore, **Hicks Island** hosts many pairs of least tern and common tern that nest undisturbed by human encroachment.

The two parks also share a natural phenomenon that fascinates both resident and visiting hikers: **The Walking Dunes of Napeague Trail.** Dunes along Napeague Bay shift with the winds, so a dune you saw in April may be somewhere else entirely by June. Every walk reveals the way the dunes have buried trees and shrubs in their path, or moved to uncover an area that lay buried for an entire season or longer. Many people hike this 0.75-mile trail regularly, just to see what may have changed since their last visit. The trail is easy to find at the end of Napeague Harbor Road between Napeague and Hither Hills State Parks on Napeague Harbor.

In about 2,000 feet after Hither Hills Park, a pull-off gives you the opportunity to see **Napeague Isthmus,** overlooking Napeague Bay. This is the last stop before you drive through more oak and pine forest to reach the town of Montauk.

If things feel much more casual here than they did in the Hamptons, it's no accident. Montauk comes from an entirely different state of mind, as do many remote towns on the farthest outskirts of populated areas. Built originally as a settlement for workers who tended to wealthy Easthampton farmers' livestock, Montauk became the site of the first American cattle ranch in the 1740s. The First House was built near Hither Hills State Park (it burned down in 1917), and the **Second House** stands in town at its original location, just as it has since the 1700s—it's a museum, so you can visit it if you like. The area's Third House now serves as the county park headquarters.

In the early 20th century, developer Carl Fisher determined that he could turn Montauk into another Miami Beach, a resort community he designed and built with tremendously successful results. He had begun construction and completed many elements of his design, including the town layout, the golf course, the Manor, a tall office building, and recreational areas, but when the stock market crashed in October 1929, his dream vanished with his funds. Nonetheless, Montauk became a favorite with tourists in the 1960s and continues to be a vacation destination, embracing a more casual—albeit still pricey—atmosphere than the towns to the west.

Here you'll find the kinds of amenities you probably expected to see all along the Montauk Highway: pancake houses, T-shirt shops, beachwear and surfboard stores, the Pink Tuna Taxi, and a lot more four-wheel-drive vehicles than BMWs. **Montauk Downs State Park golf course**—a holdover from Carl Fisher's day—attracts many golfers who want to play by the ocean, and **Shadmoor State Park** features more than 2,400 linear feet of unspoiled ocean beach skirted by high, shadbush-covered sand bluffs. At the very end of the road at Montauk Point, the state saved the last of this undeveloped coastline for visitors and residents to enjoy by making it a state park.

Before you enter **Montauk Point State Park,** make a stop at **Camp Hero State Park,** a World War II military base with a remarkable story. Back in the 1940s, the US built a number of coastal defense points to guard against European invasion. Camp Hero might have played a pivotal role if the country were ever attacked, so to keep the enemy from detecting this important base, they built it to look like a New England fishing village from the air. Happily Camp Hero never saw action, but its National Historic Landmark status allows it to remain a testament to American ingenuity. Today this park features some of the best surf fishing in the US, as well as pristine beaches, maritime forest, and exemplary bird habitat.

Your journey ends at **Montauk Lighthouse** in Montauk Point State Park. The oldest lighthouse in New York State, Montauk was authorized by the Second Congress under President George Washington in 1792, and it began to guide ships along the coast in 1796. It still operates as an aid to navigation, now with the added distinction of National Historic Landmark status. The Montauk Historical Society conducts tours and operates the museum and gift shop just down the park road from the lighthouse.

The very end of Long Island, directly in front of the lighthouse at **Look Out Point,** affords you a view of Block Island, Rhode Island, and Connecticut across the water. This is the best place on Long Island to watch for seabirds as well: common eider, white-winged and surf scoter, northern gannet, and many other birds overwinter in the waters just off the Montauk coast.

If you've reached this point, linger a while and stretch your legs in one or more of these scenic state parks before getting back in your car and fighting the traffic back down the island.

Montauk Light signals the eastern end of Long Island.

28

North Fork

Riverhead to Orient Point

General description: Small towns, open cropland, acres of grapevines, and dozens of wineries—this 29-mile drive reveals a side of Long Island many people never discover.

Special attractions: Long Island Wine Trail, Railroad Museum of Long Island, Long Island Science Center, Atlantis Marine World: Long Island Aquarium, Bayview Market and Farms, Jamesport Country Store, Gabrielsen's Country Farm, Hallock Homestead, Hallock's Cider Mill, The Old House (National Historic Landmark), Old Burying Ground cemetery, Southold Indian Museum, Horton's Point Lighthouse, Custer Institute, Museums of Historic Southold, ferry to Shelter Island, East End Seaport Museum, Oysterponds museums, Poquatuck Park

Location: The North Fork of Long Island, on the northeastern end of the island in Suffolk County

Route number: NY 25 East

Travel season: Spring, summer, and fall; passable in winter, but snow may make roads slippery, especially toward the end of the route

Camping: Cliff and Ed's Campground, Cutchogue; Cupsogue Beach County Park, Westhampton; Eastern L. I. Kampgrounds, Greenport

Services: In Riverhead, Jamesport, Southold, Greenport, and Orient

Nearby attractions: The Big Duck, Shelter Island

The Route

Where do Long Islanders go to get away from all the congested roadways and commercial areas on the western part of the island?

It turns out that they don't have to head to the mainland—there are plenty of scenic views, open spaces, and country roads on the North Fork. This northeasternmost stretch of Long Island presents visitors with rolling cropland, thick woods, and a remarkable concentration of grape-growers producing the island's most famous and celebrated vintages. Even if you're not a wine drinker, the hillsides covered with flourishing vines provide enough verdant, visual relief that you will want to visit here more than once.

The 29-mile drive on NY 25 may appear short, but the route offers so many places to stop and sample the North Fork's bounty that you won't want to rush to the scenic lookout at the end. Unlike its counterpart on the South Fork, this route provides abundant farm stands full of seasonal fresh fruit and vegetables in summer and fall, and loaded with jellies, honey, syrups, juices, baked goods, and other home-cooked and packaged products year-round. In between, the North Fork's towns work to preserve their lengthy heritage by saving and renovating some of

North Fork: Riverhead to Orient Point

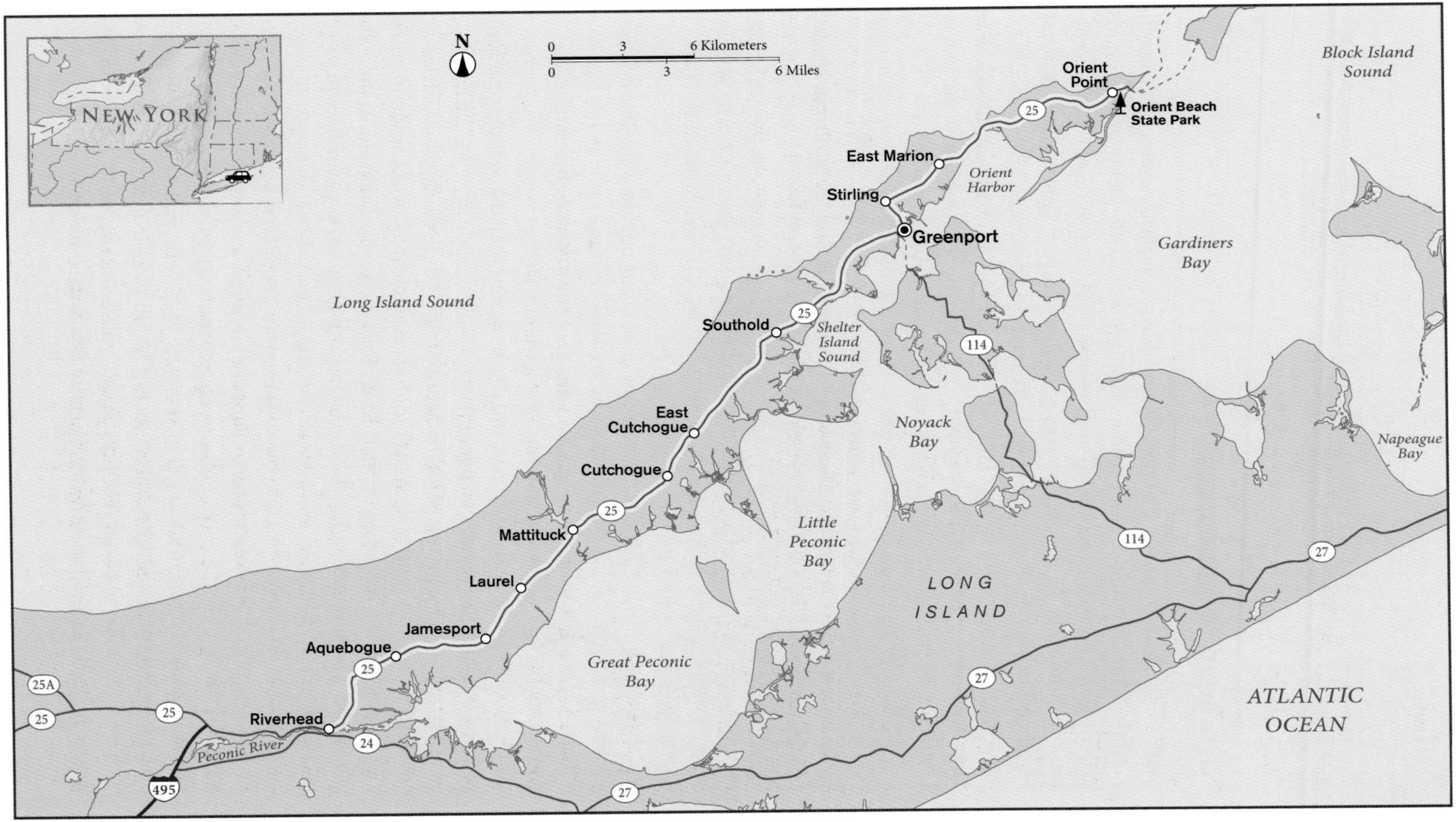

the oldest buildings in the entire state. You'll find homesteads, mansions, and churches to tour, as well as volunteer docents who are delighted to chat with you about their hamlet's heritage.

Riverhead to Jamesport

Your scenic drive begins in Riverhead, named for its position at the mouth of the Peconic River. Not only is Riverhead a charming town with plenty of restaurants, galleries, and tourist attractions to keep you busy, but it also serves as an excellent introduction to the North Fork and its agricultural thrust. **Green Earth Natural Foods Market** offers healthy options from an all-organic sensibility, as well as knowledge and advice to help you make the best choices for your own body. **Farm Country Kitchen,** in the same neighborhood, provides fresh-made dishes in a late 1800s former colonial home overlooking the Peconic River.

In Riverhead, you'll also find more museums than you would expect in a town of this size; Riverhead serves as a mini-cultural center for the North Fork, with the **Long Island Science Center, Long Island Aquarium,** and the **Railroad Museum of Long Island** all stationed here. Geared primarily to children, the highly interactive science center exhibits allow young people to explore many of the basic facts that make up our physical world. The Railroad Museum's site in Riverhead houses most of the museum's rolling stock, as well as its World's Fair Miniature Train, which gives rides to visitors when weather permits.

At the Long Island Aquarium, you can take a tour boat into the Peconic Estuary and learn about Long Island waterway ecology, or wade into the salt marsh and get a close look at the marine life that makes the saltwater and sandy bottom its home. The aquarium features a pavilion for African penguins, a reptile exhibit populated by snakes, lizards, and dragons, and the Lost Temple of Atlantis, guarded by four Japanese snow monkeys.

When you're ready to explore the rest of the North Fork, take NY 25 east out of town. Almost immediately, farm stands and garden centers begin to come into view, as do the first of more than 25 wineries you will see on this route. Long Island's fairly young but highly successful winemaking industry focuses on producing wines from vinifera wine grapes, or species specifically native to southern Europe. Here on the North Fork, the maritime climate tempers the weather to create a long growing season for grapes native to the Mediterranean region, including Cabernet Sauvignon, Cabernet Franc, Merlot, Pinot Noir, Chardonnay, Riesling, and Sauvignon Blanc. (You will see other varieties of wine as you travel through the region, but these are the most popular of Long Island's offerings.) The North Fork hosts 55 of Long Island's 90 wineries, so you will have plenty from which to choose if you'd like to stop and sample some excellent vintages.

Comtesse Therese Winery also features a bistro, so this may be a good place to stop for lunch. Set in a restored 1830s house, the restaurant features specialties by a Cordon Bleu-trained chef and outdoor dining on the nicest days. The winery's Hungarian Oak Merlot has been acclaimed as the best Merlot on Long Island, and the Russian Oak Chardonnay also earns high ratings from critics.

You can't miss **Bay View Farm Market,** with the bright pink McCormick-Deering Farmall tractor in front and the fields of wildflowers extending for many acres beyond the building. Brilliantly colored fruits and vegetables displayed here will make you slow down even if you don't need any peppers or squash. Here we discovered fresh-roasted corn, a favorite farm market offering all along this route, and we hopped out of the car to meet the dairy cows that came right up to the fence.

More wineries line the road as you approach Jamesport: the aptly named **Jamesport Vineyard** with its rustic, pine-paneled tasting room and its long list of award-winning wines, produced using strictly sustainable practices; and **Sherwood House Vineyards,** where house winemaker Gilles Martin directed the production of wines at some of France's most highly regarded vineyards and California's internationally recognized sparkling wines before coming to Long Island. The diminutive **Diliberto Winery** has produced award-winning wines since its inception, serving guests of the tasting room at bistro tables overlooking the vineyard, and **Jason's Vineyard** wines are made by Jason, who worked in the Medoc, Premiere Cote de Bordeaux, and Cadiallac regions of France before planting his own Chardonnay, Merlot, and Cabernet grapes. **Paumanok Vineyards** produces fewer than 12,000 cases of each of its wines annually, so sampling each may give a clue to why this winery was nominated as American Winery of the Year by *Wine Enthusiast* magazine in 2013.

Be sure to stop at the **Jamesport Country Store,** where locally made candy, soaps, and jams crowd shelves and fill baskets alongside all manner of country gift items. Locals come here to fill their Easter baskets with jellybeans and chocolate bunnies, and to plunder the bowls of Christmas ornaments under the store's trees in November and December.

Still need more country? **Gabrielsen's Country Farm** serves the area's gardens with large selections of annuals, perennials, shrubs, and garden decorations. In fall, Gabrielsen's mounts an ongoing festival that features an 11-acre corn maze, where you can lose yourself and your traveling companions among the tightly packed corn stalks, or come face-to-face with dairy cows, goats, and alpacas—my personal farmyard favorite.

Why a Big Duck? More to the point, if building a big cement duck will get you on the National Register of Historic Places, why not do it? That wasn't the first thing that went through the mind of Martin Maurer, the duck farmer who had this sculpture designed and built in 1930 and 1931, but his Big Duck launched a

The Big Duck.

dubious tradition in advertising that has spread around the world. Today, the term "duck architecture" applies to any such piece of novelty architecture in which a product is represented literally by a building.

Maurer built the duck to bring attention to his duck farm, from which he sold duck eggs and farm-raised white Pekin ducks as poultry. He engaged the talents of the Collins brothers, a team of Broadway set designers, and worked with a trio of local residents to execute the design. Twenty feet high, 30 feet long, and 18 feet wide, the duck sports eyes made from a Ford Model T's taillights, and its structure uses a technique called ferrocement, or spreading a mixture of cement and sand over steel mesh.

To find the duck from NY 25 in Riverhead, take Cross River Drive (County Route 105) south to NY 24, which is Flanders Road. Turn left (east) onto NY 24 and continue to Big Duck Park. Believe me, you won't miss it. Be sure to stop at the Big Duck during business hours, so you can go inside and visit the gift shop.

Bay View Farm Market is unmistakable as you start your North Fork journey.

Jamesport to Cutchogue

A left turn onto Herricks Lane as you pass through Jamesport will take you to the **Hallockville Museum Farm,** a 28-acre farm on Sound Avenue that preserves 19 buildings spanning hundreds of years of agricultural heritage. Hallock Homestead, built in 1765, became the property of the Hallock family after the Revolutionary War and passed from one generation to the next until 1979. So many of the original family's descendants lived in the surrounding homes that the entire area became known as Hallockville. When Eastern European immigrants moved in and bought many of the homes along Sound Avenue, names like Cichanowicz, Sydlowski, and Trubisz blended with the Anglo-Saxon Hallocks, making this town a fine example of the "melting pot" that so much of New York became in the 19th and 20th centuries.

The Hallocks continue to have a presence in the area, as evidenced by the very popular **Hallock's Cider Mill** back on NY 25. Cider in season, homemade soups at any time of year, and fresh-from-the-oven baked goods make this farm market a favorite stop for locals and visitors, especially after what one tourist called "a hard day of wine tasting." We picked up several jars of horseradish jam and plan to go back for more.

If the name of **Clovis Point Wines** doesn't intrigue you—and if you're not a fan of ancient Native American history, you may miss the "point"—then the wines certainly will. In fact, its specialty blend, Archaeology, may be the one that you decide to take home with you. Made only in the years with the very best fruit, it combines Merlot, Cabernet, Petit Verdot, and Syrah grapes in a blend that will last for years in your wine cellar.

You'll know you've reached the hamlet of Laurel when you see **Laurel Lake Vineyards,** where you are encouraged to linger on the two-story deck and enjoy a glass of wine from the antique bar. The owners have chosen some of the most labor-intensive methods for making wine, but the result is high marks in international wine competitions and gold and silver medals at the annual New York Wine & Food Classic. Even better, these artisanal wines are surprisingly affordable.

Hand-sorting the grapes to remove every last imperfect one, **Gramercy Vineyards** produces just three varieties of wine from its own 3.5 acres of Merlot vines, with an eye toward becoming a premier vintner of estate Merlot. Resident winemaker Roman Roth began his winemaking career at 16 in Germany, eventually finding his way to Wölffer Estate Vineyards on Long Island, where the American Sommelier Society named him Winemaker of the Year. Today he strives to make "interesting" wines, in his own words.

YOUR ICE CREAM STOP:
MAGIC FOUNTAIN HOMEMADE ICE CREAM

Have you ever had lavender ice cream? How about ginger, or cucumber, or kulfi—flavored with rosewater, pistachio, and cardamom? Intense flavors, freshly made on premises using local ingredients, make every trip to Magic Fountain an opportunity for a new discovery. Whether it's black cherry bourbon, honey cinnamon, or goat cheese with walnuts and cranberries, you're sure to find something you love here. If you're watching your diet, the nonfat/no-sugar hard yogurts deliver lots of flavor as well with varieties like cherry vanilla and butter pecan. Sorbets and smoothies made from seasonal fruits gathered from local farms round out the extensive menu. You may want to stop here again when you come back through on NY 25 on your way home.

The hamlet of Mattituck turned out to be full of nice surprises. Here you'll find **Love Lane Kitchen,** a locavore-themed eatery that serves breakfast until 2 p.m. daily—and what a breakfast! The fresh produce available from local farms determines specials, and the recipes (pastrami hash, or lemon ricotta pancakes served with fresh blueberries, for example) bring inspiration to the table. There's no waiting for your server to remember to bring you coffee—just help yourself to one of several flavors at the self-serve coffee bar. Before you get back on the road, stop at the **Village Cheese Shop** for some American or European cheeses, pate, and crusty bread to accompany your next wine tasting.

More wineries appear in quick succession as you head toward the town of Cutchogue. **Roanoke Vineyards'** wines are available only from the winery itself—not in stores anywhere in New York State—so if you want to sample the wine the *New York Times* cited with the words, "Roanoke has mastered Cabernet Franc," you'll need to stop here on your way east. (You can also find their wines at the Roanoke Vineyard Wine Bar in Mattituck, on Love Lane.)

At **Pellegrini Vineyards,** the selections of red wines and the winery's Chardonnay have received glowing reviews from *Food & Wine, Wine Enthusiast,* and the *New York Times.* The raves result from the winery's combination of modern winemaking techniques—including Long Island's first stainless steel punch down system, used to extract tannins gently from the grapes—and deep cellars where aging Merlot and Cabernet Sauvignon rest in Hungarian oak barrels. Just down the road, **McCall Wines** tends the largest Pinot Noir vineyard on Long Island, on land that owner Russell McCall saved from development by partnering with the Peconic

Land Trust. He followed this by becoming the first wind-powered farm on the island, and his organic ranch-fed cattle graze next to the winery. Producing a limited number of varieties each year, the winery is best known for its pinots—and its long list of awards led McCall Wines to be named Winery of the Year at the 2013 New York Wine & Food Classic.

Macari Vineyards, where sustainable agriculture has been in practice since its opening in 1995, showcases the family's hands-on operation and holistic approach to winemaking. Among its award-winning wines is Sauvignon Blanc Lifeforce, aged in concrete and stainless steel and lauded by *The Daily Meal* as "a stunning example of what can be accomplished on Long Island."

As you enter the hamlet of **Cutchogue,** watch for signs for historic buildings to your right. This community takes its history seriously—tours of the cluster of 17th- and 18th-century houses, carriage houses, and other structures are given through the summer on weekends, led by volunteer docents of the Cutchogue-New Suffolk Historical Council, who preserve the tales of days' past both orally and in writing. The 19th-century **Carriage House,** where tours begin, holds a small gift shop with a number of books on local history.

This town square may be best known for **The Old House,** the oldest structure on Long Island and one of the oldest in the eastern US—built on a pond in Southold in 1649 by John Budd, it was moved to this spot in 1660 by Budd's daughter, Anna, and her husband after they received it as a wedding gift. Of the six families to which The Old House provided a home over a number of generations, Parker Wickham stands as the most notorious—a Southold town supervisor in the 1770s, he was kidnapped for being a Loyalist to the British crown in 1777 by Connecticut rebels, and was forced by the New York state legislature to give up his property in Southold two years later. The legislature went on to banish him from the state—a questionable edict at best, even for the days before the US Constitution. Wickham moved to Connecticut, where he died shortly thereafter.

The town square also contains a schoolhouse from the 1840s, the Wickham Farmhouse built in 1704, and the **Old Burying Ground,** which dates back to 1717. If you want to know more about the early history of this area, the **Cutchogue New Suffolk Free Library,** a 19th-century building in its own right, contains a whole room dedicated to local history.

Wineries line the road once again as you leave Cutchogue on your way to the town of Southold. One of the oldest wineries on Long Island, **Pugliese Vineyards** is best known for its ports and its sparkling wines—including an unusual sparkling Merlot, which makes a lively dessert wine.

If you've heard of one winery on Long Island, chances are it's **Bedell Cellars,** long established as "a world-class estate," according to the *New York Times.* Bedell has the distinction of receiving a 91 score from *Wine Spectator* for its well-known

Visit the oldest house on Long Island, rightfully called The Old House.

red blend, Musée, the highest score any eastern American red had ever received from the magazine. Just down the road, **Pindar Vineyards** grew from an original 30-acre vineyard to its current 550 acres, and it's still owned by the family that founded it in 1979. A massive composting program conducted on the farm enriches the soil naturally, producing exceptional grapes and a robust selection of wines.

Lenz Winery will appear on your left. This winery has such confidence in its wines that it holds a blind tasting periodically, pitting Lenz wines against some of the finest French vintages and daring the profession's most well-known critics to tell the difference. Each year since the first such tasting in 1996, Lenz wines have received high marks, even when the next sip is something French. See for yourself if these wines are as good as the connoisseurs say.

Raphael is as well known for its tours as it is for its wines, offering a per-person price that includes the tour of the vineyard and production facility and a tasting featuring four wines—along with cheeses, olives, and fresh breads if you wish.

Corey Creek Vineyard offers an award-winning Gewürztraminer.

A stop at **Osprey's Dominion Winery** gives you the opportunity to sample a selection of the most varietals on Long Island—a whopping thirteen different grapes, including Carmenere, Edelzwicker and Spice wines, the only place you'll find these on the island. **Duck Walk Vineyards** maintains a tasting room here on the North Fork, though its vineyard thrives on Long Island's South Fork in Water Mill (see the Southampton to Montauk Point route earlier in this book).

If you're a birder, you may find yourself mysteriously drawn to wines named after your favorite species—so a stop to sample Great Blue Heron Merlot/Cabernet Franc blend or Night Heron Merlot at **Onabay Vineyard** will be particularly satisfying. **Croteaux Vineyard** prides itself on its wide selection of "summer in a glass" rosés, served in a 19th-century carriage barn with a pebble courtyard surrounded by blooming flowers.

The last winery in this cluster is **Mattebella Vineyards,** a 22-acre family farm that produces Chardonnay, Rosé, and a blend of reds. This signature red is the vineyard's Old World Blend, of which fewer than 1,000 cases are produced from the estate's own Merlot, Cabernet Sauvignon, Petit Verdot, and Cabernet Franc grapes.

Southold to Orient Point

The oldest English settlement in New York State (though a handful of individuals came to Long Island the previous year, probably to determine its possibilities for settlement), **Southold** became a town in 1640 when a small group of Puritans from Connecticut settled here, led by Reverend John Youngs. They laid out the town beginning at what is now Town Creek, building a church on the northeast corner of the current cemetery of the First Church of Southold. Very committed to the Puritan ethic, the settlers adopted the Ten Commandments—what they called the Mosaic Code—as their system of law, and maintained a close unity between church and government right up through the Revolutionary War, when many residents took their families and belongings and fled to fight for freedom from England. The British moved in and occupied the area until the end of the war, but not without challenges: a daring 1777 raid on British ships in Sag Harbor moved directly across Southold to reach the moored ships, ending the raid with 90 prisoners. The British later skirmished with members of the Cutchogue militia, firing on houses along Hog Neck from their ship in Peconic Bay.

The Southold Historical Society has done a masterful job of locating, identifying, and collecting many 18th- and 19th-century buildings that represent the hamlet's past. The **Maple Lane Museum Complex** features homes that date back as far as 1750, as well as an 1840 print shop, a blacksmith shop, a barn, corncrib, a school, a farm equipment shed, and even an outhouse. You may enjoy a stop at the **Reichert Family Center and Cosden Price Gallery,** which comes into view on the north side of NY 25 as you drive through Southold. First constructed before 1850, the building served as a store from the 1860s until the mid-20th century, when locally renowned painter Joseph Beckwith Hartranft used it as his studio and gallery. Today the building bears the name of the family that helped to fund its restoration, and it serves as exhibition space for the historical society.

The 58-foot-tall **Horton Point Lighthouse** should be your next stop, both to see the fine views of Long Island Sound and to visit the recently renovated Nautical Museum in the lower level of the Keeper's House. Turn left onto Youngs Avenue and continue to Old North Road to reach the lighthouse. The museum exhibits include artifacts from the War of 1812, the whaling industry, and the history of the lighthouse, as well as paintings of nautical scenes. It's only 120 steps down a wooden staircase to the beach, so this may be a place to stretch your legs for a bit—and if the stairs are too daunting, there's a very pleasant (and flat) nature trail here as well.

Just off NY 25 to the right on Main Bayview Road, the **Southold Indian Museum** tells a different story about this area's heritage, presenting exhibits of pottery, spearheads, soapstone, and tools used by the Long Island Algonquin Indians, nearly all of which were collected by area archaeologists. Special exhibits during the summer months often reveal artifacts in the museum's collection, but not normally on display.

Also on Bayview Road, the **Custer Institute and Observatory** opens to the public on Sat evenings from dark until midnight, with volunteer astronomers available to help you find and identify stars, planets, and other celestial objects in the night sky. The observatory uses a 25-inch, 11-foot-tall Newtonian-style telescope, the largest one in any Long Island public observatory, to look at the sky and bring far-distant objects into focus.

If you're thinking about finding dinner and staying the night to better explore the Southold town center, the **North Fork Table & Inn** preserves the sense of history and country elegance you've enjoyed on your way up the island. The restaurant serves a menu that features freshly caught seafood and local seasonal produce, as well as a selection of Long Island's best wines and artisan cheeses. You'll find Long Island's famous duck on the menu as well. Remarkably, the Inn's well-appointed rooms are no more expensive than some of the island's far less attractive roadside hotels.

As you leave Southold, you'll spot the **Old Field Vineyards,** a fruit farm established in 1974 that turned from selling fruit to winemaking in 1997. Only the fourth family to own and farm this land since the Puritans first arrived here in 1640, the Baiz family—descendants of the Langs, who purchased the land at the end of World War I—planted Merlot and Cabernet Franc vines in the late 1990s, and they now produce Chardonnay, Pinot Noir, and Blanc de Noir wines as well. Just a note: If you have somehow resisted stopping for a tasting on your drive, this is the last winery on this route.

Now the foliage and development on the southern side of the road opens up, and you can see inlets and marinas as Gardiner's Bay extends to your right. Restaurants, clam bars, and occasional galleries appear as you approach Greenport, the last hamlet before Orient Point and the end of the North Fork.

In Greenport, you can take a shortcut to the end of the South Fork by driving onto the ferry to **Shelter Island,** and then driving across the island to take a ferry from its south shore to the Hamptons, all for a fairly nominal price. This summer resort island nearly quadruples its population in the summer months, so the line to board the ferry can be very long; this may be a route you'd rather take in the off-season.

The Horton Point Lighthouse is just 120 steps from the beach.

There's enough going on in Greenport to make you want to stop and explore. The town center features lots of shops with unusual items, from **Greenport Jerky Company** with a wide selection of flavors and gift packages, to nearly a dozen stores with antiques and collectibles. **Lydia's Antiques and Stained Glass,** for example, specializes in handcrafted glass, as well as a personal welcome from one of Lydia's calm, friendly golden retrievers. Plenty of restaurants, T-shirt and souvenir shops, and funky boutiques round out the town's fun shopping district.

Perhaps it's ironic that the **East End Seaport Museum,** near the enclosed carousel on the southern waterfront, inhabits a former railroad station—but there's no ambiguity about the area's long fishing industry history once you're inside. A collection of Fresnel lenses from a number of area lighthouses fascinates many visitors with their facets and their impressive size, as do exhibits about menhaden fishing—a species that is still used for fishmeal, a livestock feed product, and for the fish oil you might purchase as a dietary supplement. (This fish oil also figures prominently in lipstick production—so think about menhaden the next time you put on makeup.)

Now you're on the last stretch of road before the end of the North Fork, lined with homes that feature many styles of early-20th-century architecture. The causeway along the Orient Harbor provides an unobstructed view of the water as you approach East Marion Orient Park and the town of Orient, the final hamlet in your scenic drive. Turn right at the **Soldier's Monument,** a sandstone obelisk, and enter Orient Point, a sleepy town with a ferry to Block Island, Rhode Island, and New London, Connecticut, a cluster of historic buildings, a country store, and a smattering of homes, presumably owned by people who snub the crush of tourist towns in favor of this remoteness on the edge of the sea.

Settled in the late 1600s at the behest of the King of England, the five families who braved the elements to make the easternmost point of Long Island their home still have descendants in the area. Back then, the town received the name Poquatuck, the name of the Indian tribe that lived in the area, but soon the residents renamed it Oysterponds because of the richness of shellfish that lived just off the coast. Some say that the town gave up that name when Oyster Bay, Long Island, became famous as the home of President Theodore Roosevelt, but it may simply have been the desire to associate the town with its most prominent landmark, Orient Point.

As you proceed to the point, a right turn at the sign for **Oysterpond Museums** will take you to a carefully assembled campus of homes and outbuildings that

Great egrets and many other long-legged wading birds fish in the salt marshes.

provide clues about the lifestyles of 18th- and 19th-century residents. A former boardinghouse, two schoolhouses, a dormitory for farm workers, a grain storage shed, and an elegant Federal-style home date back as far as 1720 (in the case of the Federal-style Webb House), and each has been meticulously restored and preserved. The stories of the rescue and relocation of each of these buildings are every bit as interesting as the history that created them.

Make your last stop on this drive at **Orient Beach State Park,** where 45,000 feet of Gardiner's Bay frontage gives you the unobstructed, long-range view of the bay and the ocean beyond for which you've been waiting through this entire trip. Here you can enjoy a maritime forest—a rarity on the eastern coast, earning it National Natural Landmark status—where the scent of red cedar almost overpowers the smells of salt spray and ocean breeze. A saltwater marsh gives you an opportunity to look for black-crowned night heron, great egret, and soaring osprey as they hunt for fish along the shore.

When you're ready, the only way back from here is to go west on NY 25. I hope you made a list of the wineries you'd like to try on your way back—with their leisurely atmosphere and their patios overlooking rows of grapevines, many of these vineyards offer delightful ways to watch the sunset on the edge of Long Island.

29

Ocean Parkway

General description: This 15.5-mile coastal highway connects two of Long Island's most popular and celebrated ocean-front parks: Jones Beach and Robert Moses State Parks.

Special attractions: Jones Beach State Park, Robert Moses State Park, Captree State Park, Gilgo State Park, John F. Kennedy Memorial Wildlife Sanctuary (if you want to hike here, you will need to obtain a permit first—see below), breeding grounds for the endangered piping plover and other seabirds

Location: Nassau County, Long Island, along the island's south shore

Drive routes: Robert Moses Causeway, Ocean Parkway

Travel season: Spring and summer; parts of the parkway often close in winter months

Camping: Nickerson Beach Park on Lido Beach is at the end of Loop Parkway, across the Meadowbrook State Parkway from Jones Beach

Services: Snack bars at beaches; otherwise, there are plenty of amenities in West Islip at the beginning of Robert Moses Causeway

Nearby attractions: Fire Island National Seashore, Gateway National Recreation Area, Bethpage State Park, Seatuck National Wildlife Refuge, Massapequa Preserve

The Route

If Long Island's parkway system represents the best of developer Robert Moses's imagination, then Ocean Parkway must have been his crowning achievement. This ribbon of roadway—from Meadowbrook State Parkway south of Freeport to the Robert Moses Causeway in West Islip—travels along a barrier island with clear, unobstructed access to the Atlantic Ocean, which is nothing short of a miracle on this tightly developed coast of Nassau County.

The short but satisfying route threads through two state parks and provides a quick route to a third, over an extension of the Robert Moses Causeway. To begin, take the Meadowbrook Parkway south to its terminus, crossing a series of islands to reach the barrier island and Jones Beach. When you reach the cloverleaf, follow the signs to Ocean Parkway (not Bay Parkway). As you come out of the cloverleaf, you will be heading east.

A special note to birders: If you want a great shorebird-watching experience, follow the Bay Parkway to the west as you come out of the cloverleaf, and continue to the Coast Guard Station. Turn right at the Coast Guard station and continue around behind it to the parking area. Get out your scope and scan the sandbar and the surrounding open sand—which will vary depending on the tide—to look for

Ocean Parkway

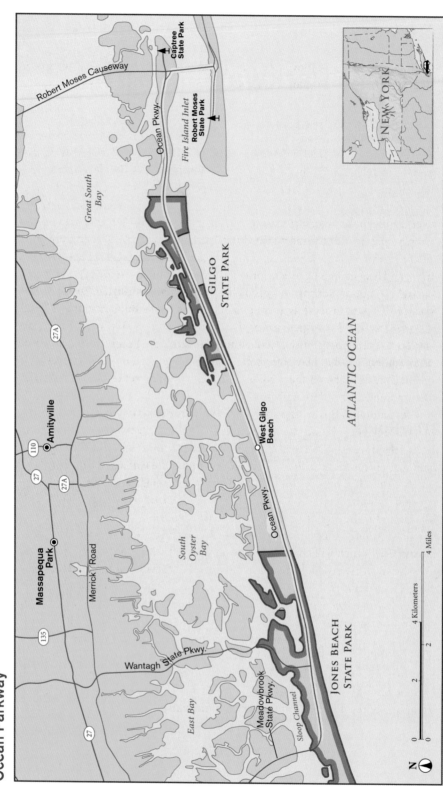

red knot, black-bellied plover, American golden plover, willet, ruddy turnstone, and all of the more common sandpipers, yellowlegs, and sanderlings.

Jones Beach State Park

Six and a half miles of white sand beach extend along the parkway, with the **Atlantic Ocean** ebbing and flowing along this pristine shoreline. If you're visiting on a hot summer day, you may see thousands of people on this beach and frolicking in the waves, a fraction of the six to eight million people who make use of this beach over the course of a normal season. Playing in the ocean is just one of the activities people enjoy here at the most visited state park in New York: Fishing from piers at field 10 (where the park provides a fully stocked bait-and-tackle shop) rivals swimming and beachcombing as a favorite pastime, and the waves are often energetic enough to support surfing and paddle-boarding. Master designer Robert Moses created this park to serve as a sort of landlubber's cruise ship, providing all manner of recreational activities for people who may never be able to afford a luxury trip on an oceangoing vessel. Here visitors can stroll the beach, learn a little history at an outdoor exhibit, play volleyball or miniature golf, go to a concert, get an ice cream cone or lunch on the sand, or take their children to the Theodore Roosevelt Nature Center for indoor activities.

As natural as this setting appears, it may surprise you to learn that Moses actually engineered Jones Island. He saw the opportunity to connect a series of small islands along State Boat Channel by dredging sand out of the channel and building up connecting dunes. This process raised the barrier islands' elevation by 14 feet. He called his creation a "people's park," one that transformed a breeding ground for biting insects into a place where millions of people can interact with the ocean for the cost of a train ticket or a parking fee.

Pass through the roundabout at the Wantaugh Parkway and continue past **Zachs Bay,** which will come into view on your left. After the bay, the grassy, marshy area that expands to your left disguises the **John F. Kennedy Memorial Wildlife Sanctuary,** a 500-acre segment of the much larger wetland you see. The town of Oyster Bay allows hiking in here with a free permit, which you can obtain at the Town of Oyster Bay Parks Department, 977 Hicksville Rd. in Massapequa. If you do go out of your way to obtain a permit, the good news is that it's good for the rest of the year. Paved or sand and gravel trails through this coastal wetland lead to views of Guggenheim Pond, where you may see a variety of long-legged wading birds and you will most assuredly encounter biting insects. Bring your bug spray and apply it before you venture into the marsh.

Shorebirds rest and feed by the thousand at Jones Beach.

Tobay Beach to Gilgo State Park

As you leave Jones Beach State Park, **Tobay Beach Park** takes over the oceanfront. This county park provides access to South Oyster Bay to the north for calm water bathing as well as the Atlantic Ocean, but on summer weekends, it's only open to residents of the Town of Oyster Bay and their guests. If you're passing through on a weekday, you are welcome to enjoy this pretty beach.

After Tobay Beach, the parkway enters Suffolk County and passes through **West Gilgo Beach,** a community created by the people displaced from the town of High Hill Beach when Robert Moses bought that town's land to create Jones Beach State Park. The resort community contained about 80 summer homes, most of which were picked up and moved to this location, either over land on the new causeway or by barge. Since the transition in 1939, many of the homes have been winterized and the residents remain there year-round. It might sound like this would be an interesting place to see up close, but West Gilgo Beach is a gated community.

The ocean beach on your right is **Gilgo Beach,** where the waves are dependable enough to attract a surfing crowd. A Town of Babylon beach, it requires a permit to enter . . . or a stiff admission fee if you're not a resident. You have plenty of state parks beaches available to you along this route if you want to get up close and personal with the ocean.

The parkway opens up to six lanes across at Gilgo Beach, a signal that you are approaching **Gilgo State Park.** This undeveloped park requires a permit and a four-wheel-drive vehicle to enter, and there's no swimming allowed in either the ocean or **Great South Bay**—but if you fish, you may want to look into gaining access (for permit information, visit parks.ny.gov/documents/regions/2020Dash boardPermitGuide.pdf), especially in fall when the striped bass migrate through here. Here you can look for nesting piping plovers (though there are easier places on this route to see them), as well as the endangered sea beach amaranth, a plant that has nearly succumbed to habitat loss that has occurred with the development of so many beaches along the Atlantic seaboard.

Oak Beach and Captree State Park

For a tiny community of mostly summer residents, **Oak Beach** has attracted more than its share of regional attention. Here the controversial Oak Beach Inn entertained thousands of guests nightly for 30 years until 1999. The OBI, as it was known, employed a bartender named Robert "Rosebud" Butt (this is not a joke), who in the 1970s invented the drink we know as Long Island Iced Tea. The uber-popular nightclub drew crowds from as far away as Connecticut and New Jersey, not to mention Manhattan, until noise, traffic, parking, and general rowdiness made OBI such an enemy of local residents that owner Robert Matherson sold it and moved to Key West, Florida, where he opened a nightclub of the same name. In 2003, the new owners had the building demolished.

If being notorious for partying too hard wasn't enough to give Oak Beach a tough rap, more recent events certainly did the job. In 2010 and 2011, while searching for a missing prostitute, police discovered ten bodies along Ocean Parkway in this area—and while the investigation continues as of this writing, police reports indicate that all of these murders look to be the work of a single serial killer over the course of eight years.

Chances are you haven't even slowed down in Oak Beach after reading all of this, so let's roll on to **Captree State Park,** home of the largest public fishing fleet on Long Island. Here you can go saltwater fishing on an open boat, on which you'll be provided with all of the gear you need. If fishing doesn't float your boat, the fleet also offers sightseeing trips. You'll see lots of people fishing from the pier as well, where crabs can be plentiful. Captree has a full-service restaurant and a refreshment stand where the chili dogs are rumored to be legendary, and an area called The Overlook with a stunning view of **Fire Island National Seashore,** just across Fire Island Inlet.

With Fire Island so close by, you may wonder why the parkway does not extend to this national park. Such an extension was part of Moses's original plan back in the 1930s, but the residents of Fire Island—which was not yet a national park at the time—blocked construction, first citing negative economic impact when their remote area became easily accessible. When the concept came up for a second time years later, the residents raised environmental objections that prevented construction once again. Once Fire Island became a National Seashore in 1964, there could be no more development there.

As you enter Captree State Park, the parkway reaches a cloverleaf interchange with the Robert Moses Causeway. Bear right on the causeway and head south.

Robert Moses State Park

There is no better or easier place on Long Island—or perhaps on the entire eastern seaboard—to see piping plovers in their nesting habitat than at **Robert Moses State Park.** Here in a protected area cordoned off from the crush of beach lovers in early summer, the tiny sand-colored plovers scrape tinier dents in the sand, lay their sand-colored eggs, and sit and wait for their tiny, fluffy, sand-colored babies to hatch. Were this area not denoted as protected habitat, these little birds most certainly would be trampled underfoot, as they seem impervious to the crowds around them and don't make a habit of getting out of the way.

What makes this behavior even more perplexing is that these little birds nest alongside much larger birds: American oystercatchers, common terns, least terns, and a number of gull species, all of which choose this particular beach to set up breeding colonies every spring. Here you can watch terns perform the most absurd mating dance we have ever witnessed, holding their wings at crazy angles and bobbing at one another like pre-adolescent middle school nerds at their first mixer. Oystercatchers—stunning black-and-white birds with bright orange bills—do not strut around so, but they are large enough and aggressive enough that they dominate the entire scene. The result is every bit as fascinating as anything on the Discovery Channel.

The endangered piping plover nests in a scrape in the sand at Robert Moses State Park.

If the mating season is not in session when you arrive, this state park still gets high marks for its 5 miles of ocean beach, its fishing piers and ample space for surfcasting, and its perfect conditions for surfing and paddle-boarding. While a summer day may attract a sea of humanity as well as saltwater, this park brings in so many people for good reason.

You have reached the end of the parkway and this scenic drive. When you're ready, you can return to Long Island by taking the Robert Moses Causeway due north to West Islip.

30

New York 39

Avon to Letchworth State Park

General description: Take a 32-mile drive along a country road to the Grand Canyon of the East, a gorge masterfully incised by the Genesee River.

Special attractions: Letchworth State Park, Glen Iris Inn, Nation's Road Important Bird Area, Tom Wahl's, Livingston County Historical Museum

Location: South of Rochester and west of I-390 in New York's Southern Tier region

Route numbers: NY 39, CR 22, NY 36

Travel season: Year-round

Camping: Letchworth State Park

Services: In Avon, Geneseo, and Mount Morris

Nearby attractions: Genesee Country Village and Museum, Silver Lake State Park, Swain Ski and Snowboarding Center

The Route

Beginning in the small town of Avon and crossing through equestrian country, this route introduces a little-known Audubon-recognized Important Bird Area and continues to one of the state's most remarkable and popular state parks. If you're a birder, a wildlife enthusiast, or a fan of livestock, this route will delight you.

Avon to Geneseo

We hope you're hungry, because you need to begin your drive with a stop at **Tom Wahl's,** a locally owned chain of burger joints that got its start here at its Avon store. Named one of the 51 great burger joints across the US by *USA Today* in 2010, Tom Wahl's serves one of the finest made-to-order cheeseburgers—excuse me, "ground steak sandwiches"—you'll find just about anywhere. The real star here, however, is the root beer, big frosty mugs of the stuff that taste almost like maple syrup with a foamy head.

Letchworth Park provides many pleasant walking opportunities.

New York 39: Avon to Letchworth State Park

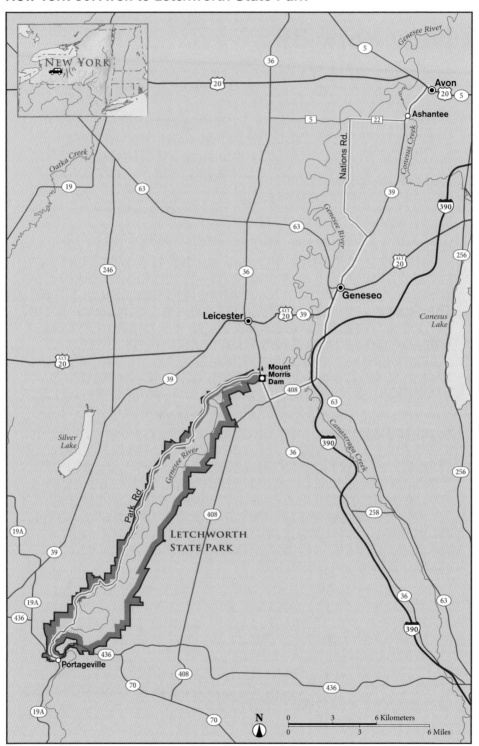

YOUR ICE CREAM STOP: TOM WAHL'S

Once you've had your ground steak sandwich and fries, you might as well go all out and top it off with a root beer float made with Wahl's famous custard. Made from a proprietary recipe that produces some of the region's creamiest soft-serve, the "twin kiss" ice cream just makes the handcrafted root beer even foamier, and the combination of vivid vanilla flavor and robust root beer creates one of the area's most iconic desserts. If you prefer one of the hard ice cream flavors, you'll still get the benefit of Wahl's homemade goodness. Seriously, though, have a root beer float.

Before you head south from Avon, check out one of the town's best known landmarks: the **statue of a white horse** at the corner of NY 15 and NY 5/US 20, a few blocks west of Tom Wahl's. Back in 1812, a man named John Pierson built the White Horse Tavern here on this corner, and the establishment became the area's stagecoach station at this centrally located spot. More than 100 years later, in 1930, Emma Rettig—the tavern owner at that time—placed this statue of a white horse in front of the tavern. The horse still stands at this spot, though the tavern succumbed to fire in 1955 and has long since been replaced with a service station.

From the rotary in the middle of Avon, take NY 39 south. Watch on your right for the **Avon Five Arch Bridge,** recently added to the National Register of Historic Places. Built in 1856–57 by the Genesee Valley Railroad, this 200-foot-long limestone bridge stood as part of the Rochester-Avon-Geneseo-Mount Morris line, and helped make Avon a railroad hub between Rochester, Buffalo, Corning, and Hornell. As other forms of transportation became more popular, this line eventually was abandoned and the rails were removed. There's a nice little park here with picnic tables if you took your Tom Wahl's lunch to go.

When you reach Fowlerville Road (County Road 22) in a moment, turn right. Continue through farmland to **Nations Road,** which will appear as the second left. Turn left onto Nations Road. This partially paved, partially gravel road leads through private farmland where owners grow corn, raise horses, cattle, and sheep, and run equestrian events including the Genesee Valley Hunt Race Meet on the second Saturday in October. Remarkably, it's also one of the most productive birding spots in western New York, in part because the landowners protect this area and maintain the habitats that are critical to a number of unusual bird species. The enormous old-growth oak trees in the fields—particularly the ones at the corner of Roots Tavern Road—have been nesting sites for redheaded woodpeckers on and off for many years, a fairly uncommon species in this area. Short-eared owls roost in these trees and sit on fence posts here in winter, and bobolinks and

Avon Five Arch Bridge once served as a railroad crossing.

eastern bluebirds are common in the fields in spring. In winter, horned larks, snow buntings, and Lapland longspurs frequent the plowed-under fields, feeding on the corn and other seeds left behind after the harvest. Northern harriers and rough-legged hawks become common in winter as well. Spring and early summer draw grasshopper and vesper sparrows to the grasslands, and this is one of the most reliable places in the area for northern harrier as well.

Drive slowly along Nations Road and give the right-of-way to any riders on horseback. Continue as the road becomes gravel and crosses a stream, and follow it around the bend until it meets up again with NY 39. When you reach that T intersection, turn right and continue through cropland to Geneseo.

A college town with a thriving town center, Geneseo is home to the State University of New York at Geneseo—as well as to the **National Warplane Museum,** where experts in World War II military aircraft restore planes of that war and the

Nation's Road provides expansive views any time of year.

Korean War. The museum hosts the annual Geneseo Airshow in July and a number of smaller events throughout the year, and the museum is open year-round, though only on Mon, Wed, and Sat from Oct through Mar.

Upstate New York has a strange attraction to quirky people selling musical instruments, and nowhere is this more apparent than at **Buzzo Music,** a long-standing institution here in Geneseo. Buzzo's the guy with the ample white beard, and he sells guitars, amps, strings, cables, CDs, and records (yes, on vinyl) at fair prices to people who are passionate about music. Even if you have no interest in the instruments, stop here for the sheer fun of a blast from the past.

Geneseo to Mount Morris

Continue on NY 39 past the SUNY Geneseo campus, and you will see the junction with NY 63. Take NY 63 south. Pass the American Rock Salt mining company and cross I-390, and continue south on NY 63 until it meets NY 408. Bear right onto NY 408, and continue through farmland until you reach **Mount Morris.**

Have you ever stopped to think about the origins of the Pledge of Allegiance? Chances are you haven't, but the man who created it—Francis Bellamy—was born here in Mount Morris. Bellamy wrote the Pledge in 1892 as part of a newspaper's campaign to place an American flag in every school in the country. The US Congress adopted a modified version of Bellamy's original pledge in 1942.

The most popular attraction in Mount Morris, aside from its charming Main Street with its plethora of shops and restaurants, is the **Mount Morris Dam.** Located deep in the **Genesee River Gorge** at the northern end of **Letchworth State Park,** the dam provides much-needed flood protection to downstream communities as far away as Rochester. It's the largest dam of its kind in the eastern US, measuring more than 1,000 feet across and nearly 250 feet from top to bottom. This feat of engineering took place in the 1950s, and it has succeeded in holding back the waters of the mighty Genesee River even in the face of hurricanes and massive snowmelt. You'll see the parking area and visitor center for the dam just after the ranger station as you enter Letchworth Park.

Letchworth State Park

Once you have enjoyed the dam, start the 17-mile drive through Letchworth State Park. The 14,350-acre park contains the Genesee River Gorge, a phenomenon rightfully called the Grand Canyon of the East, carved by the river's flow through solid rock to its current depth of more than 600 feet. The river rushes below as you follow the canyon rim, providing some of upstate's best whitewater rafting in spring and early summer, while more than 60 miles of hiking trails take walkers to

One of the best views in the park is from Great Bend Overlook.

unparalleled views of the gorge and into the northern hardwood forest along either side.

Turkey vultures swoop and dodge in the air above the gorge, often in kettles of 15 to 20 birds, prompting many visitors to believe that they are eagles (they're not—look at their featherless red heads). Chipmunks and colonies of squirrels chase through the woods collecting nuts and seeds, and rabbits, skunks, and groundhogs occasionally show themselves along the road or in meadows at either end of the park.

As you drive through the park, make a point of stopping at **Tea Table Rock** for wonderful views and some of the park's best picnic areas, and at **Wolf Creek Cascade** for canyon and waterfall views and an excellent short woodland hike. **Great Bend Overlook** provides one of the finest views of the canyon in the entire park.

At the southern end of the park, three waterfalls await you: **Lower, Middle,** and **Upper Falls.** Walking paths trimmed with stacked stone walls take you down carved stone steps to flat stone viewing areas where you can enjoy unobstructed views of these cataracts. Measuring 71, 107, and 70 feet respectively, these falls formed sequentially as the glaciers melted during the last ice age, retaining the meltwater in temporary lakes until erosion took the flow over the side. Sandstone held the falls in place, resisting the water's power, while layers of shale and sandstone form the supporting natural structure.

In addition to the three waterfalls, this end of Letchworth Park offers the **Glen Iris Inn**—a historic hotel and restaurant created in the home originally owned by William Pryor Letchworth, who made a gift of this magnificent park to the State of New York in 1906. You'll also find concessions in season, picnic areas, a gift shop, and modern restrooms. During the rainy seasons you may see many other waterfalls along the length of the gorge and on a variety of tributary streams throughout the park. Most of the horsetail cascades and curtain falls in the gorge disappear in the dry days of summer, but it's always worth exploring the area for more falls, woodland creatures, birds, wildflowers, and other delights that Letchworth offers.

Once you've reached the inn and the waterfalls, your drive continues past a very high steel arch railroad bridge. This bridge replaced an iron trestle bridge that stood here rather miraculously from 1875 to 2017, a hastily built replacement for a wooden bridge that burned to a crisp in May 1875. The newest bridge opened in December 2017, and crews disassembled the old iron bridge piece by piece over the following months.

You'll exit the park through its southern exit in Portageville. From here, you may want to consider continuing down NY 19 toward Wellsville, especially in fall—a route that takes you through a number of small towns and some of the Southern Tier's rolling, wooded hills.

This is the last scenic route described in this book, but it's far from the last exciting driving experience you can have in New York. Continue southwest into the Allegheny Mountains to explore famous retreats like Chautauqua Institution, or head for the backcountry in which naturalist Roger Tory Petersen first discovered the thrill of seeing and identifying wild birds. Go east to find New York's bounteous agricultural lands and the hidden, smaller lakes the glaciers left behind more than 10,000 years ago. Encounter more scenery in the southern Adirondacks, where Great Sacandaga Lake becomes the backdrop for sweet mountain villages and hunters' retreats. Head downstate to find the most dramatic view of the Manhattan skyline, or ride a ferry to see the nation's greatest metropolis the way arriving immigrants first viewed it from New York Harbor.

There's no limit to the experiences you can have as you drive the scenic routes of the Empire State. Still don't know why we love New York? Get in your car and find out.

APPENDIX A
SOURCES OF MORE INFORMATION

Avon Chamber of Commerce
74 Genesee St.
Avon, NY 14414
(585) 226-8080
avon-ny.org

Blue Mountain Lake/Indian Lake Chamber of Commerce
PO Box 245
Blue Mountain Lake, NY 12812
(518) 352-7659

Bronx Chamber of Commerce
1200 Waters Place #106
Bronx, NY 10461
(718) 828-3900
bronxchamber.org

Buffalo Niagara Partnership
257 W. Genesee Street
Buffalo, NY 14202
(716) 852-7100
thepartnership.org

Canandaigua Chamber of Commerce
113 S. Main St.
Canandaigua, NY 14424
(585) 394-4400
canandaiguachamber.com

Capital Region Chamber of Commerce
1473 Erie Blvd.
Schenectady, NY 12305
(518) 431-1400
capitalregionchamber.com

Cazenovia Chamber of Commerce
59 Albany St.
Cazenovia, NY 13035
(315) 655-9243
cazenovia.com

Cedar Grove-Thomas Cole National Historic Site
218 Spring St.
Catskill, NY 12414
(518) 943-7465
thomascole.org

Colchester Chamber of Commerce
PO Box 506
Downsville, NY 13755
(607) 363-2422
colchesterchamber.com

Columbia County Chamber of Commerce
1 N. Front St.
Hudson, NY 12534
(518) 828-4417
columbiachamber-ny.com

Cooperstown Chamber of Commerce
31 Chestnut St.
Cooperstown, NY 13326
(607) 547-9983 ext. 3
wearecooperstown.com

Dutchess County Regional Chamber of Commerce
1 Civic Center Plaza
Poughkeepsie, NY 12601
(845) 454-1700
dcrcoc.org

East Hampton Chamber of Commerce
58B Park Place
East Hampton, NY 11937
(631) 324-0362
easthamptonchamber.com

Ellenville Wawarsing Chamber of Commerce
124 Canal St.
Ellenville, NY 12428
(845) 647-4620
ewcoc.com

Geneva Area Chamber of Commerce
One Franklin Square, Ste. 202
PO Box 587
Geneva, NY 14456
(315) 789-1776
genevany.com

Hammondsport Chamber of Commerce
47 Shether St.
Hammondsport, NY 14840
(607) 569-2989
hammondsport.org

Harlem Valley Chamber of Commerce
PO Box 376
Amenia, NY 12501
(845) 453-0415
harlemvalleychamber.com

Hyde Park Chamber of Commerce
4389 Albany Post Rd.
Hyde Park, NY 12538
(845) 229-8612
hydeparkchamber.org

Lake Placid Visitors Bureau
2608 Main St.
Lake Placid, NY 12946
(518) 523-2445
lakeplacid.com

Livingston County Chamber of Commerce
4635 Millennium Dr.
Geneseo, NY 14454
(585) 243-2222
livingstoncountychamber.com

Malone Chamber of Commerce
497 E. Main St.
Malone, NY 12953
(518) 483-3760
malonechamberofcommerce.com

Massena Chamber of Commerce
16 Church St.
Massena, NY 13662
(315) 769-3525
massenachamber.com

Montauk Chamber of Commerce
742 Montauk Hwy.
Montauk, NY 11954
(631) 668-2428
montaukchamber.com

Naples Valley Visitor Association
130 S. Main St.
Naples, NY 14512
(585) 374-2629
naplesvalleyny.com

Narrowsburg Chamber of Commerce
PO Box 44
Narrowsburg, NY 12764
narrowsburg.com

New Paltz Regional Chamber of Commerce
257 Main St.
New Paltz, NY 12561
(845) 255-0243
newpaltzchamber.org

New York State Canals
30 S. Pearl St.
PO Box 189
Albany, NY 12207
(518) 449-6036
canals.ny.gov

Niagara Falls Chamber of Commerce
1220 Main St.
Niagara Falls, NY 14301
(716) 285-5345
nfnycc.com

Niagara River Region Chamber of Commerce
895 Center St.
Lewiston, NY 14092
(716) 754-9500
niagarariverregion.com

North Country Chamber of Commerce
7061 Route 9
PO Box 310
Plattsburgh, NY 12901
(518) 563-1000
northcountrychamber.com

Old Forge Town of Webb Visitor Information Center
PO Box 68
3140 State Route 28
Old Forge, NY 13420
(315) 369-6983
oldforgeny.com

Oswego-Fulton Chamber of Commerce
121 E. First St.
Oswego, NY 13126
(315) 343-7681
oswegofultonchamber.com

Rensselaer County Regional Chamber of Commerce
90 Fourth St., Suite 200
Troy, NY 12180
(518) 274-7020
renscochamber.com

Rhinebeck Area Chamber of Commerce
23F E. Market St.
Rhinebeck, NY 12572
(845) 876-5904
rhinebeckchamber.com

Riverhead Chamber of Commerce
59 E. Main St.
Riverhead, NY 11901
(631) 727-7600
riverheadchamber.com

Rochester Convention and Visitors Bureau
45 East Ave., Ste. 400
Rochester, NY 14604
(800) 677-7282, (585) 279-8300
visitrochester.com

Saratoga Convention and Tourism Bureau
60 Railroad Place, Ste. 301
Saratoga Springs, NY 12866
(844) 947-4922, (518) 584-1531
discoversaratoga.org

Saratoga National Historical Park
648 Route 32
Stillwater, NY 12170
(518) 664-9821 ext. 224
nps.gov/sara

Seneca County Chamber of Commerce
1 W. Main St., PO Box 350
Waterloo, NY 13165
(315) 568-2906
senecachamber.org

Sodus Chamber of Commerce
PO Box 187
Sodus, NY 14551
(315) 576-3818
sodusny.org

Southampton Chamber of Commerce
76 Main St.
Southampton, NY 11968
(631) 283-0402
southamptonchamber.com

Ticonderoga Area Chamber of Commerce
94 Montcalm St., Ste. 1
Ticonderoga, NY 12883
(518) 585-6619
ticonderogany.com

Tompkins County Chamber of Commerce
904 E. Shore Dr.
Ithaca, NY 14850
(607) 273-7080
tompkinschamber.org

Tupper Lake Chamber of Commerce
121 Park St.
Tupper Lake, NY 12986
(518) 359-3328
tupperlake.com

Ulster County Chamber of Commerce (Kingston)
214 Fair St.
Kingston, NY 12401
(845) 338-5100
ulsterchamber.org

Warrensburg Chamber of Commerce
3839 Main St., Suite 2
Warrensburg, NY 12885
(518) 623-2161
warrensburgchamber.com

Waterford Harbor Visitor Center
One Tugboat Alley
Waterford, NY 12188
(518) 223-9123
town.waterford.ny.us

Watertown North Country Chamber of Commerce
1241 Coffeen St.
Watertown, NY 13601
(315) 788-4400
watertownny.com

Yates County Chamber of Commerce
2375 Route 14A
Penn Yan, NY 14527
(315) 536-3111
yatesny.com

APPENDIX B
GUIDE TO ROADSIDE
WILDFLOWERS AND PLANTS

How many times have you passed a field or ditch filled with blooming wildflowers and wondered what the flowers were? This guide will help you identify the most common blooms you'll see on scenic drives throughout New York State. We've noted the months in which you may see these flowers to help you narrow down the identification. If you're thinking about planting some of these flowers in your own garden, we've noted which ones are native to New York and which are invasive. Please choose from the native varieties, because invasive species crowd out so many native plants that provide food for local birds, butterflies, and bees.

American Cranberrybush
(Viburnum trilobum)
Blooms May–June
Native

Common Boneset
(Eupatorium perfoliatum)
Blooms August–October
Native

Field Bindweed
(Convolvulus arvensis)
Blooms June–August
Invasive

Hobblebush
(Viburnum alnifolium)
Blooms May–June
Native

Multiflora Rose
(Rosa multiflora)
Blooms June–August; also may be pink
Invasive

Oxeye Daisy
(Leucanthemum vulgare)
Blooms June–August
Invasive

Queen Anne's Lace
(Daucus carota)
Blooms June–October
Invasive

White Snakeroot
(Ageratina altissima)
Blooms August–October
Native

White Sweet Clover
(Melilotus albus)
Blooms June–August
Invasive

Japanese Knotweed
(Fallopia japonica)
Blooms August–September
Invasive

Common Fleabane
(Erigeron philadelphicus)
Blooms June–September
Native

Common Milkweed
(Asclepias syriaca)
Blooms June–July
Native

Crown Vetch
(Securigera varia)
Blooms May–June
Invasive

New York Aster
(Symphyotrichum novea-belgii)
Blooms August–October
Native

Pennsylvania Smartweed
(Polygonum pensylvanicum)
Blooms August–October
Native

Purple Coneflower
(Echinacea purpurea)
Blooms August–October
Native

Purple Loosestrife
(Lythrum salicaria)
Blooms August–October
Invasive

Red Clover
(Trifolium pretense)
Blooms June–July
Nonnative

Joe-Pye Weed
(Eupatorium maculatum)
Blooms August–September
Native

Sweet Pea
(Lathyrus latifolius)
Blooms June–July
Invasive

Woodland Phlox
(Phlox divaricata)
Blooms April–May
Native

Dame's Rocket
(Hesperis matronalis)
Blooms May–June
Invasive

New England Aster
(Symphyotrichum novea-anglia)
Blooms August–October
Native

Wild Bergamot
(Monarda fistulosa)
Blooms June–July
Native

Brown Knapweed
(Centaurea jacea)
Blooms June–July
Invasive

Spear Thistle
(Cirsium vulgare)
Blooms August–September
Invasive

Wild Teasel
(Dipsacus fullonum)
Blooms August–September
Invasive

Common Chicory
(Cichorium intybus)
Blooms July–September
Nonnative

Black-eyed Susan
(Rudbeckia hirta)
Blooms July–October
Native

Brown-eyed Susan
(Rudbeckia trilobum)
Blooms August–October
Native

Blanketflower
(Gaillardia aristata)
Blooms April–October
Native

Dandelion
(Taraxacum officinale)
Blooms April–May
Invasive

Wild Parsnip
(Pastinaca sativa)
Blooms June–July
Invasive

Bird's Foot Trefoil
(Lotus corniculatus)
Blooms June–July
Invasive

Giant Goldenrod
(Solidago giantea)
Blooms August–October
Native

Canada Goldenrod
(Solidago canadensis)
Blooms August–October
Native

Gray Goldenrod
(Solidago nemoralis)
Blooms August–October
Native

Tiger Daylily (Ditch Lily)
(Hemerocallis fulva)
Blooms June–July
Nonnative

Jewelweed
(Impatiens capensis)
Blooms August–September
Native

Staghorn Sumac
(Rhus typhina)
Blooms May–June, fruit September–October
Native

Common Cattail
(Typha latifolia)
Spike appears in June–July
Native

Common Reed
(Phragmites australis)
Blooms in August–September
May be native or invasive

INDEX